SKULL
TATTOOS

Johnny Karp

Skull Tattoos
by Johnny Karp

ISBN 978-1-926917-00-9

Printed in the United States of America

Copyright © 2010 Psylon Press

All rights reserved. Except for use in a review, no portion of this book may be reproduced in any form without the express written permission of the author. For information regarding permission, write to admin@psylonpress.com

Neither the author nor the publisher assumes any responsibility for the use or misuse of information contained in this book.

Other Books in the Series

- Cross Tattoos
- Angel Tattoos
- Butterfly Tattoos
- Fairy Tattoos
- Zodiac Tattoos
- Lettering Tattoos
- Scorpion Tattoos
- Hummingbird Tattoos
- Dragonfly Tattoos
- Kanji Tattoos
- Dolphin Tattoos
- Cherub Tattoos

Other titles are in preparation.

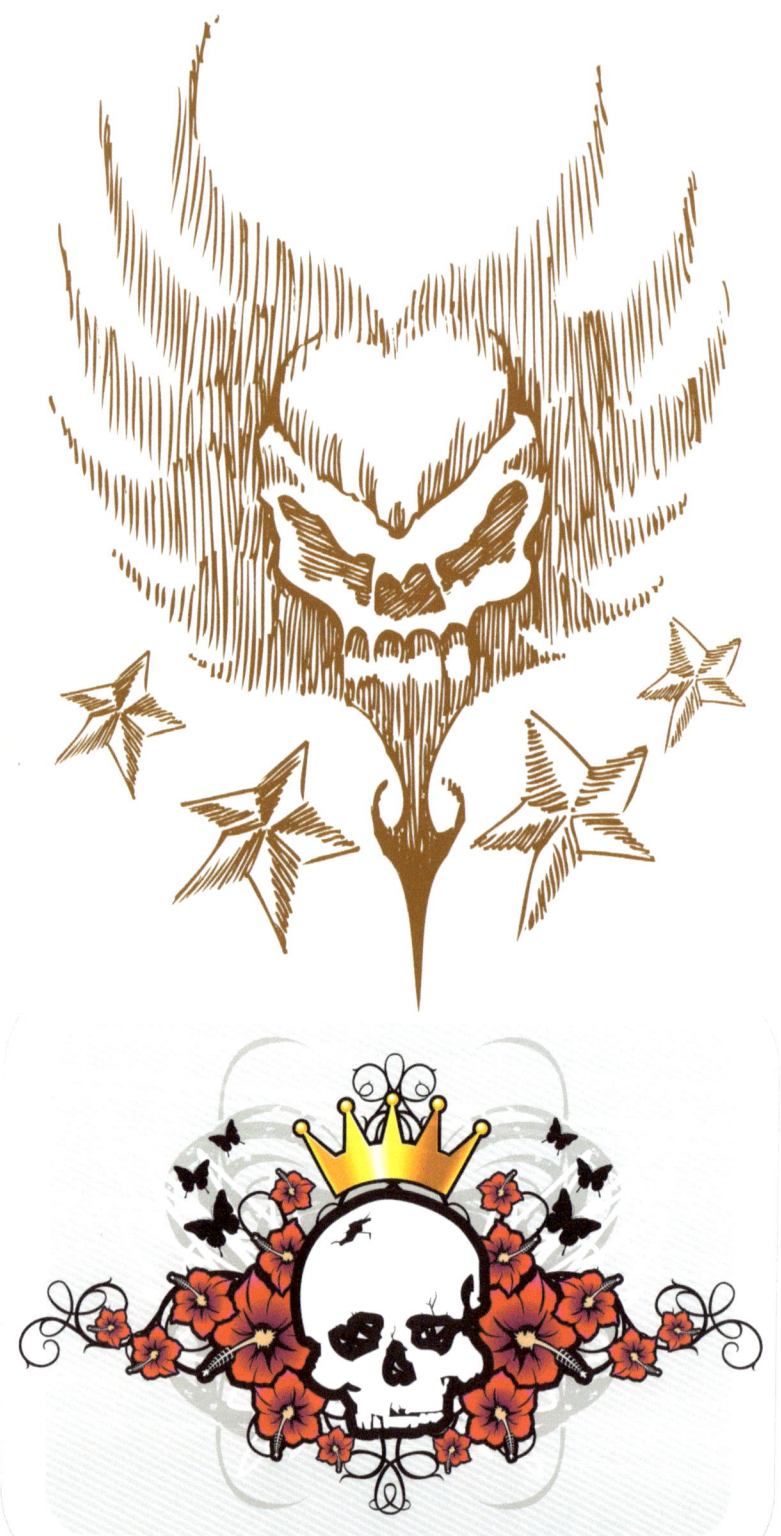

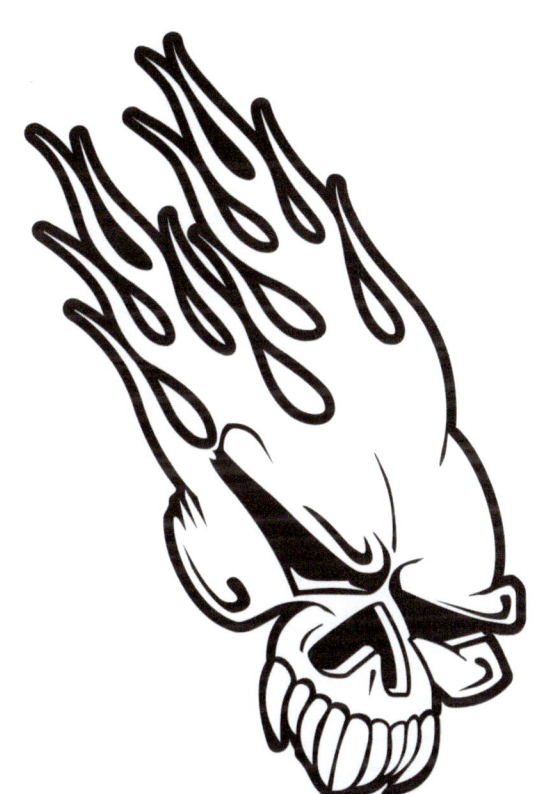

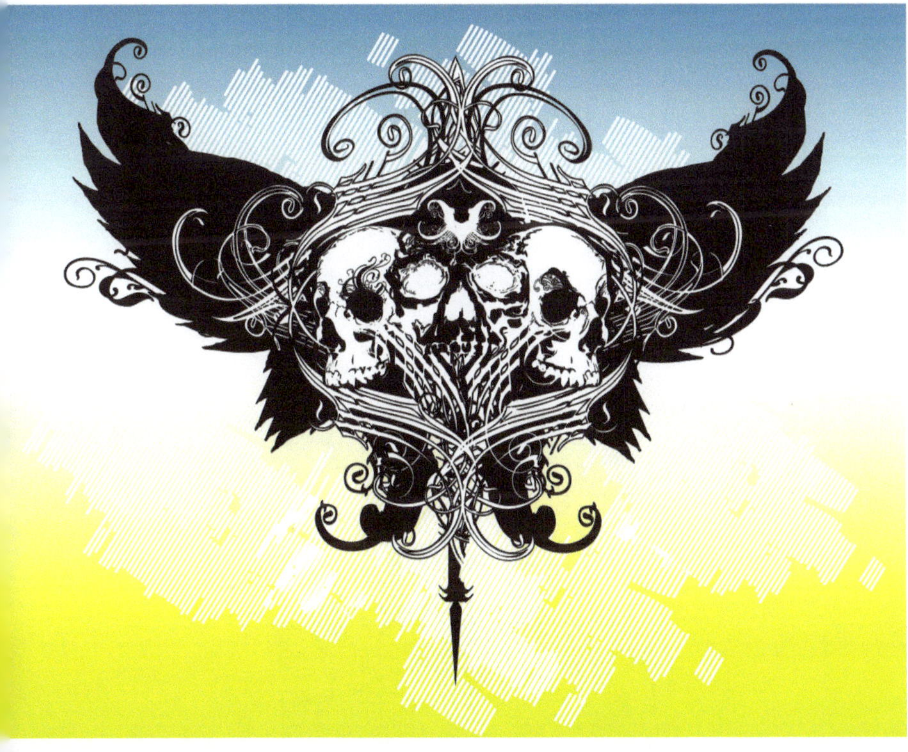

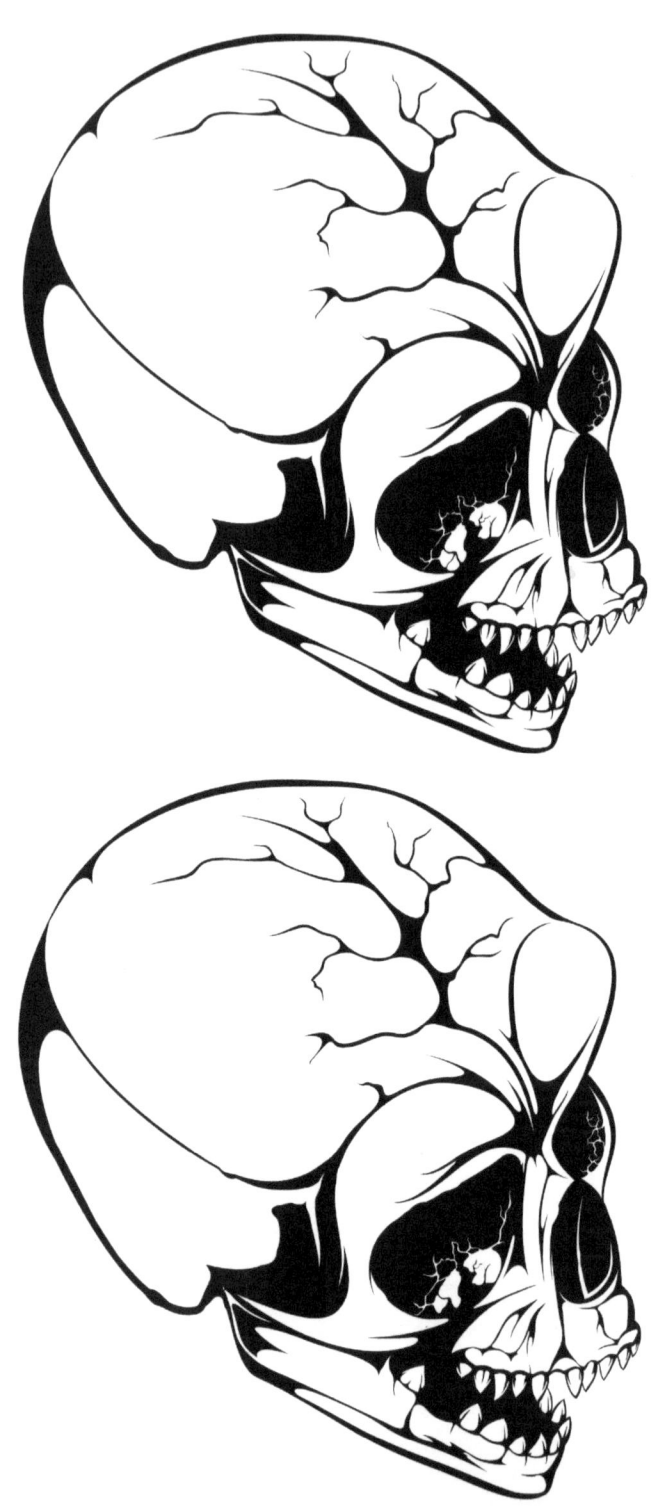

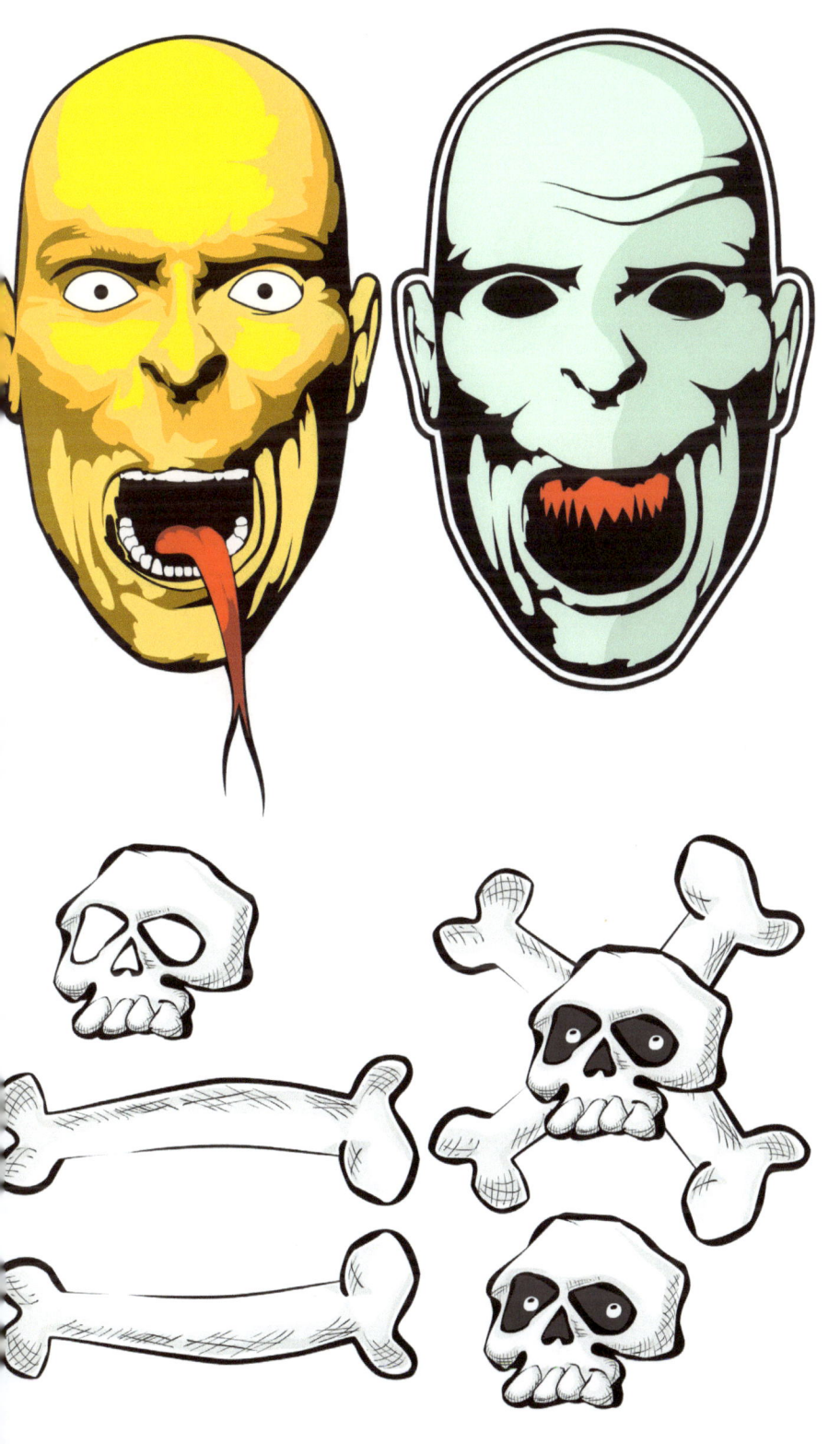

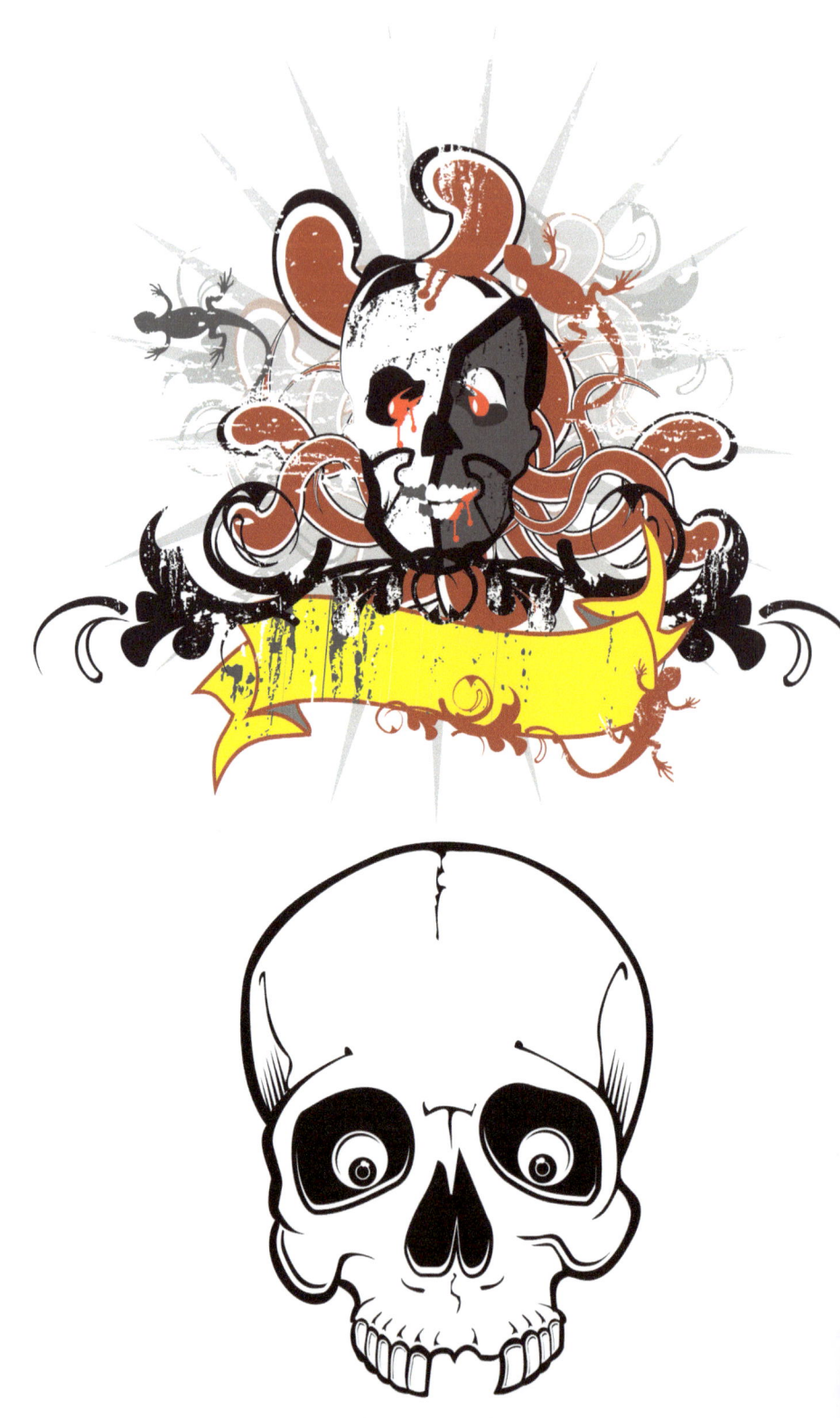

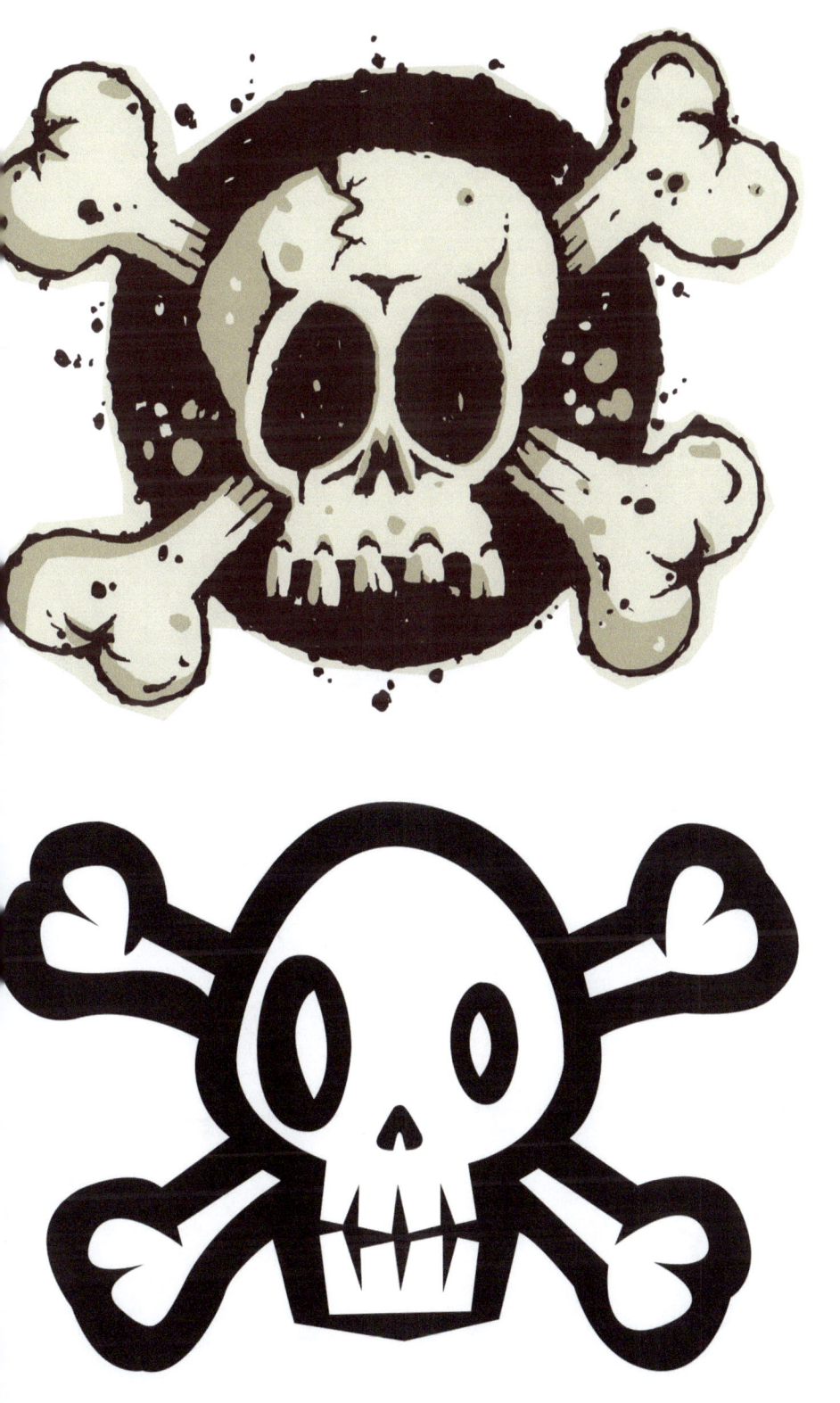

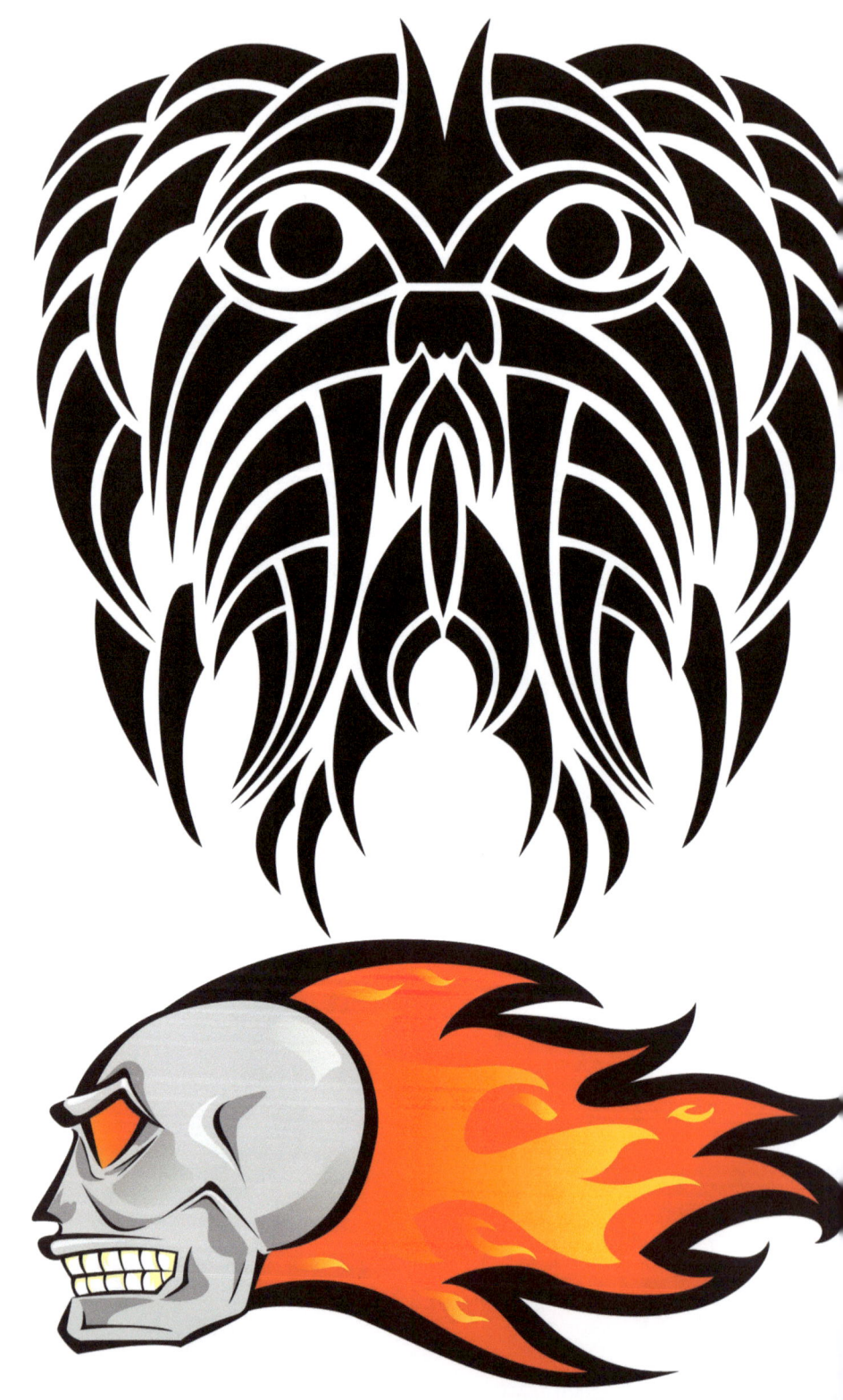

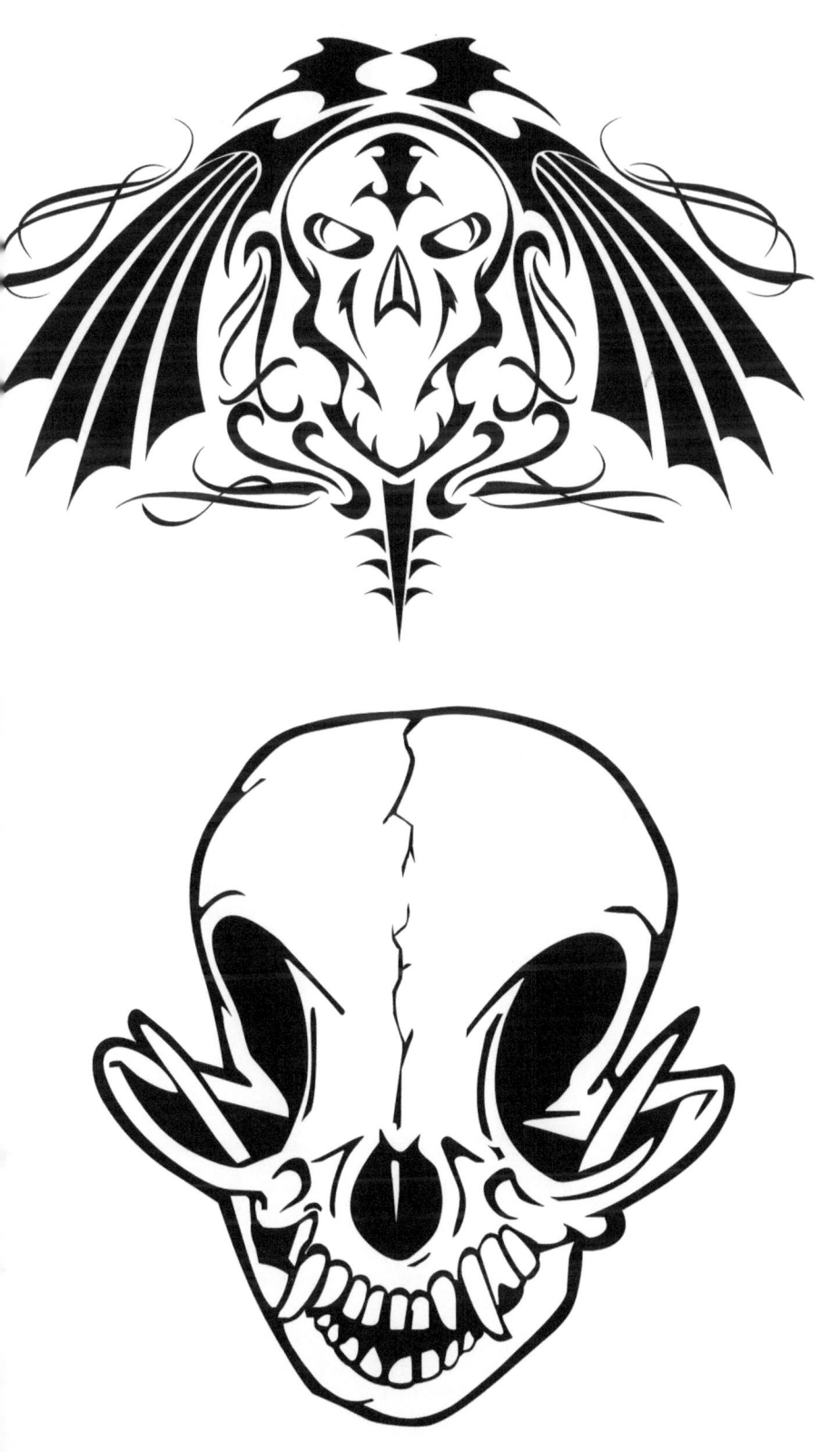

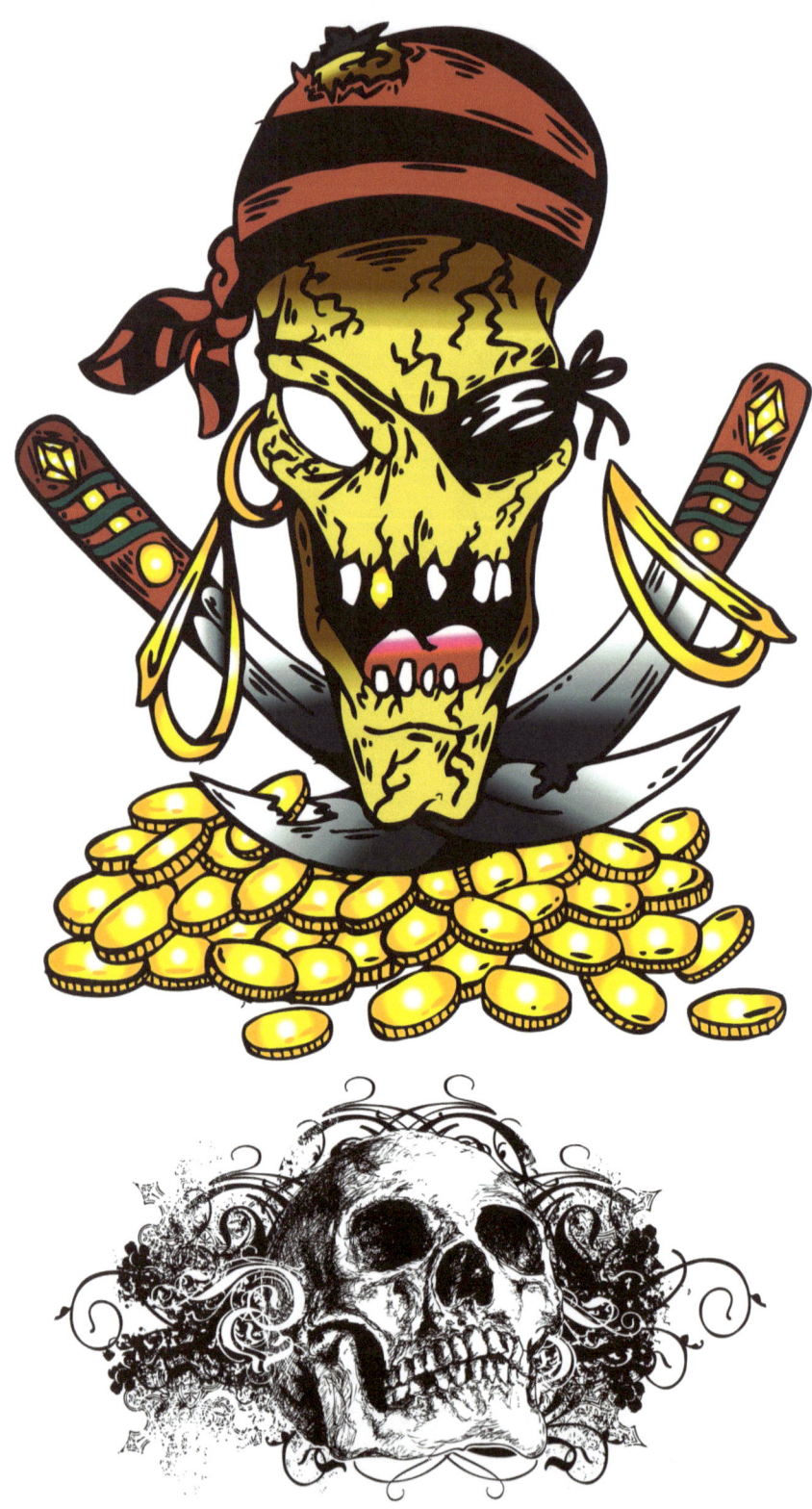

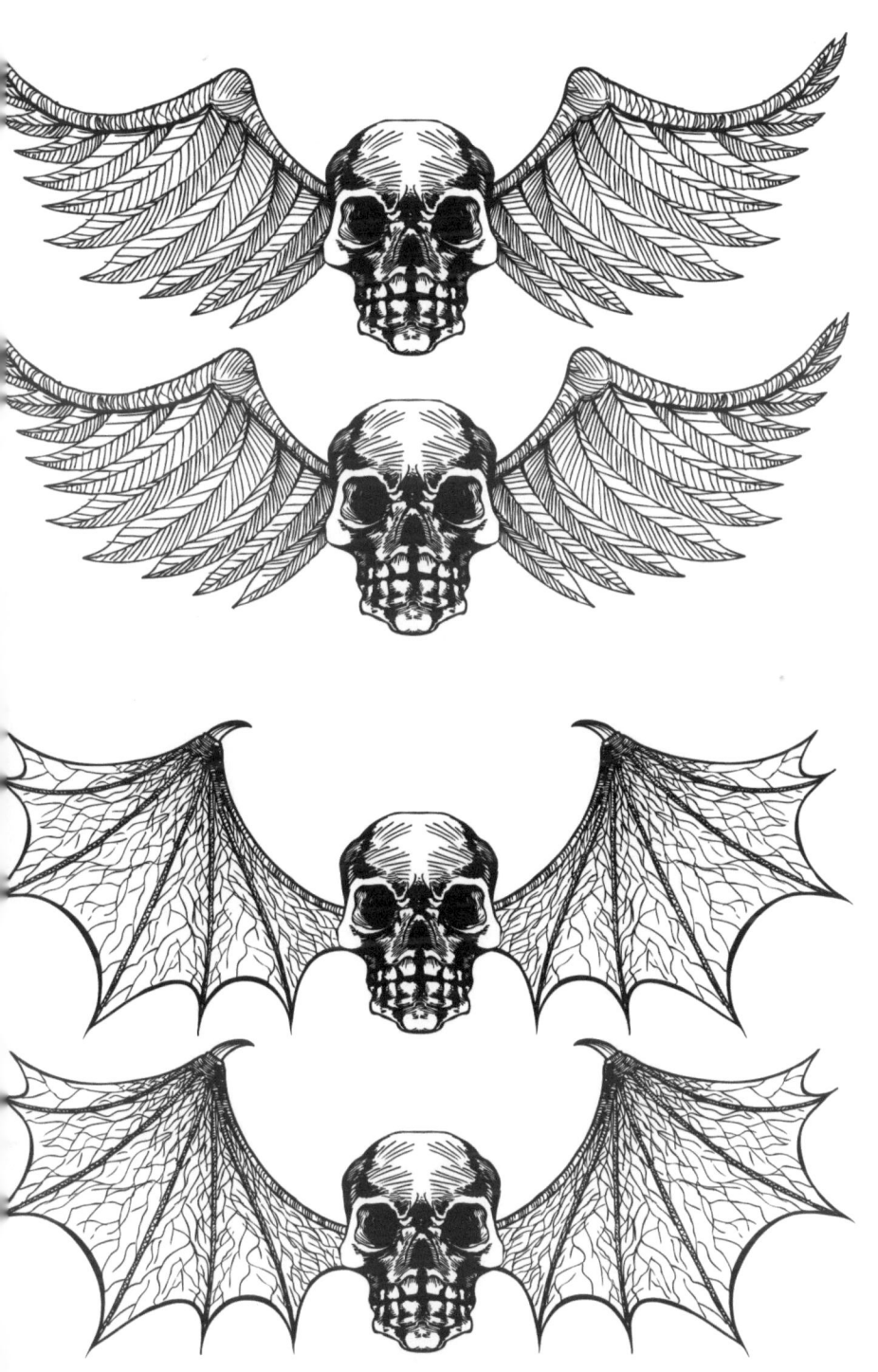

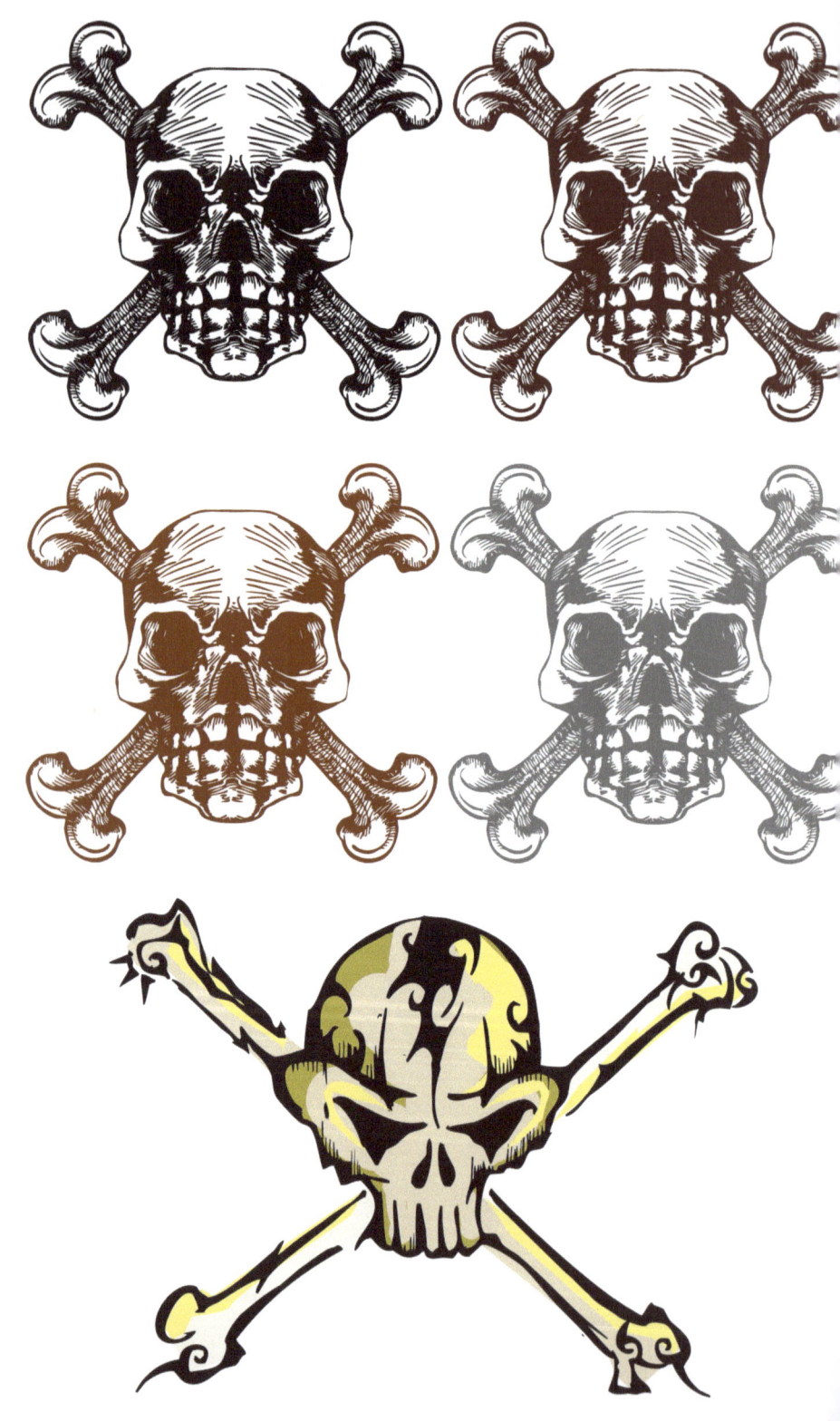

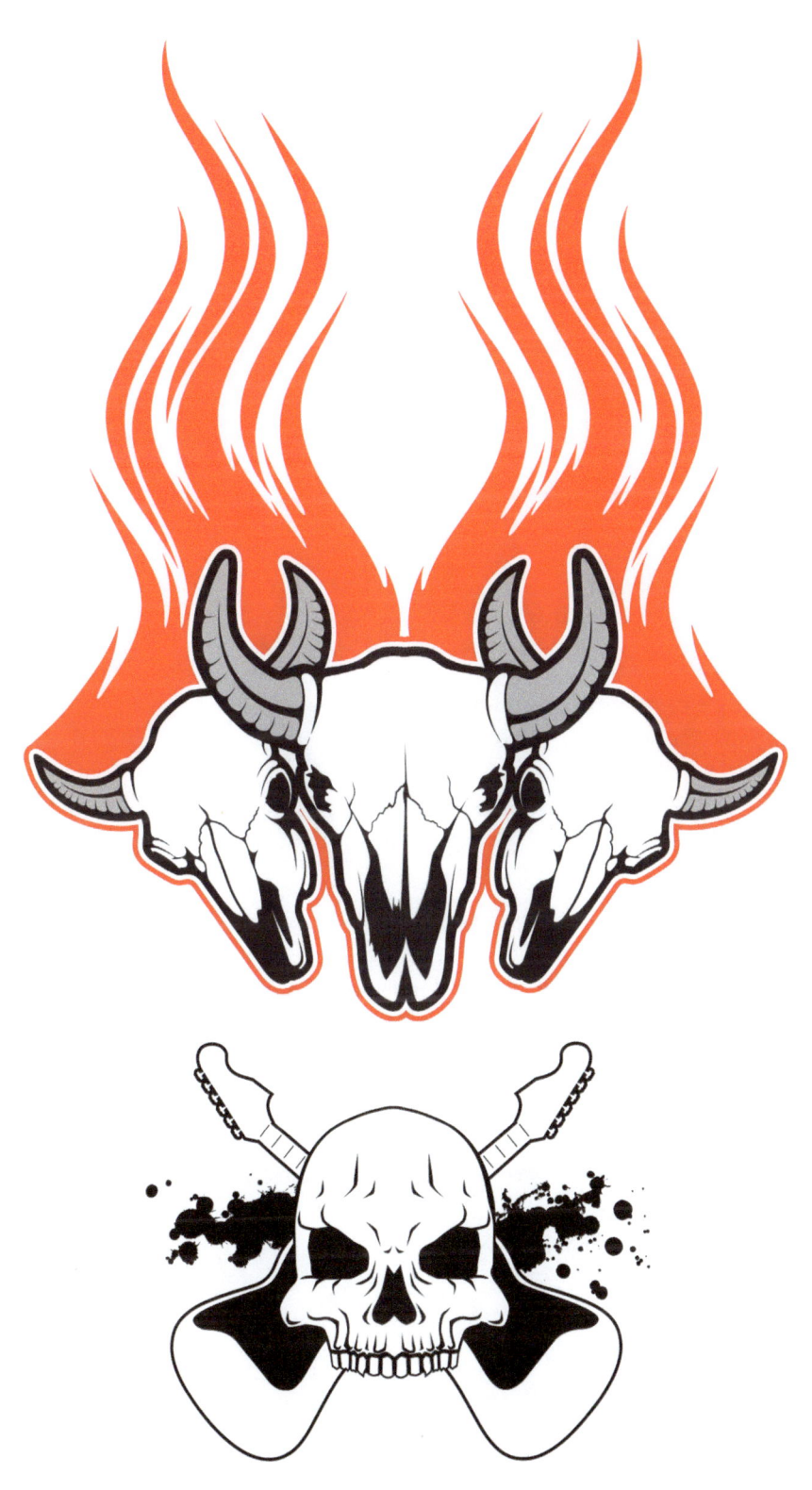

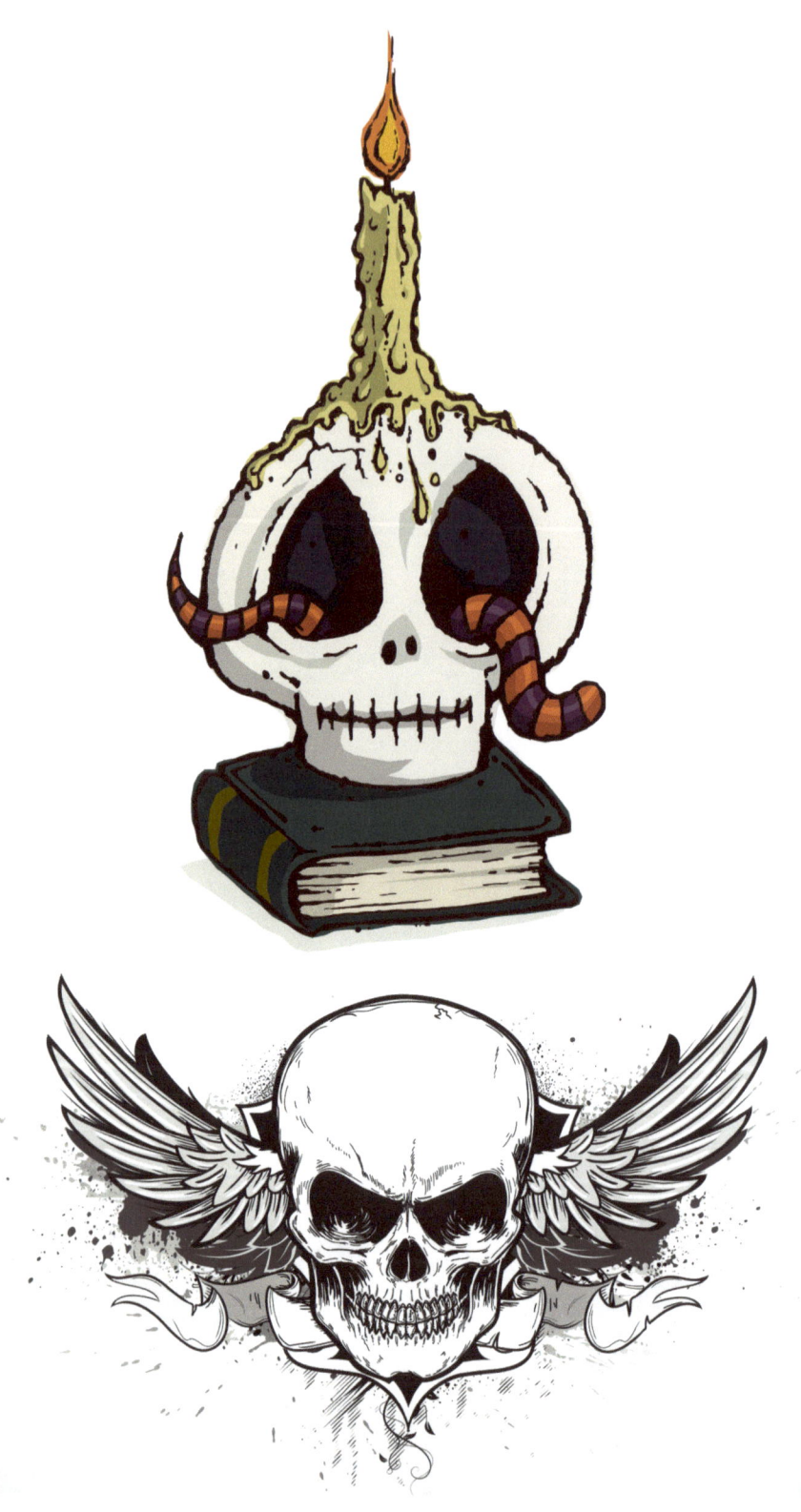

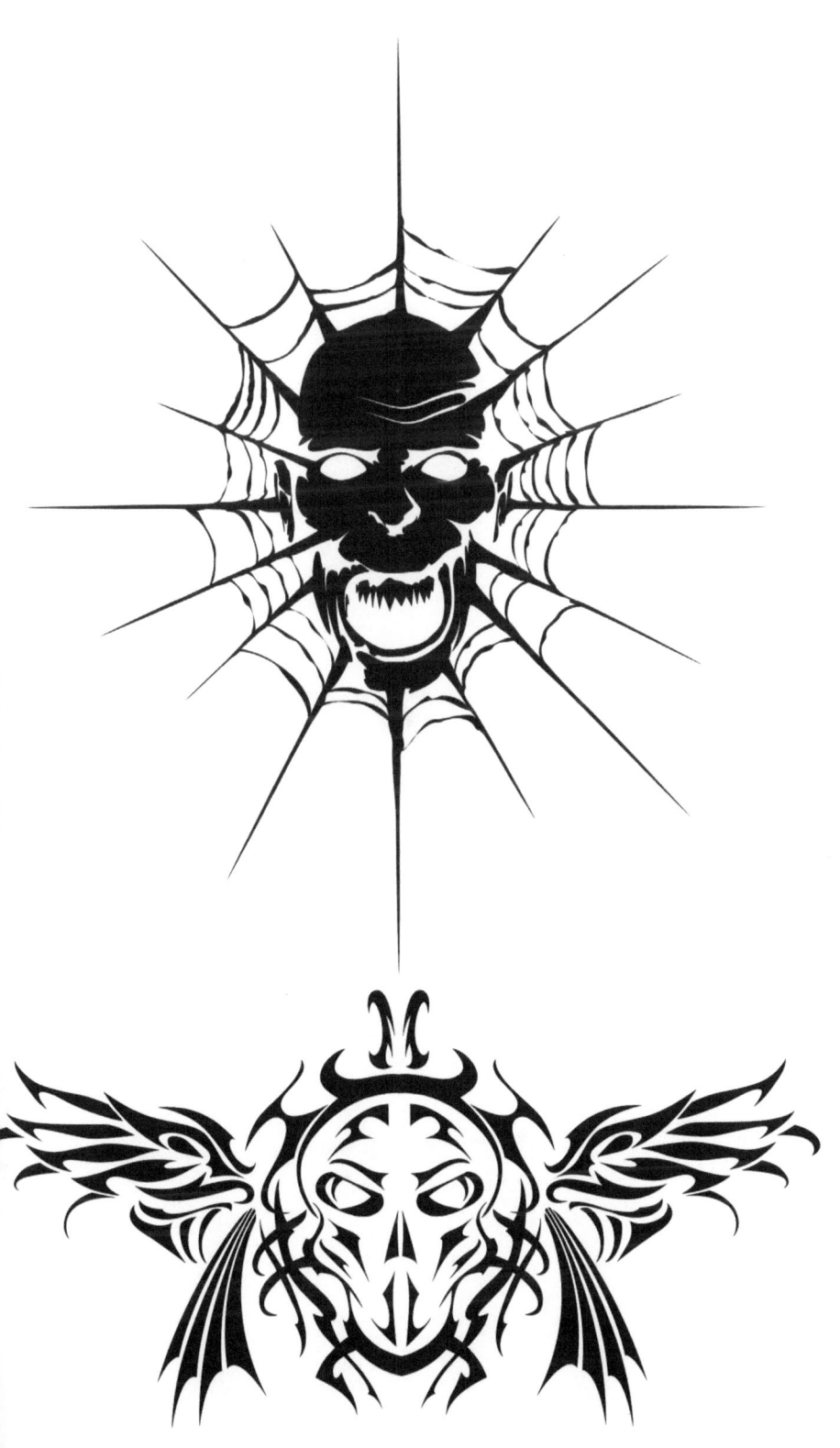

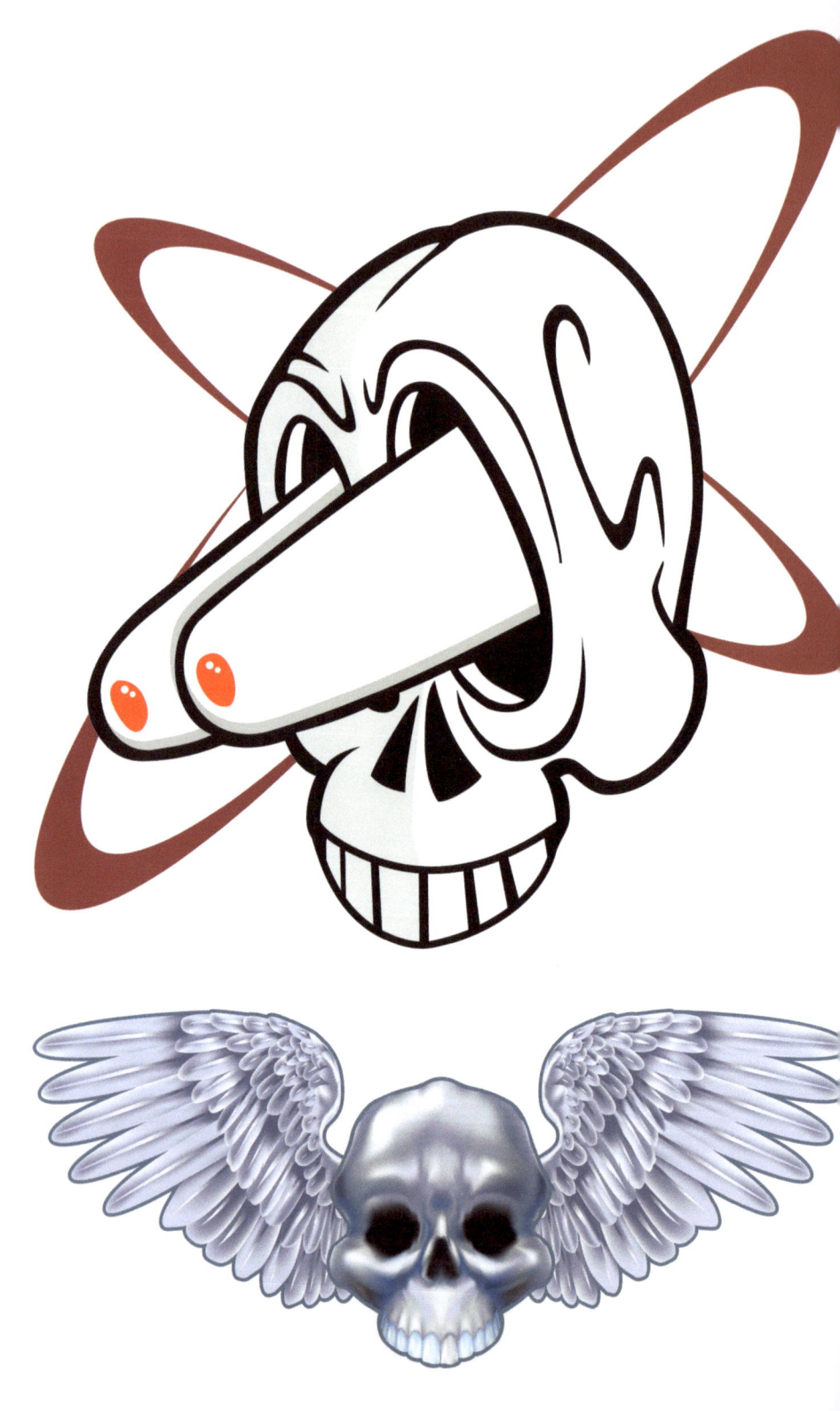

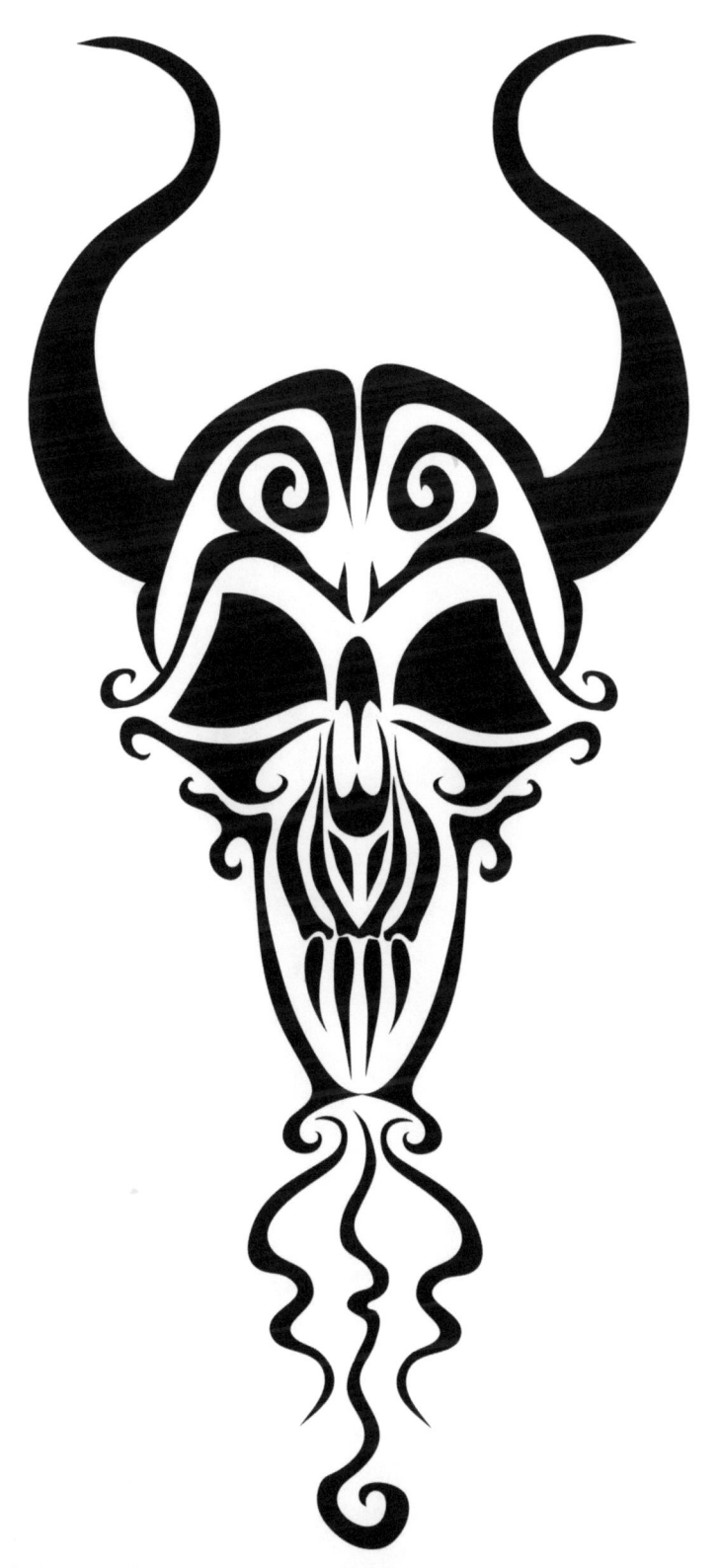

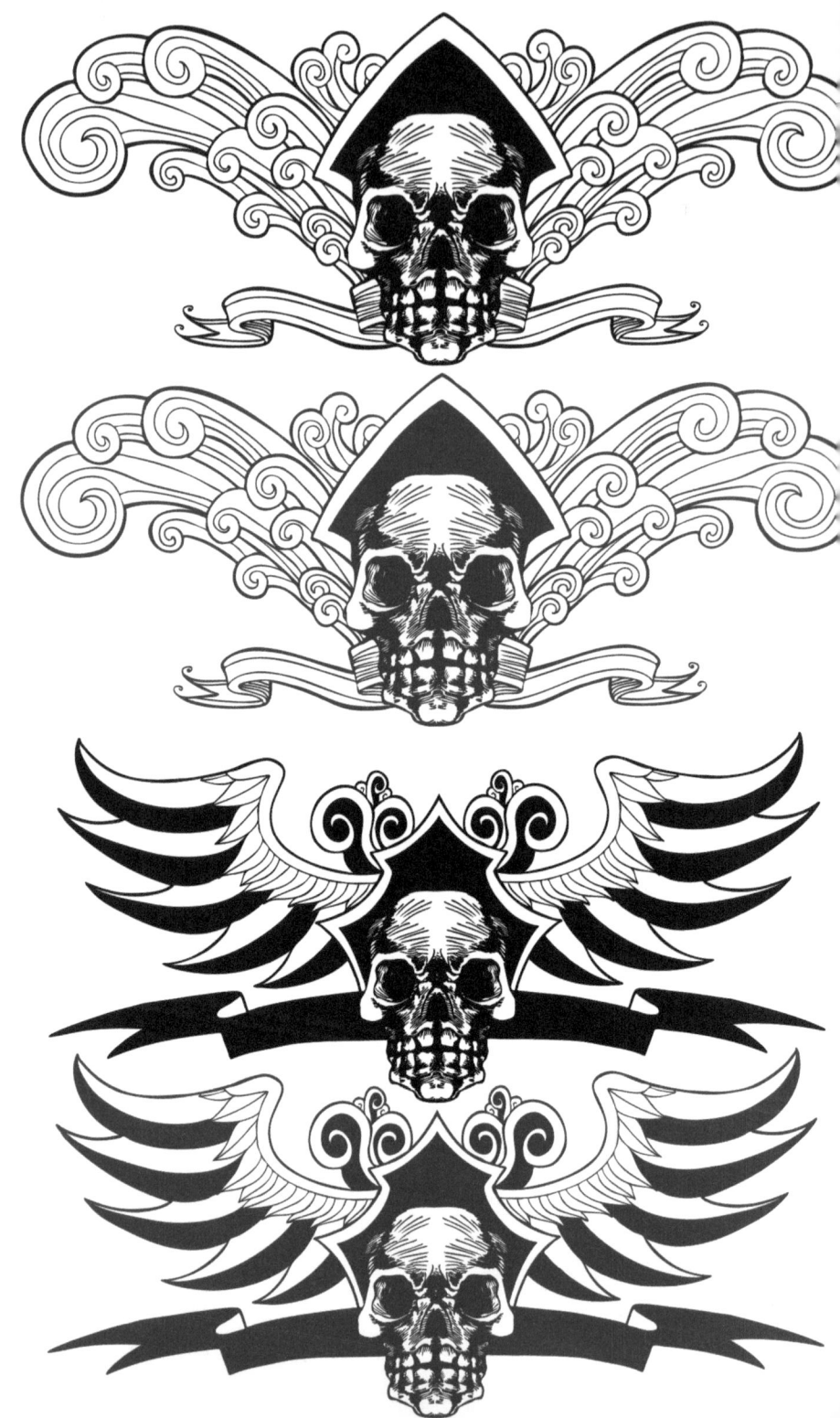

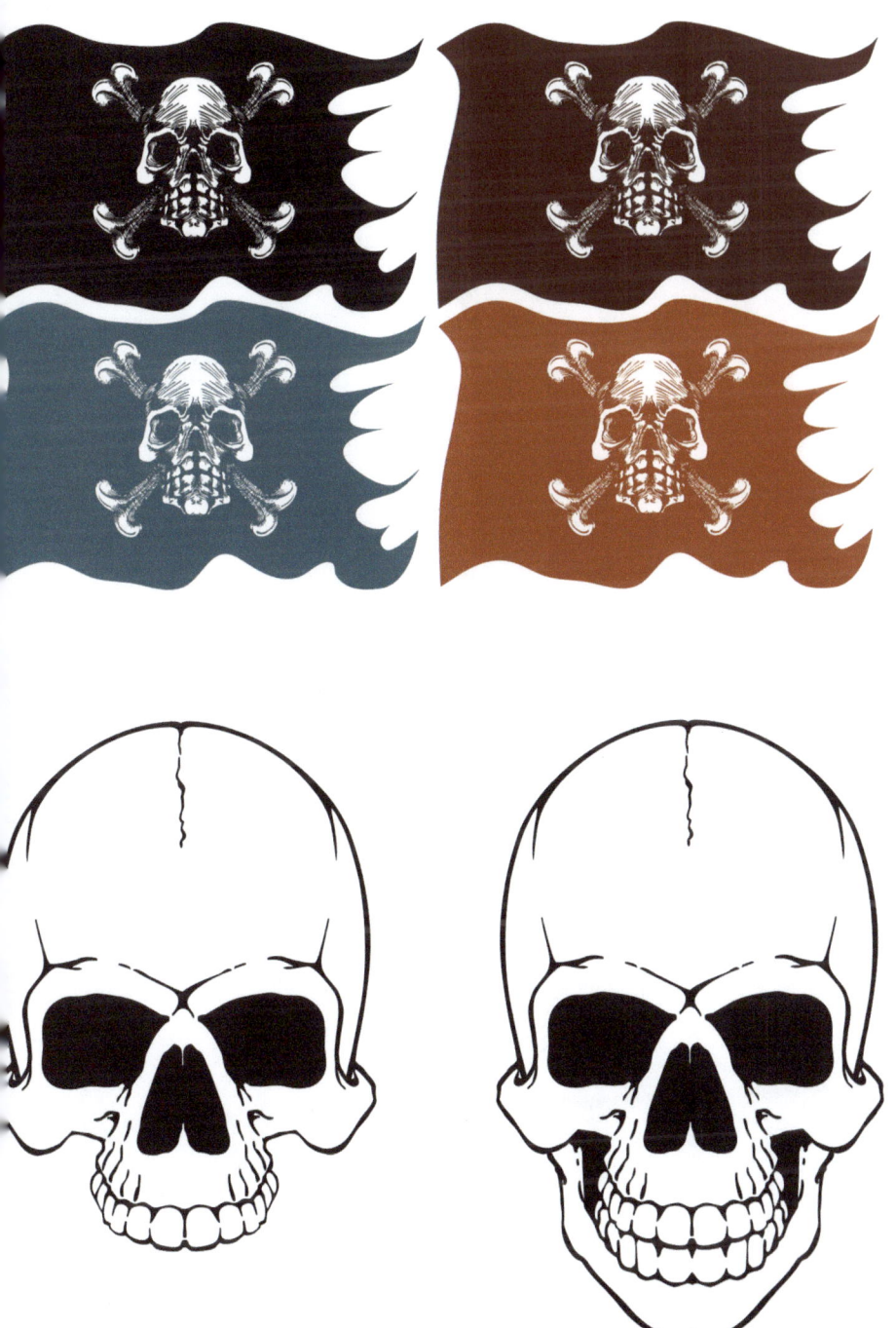

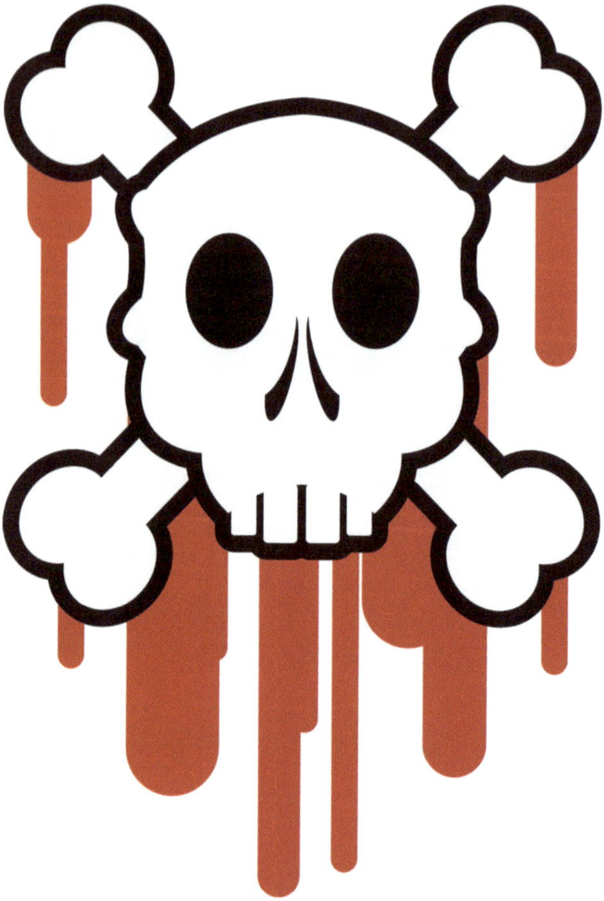

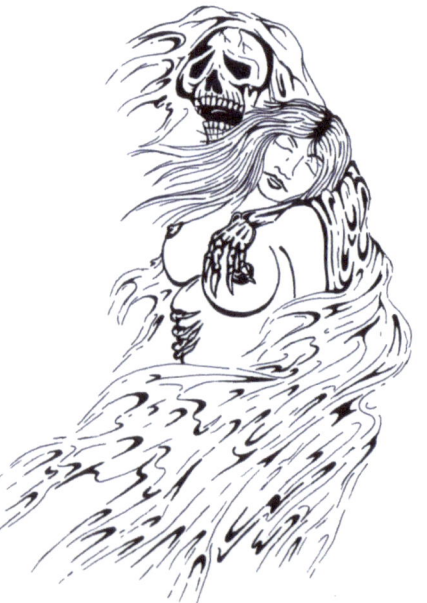
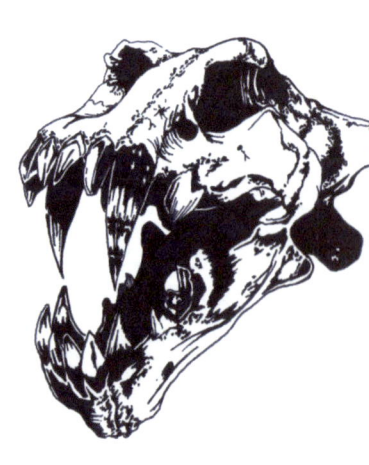

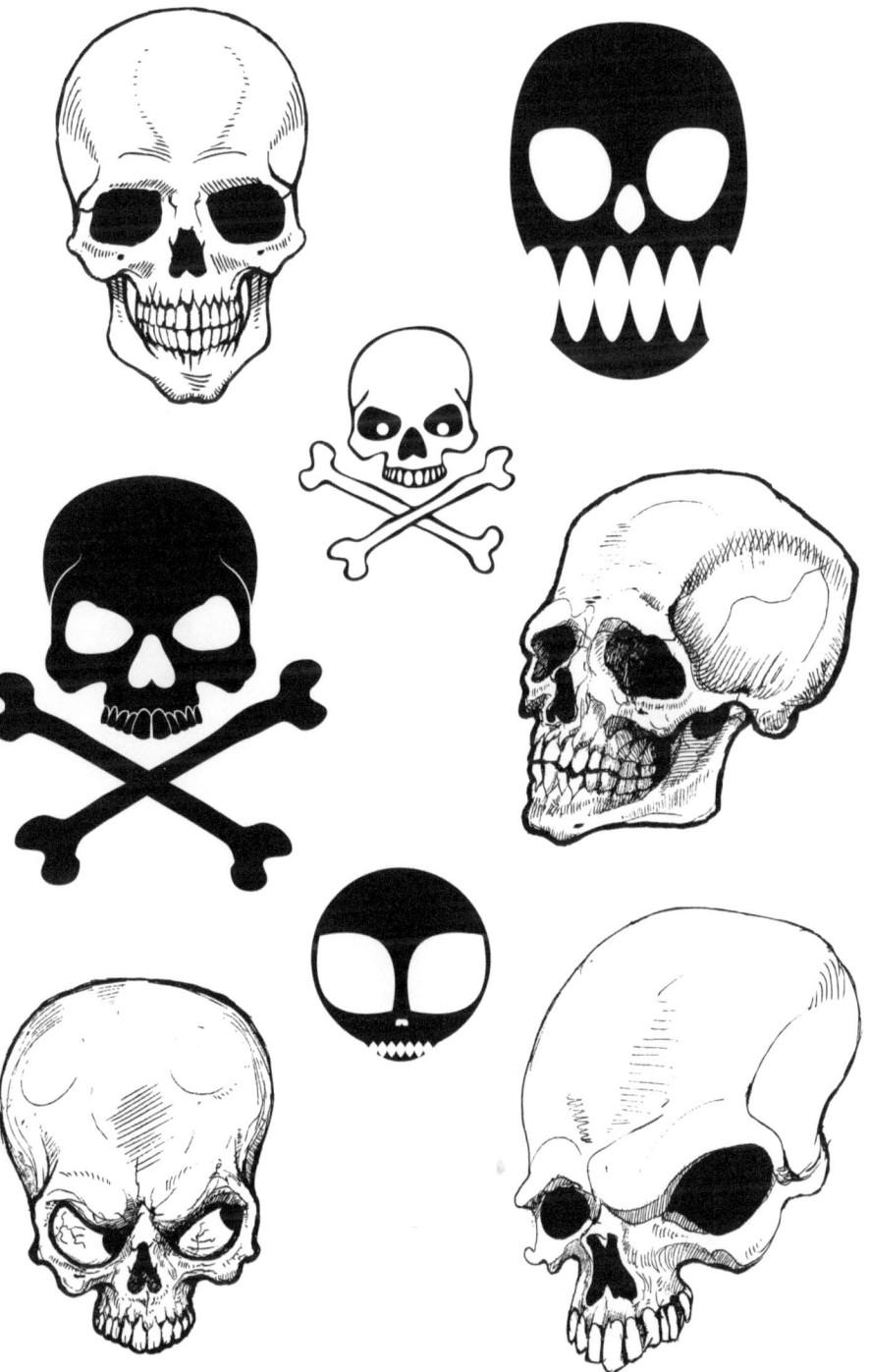

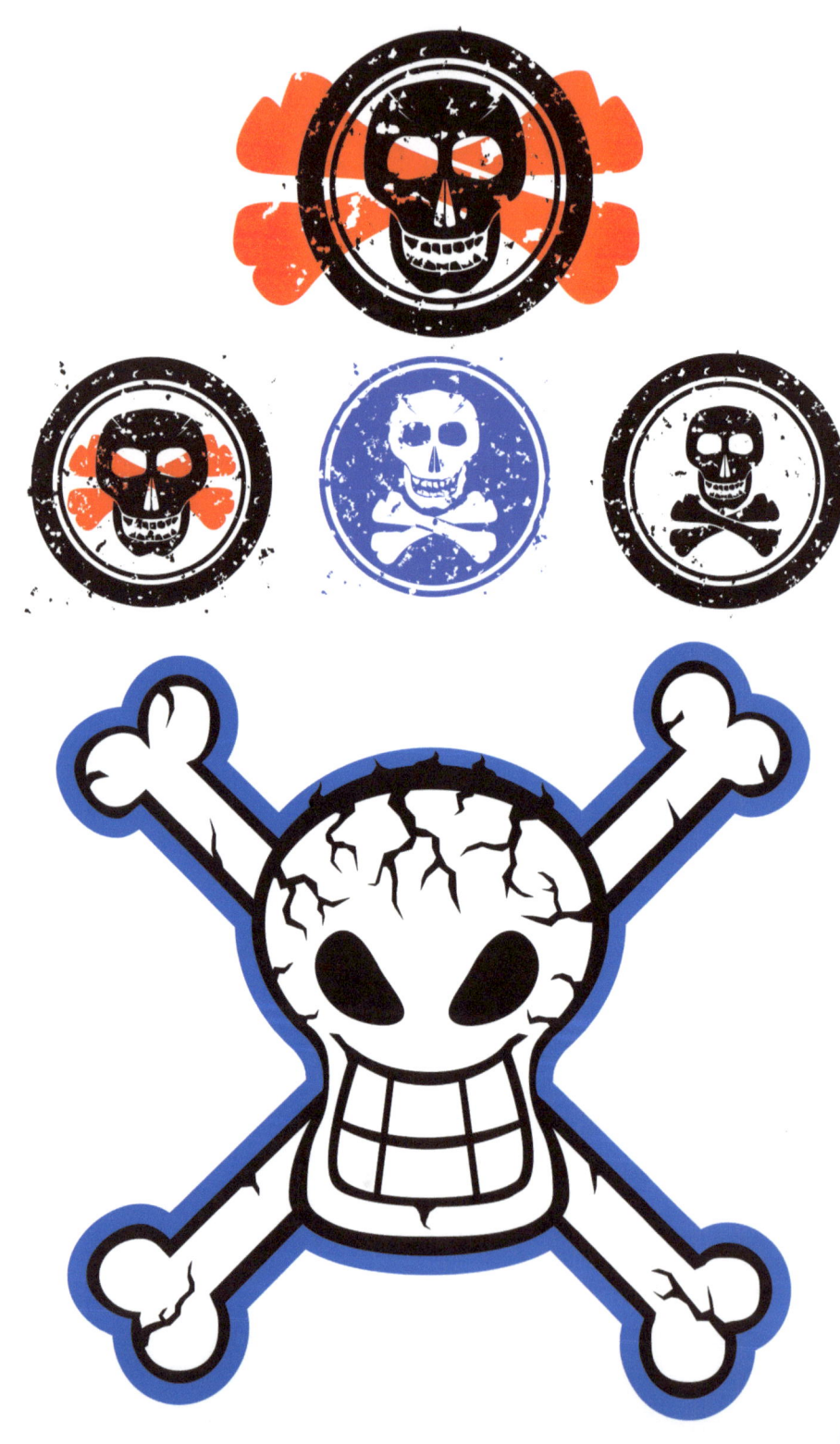

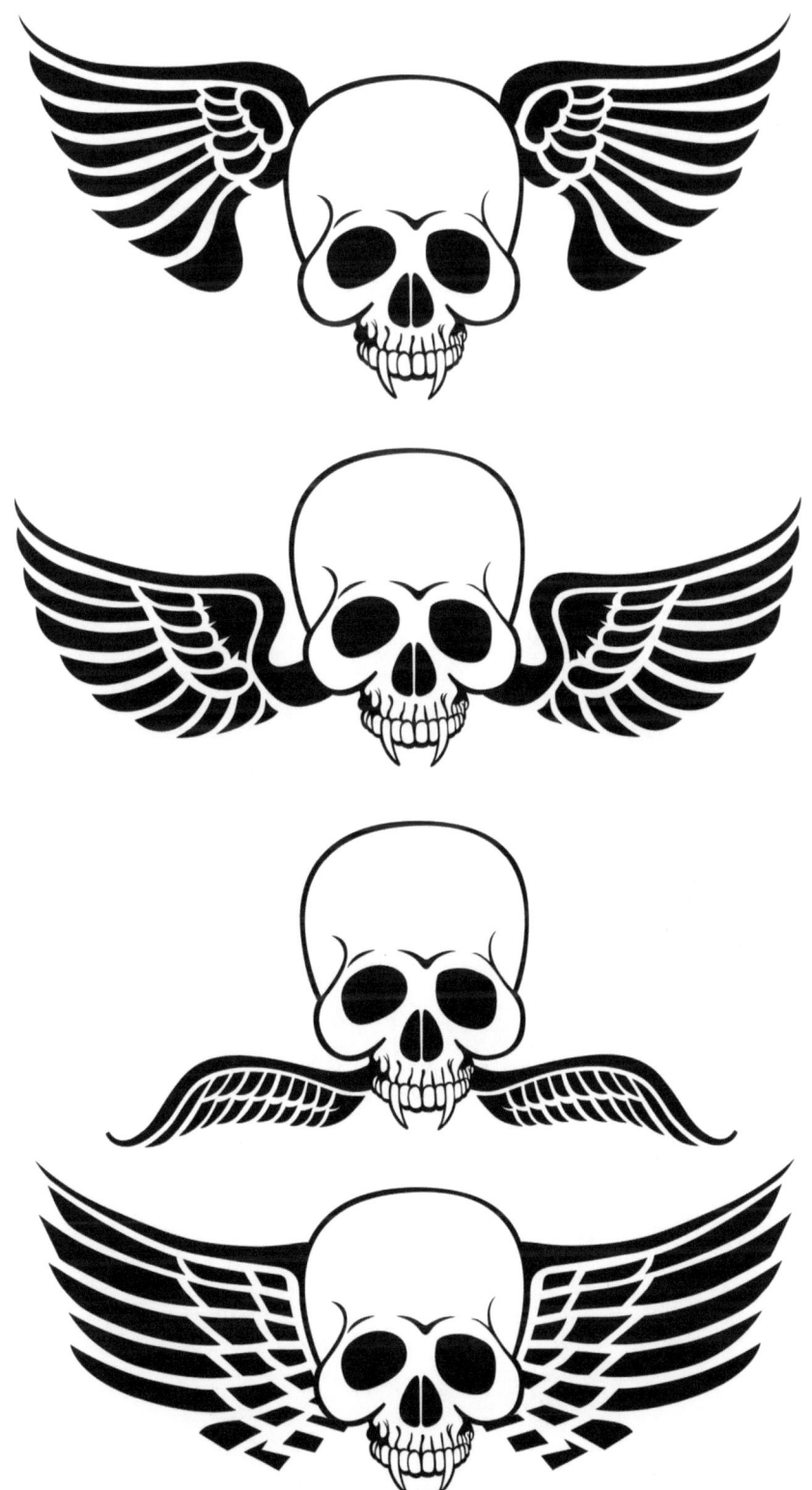

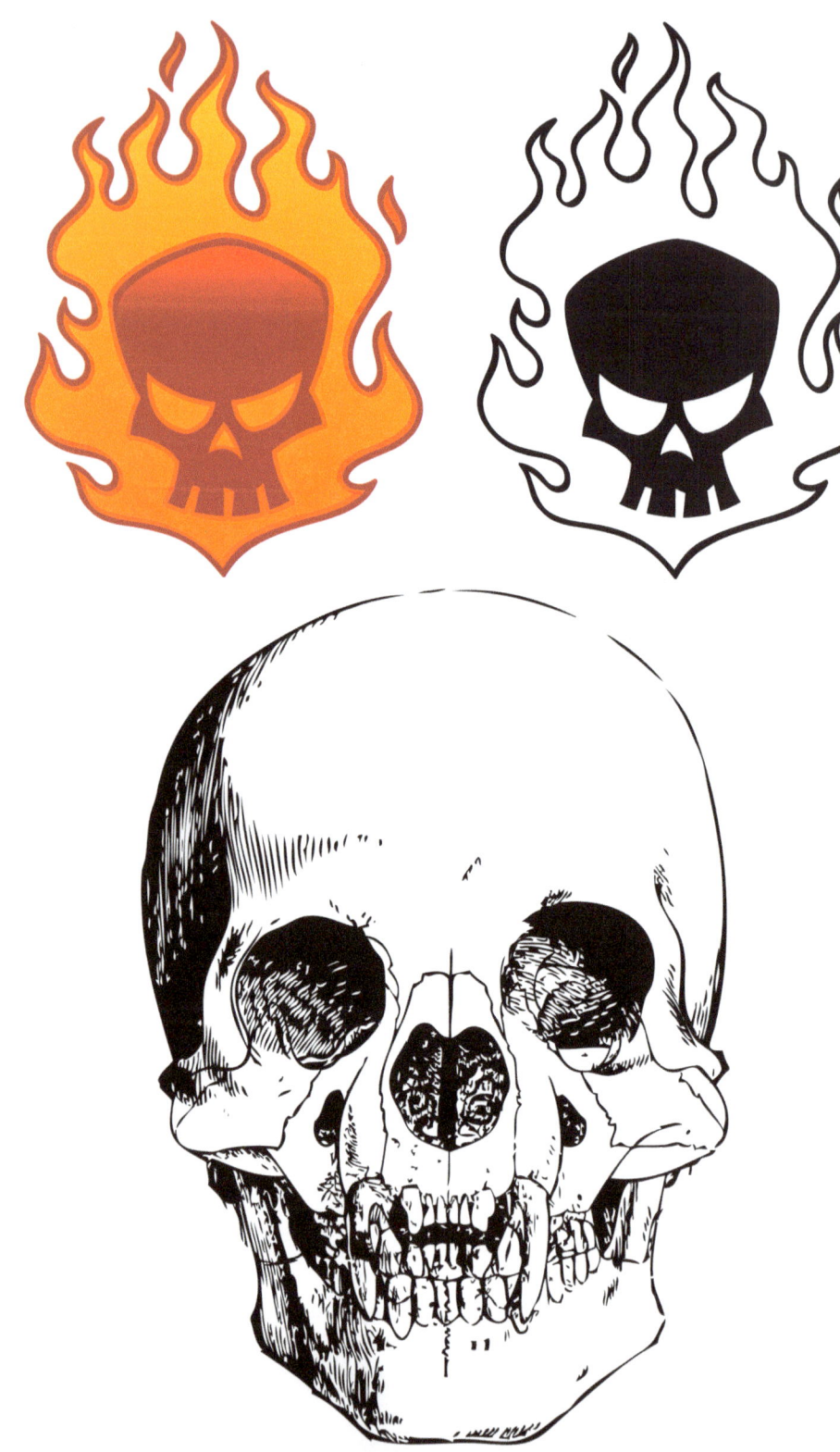

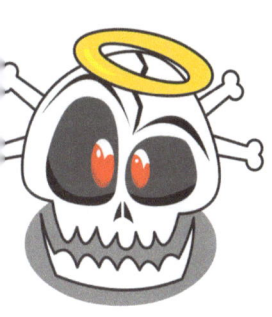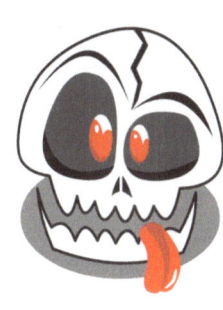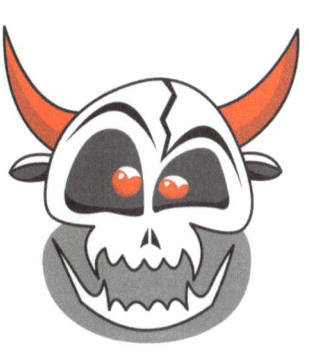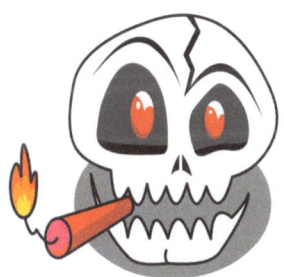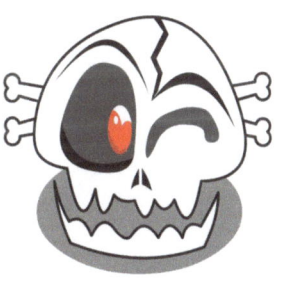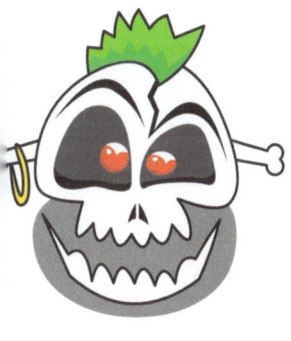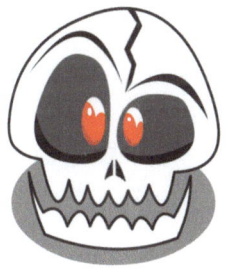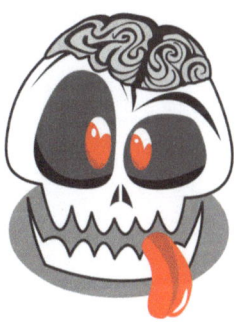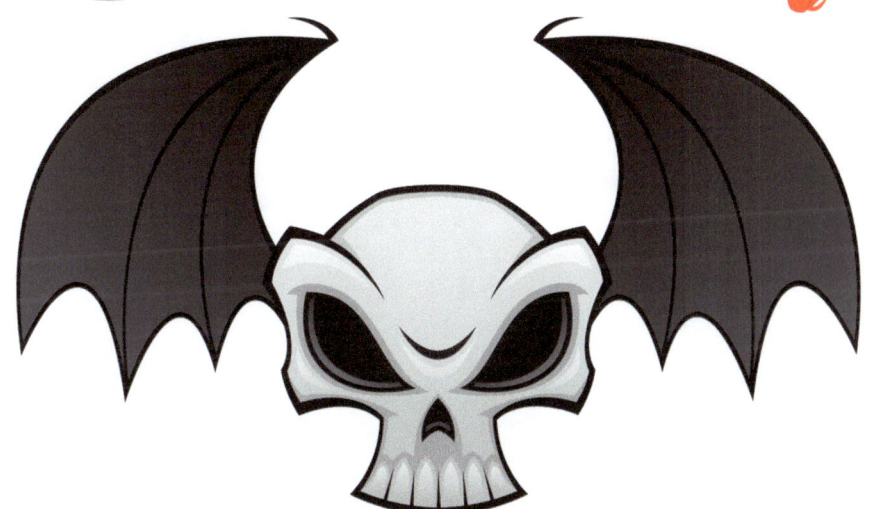

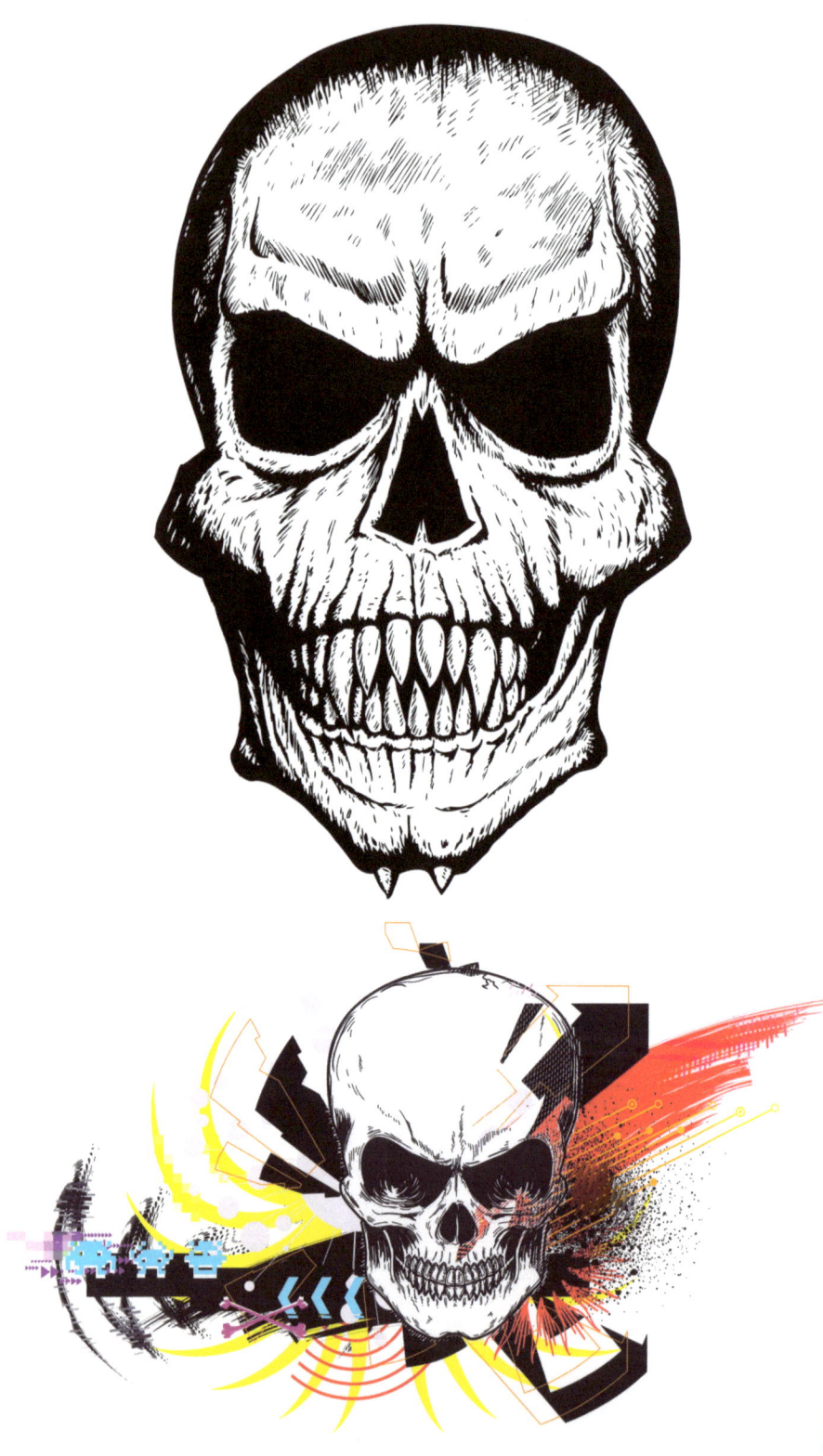

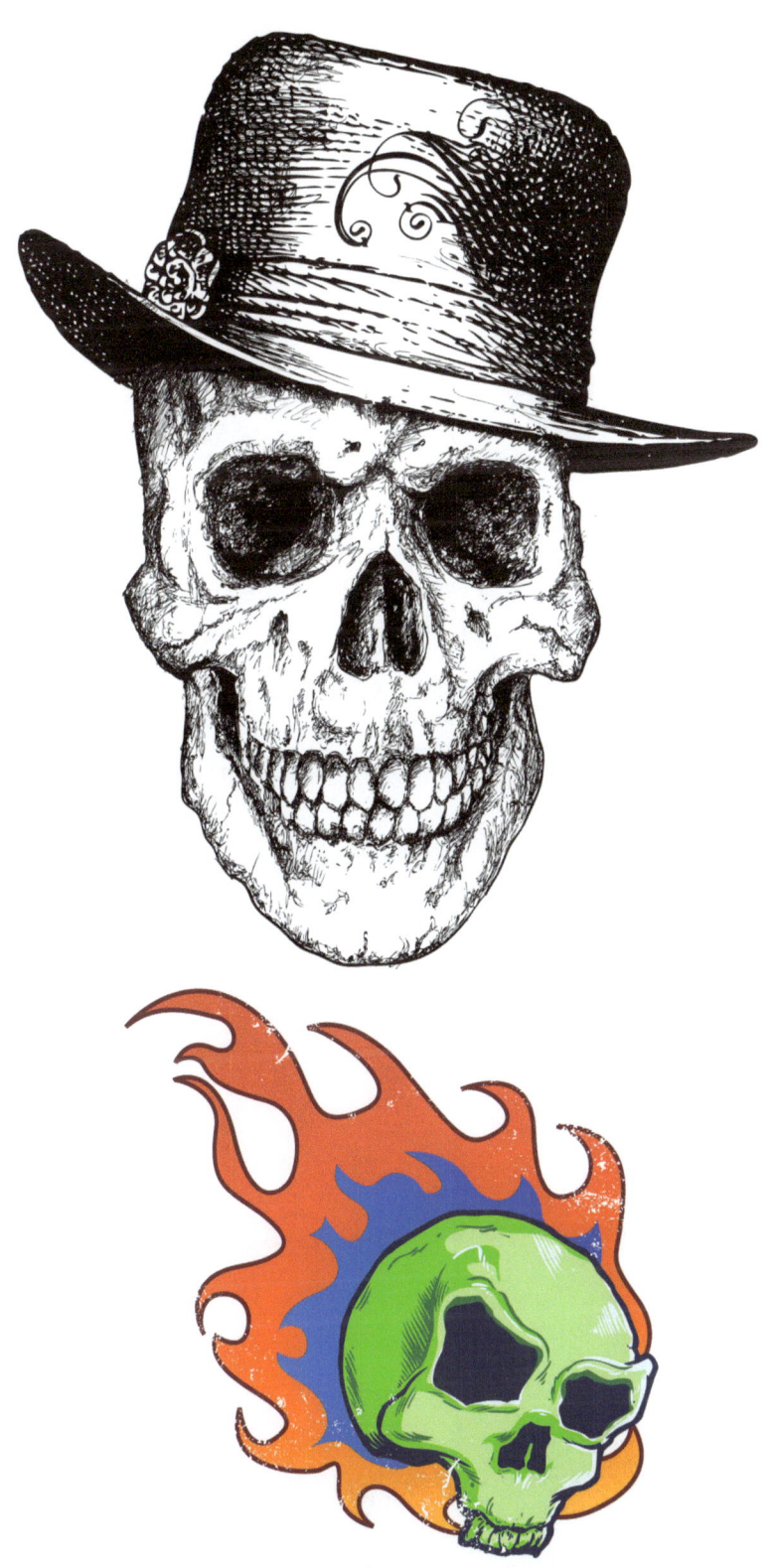

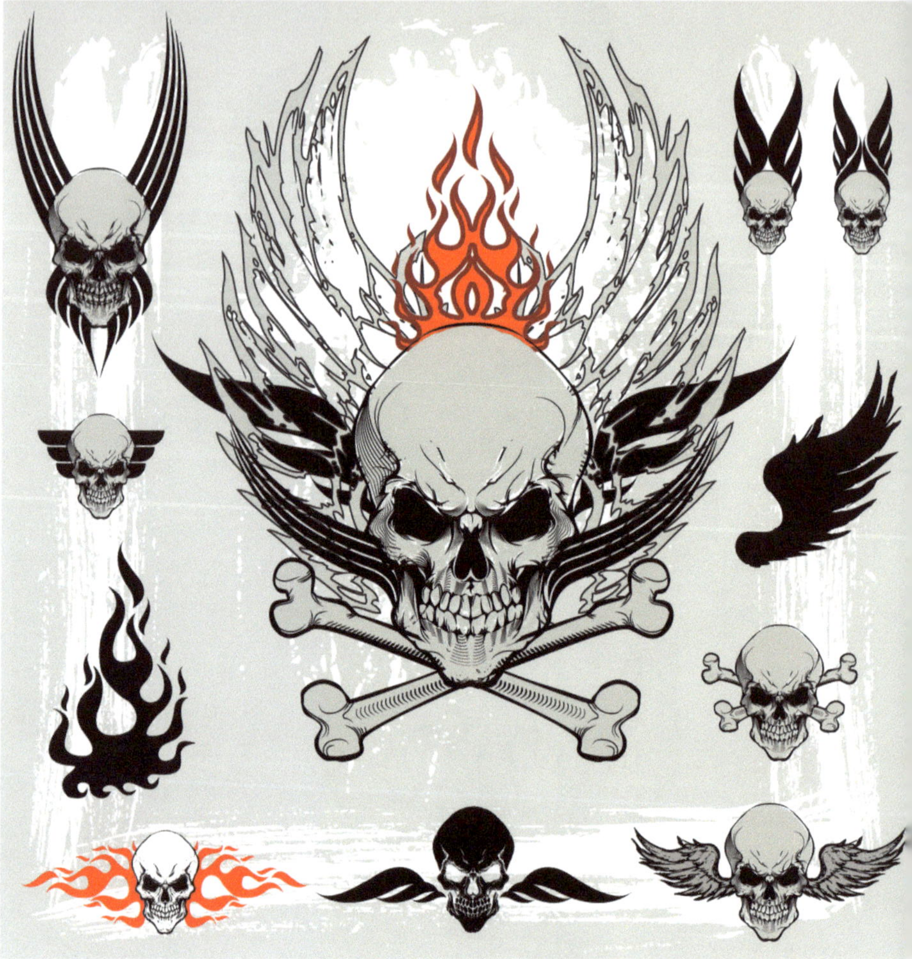

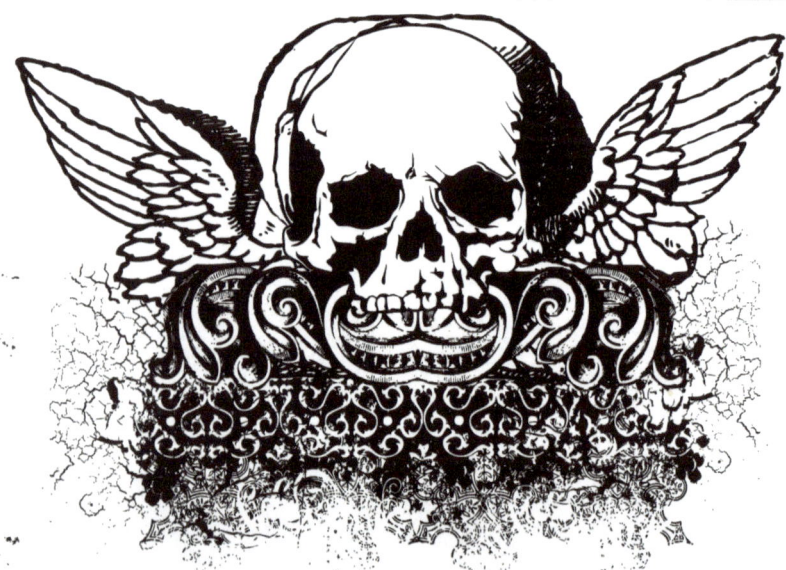

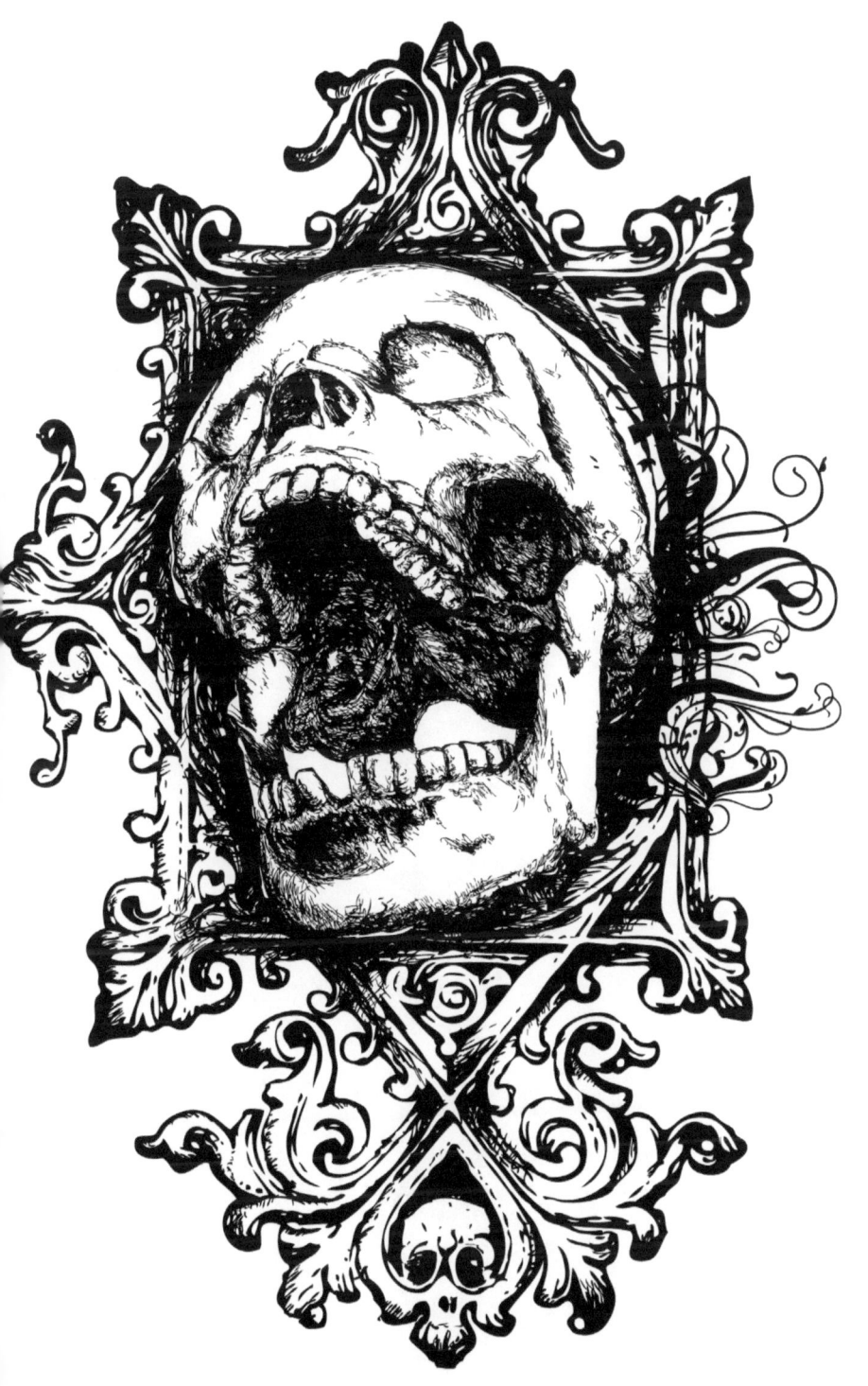

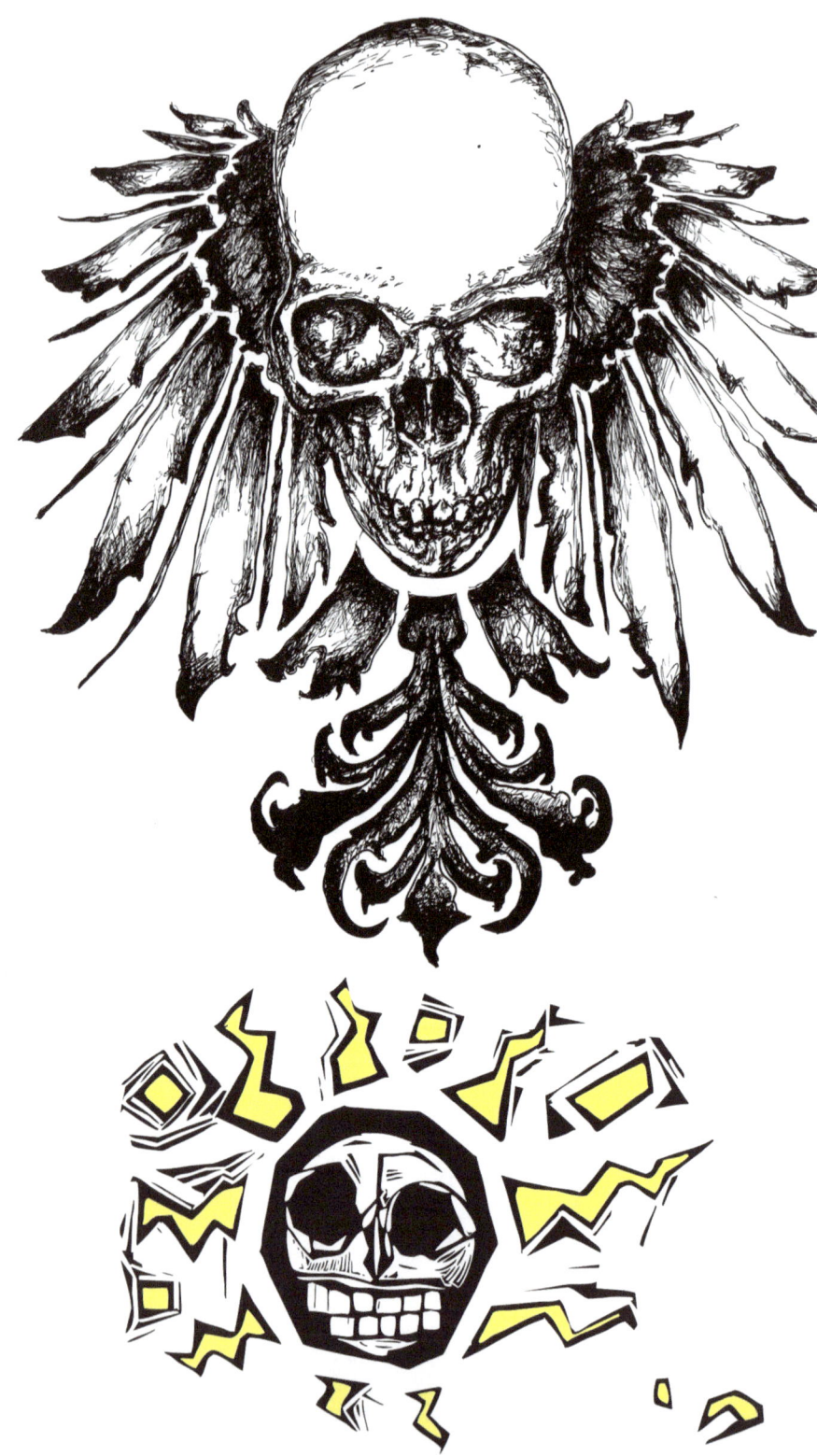

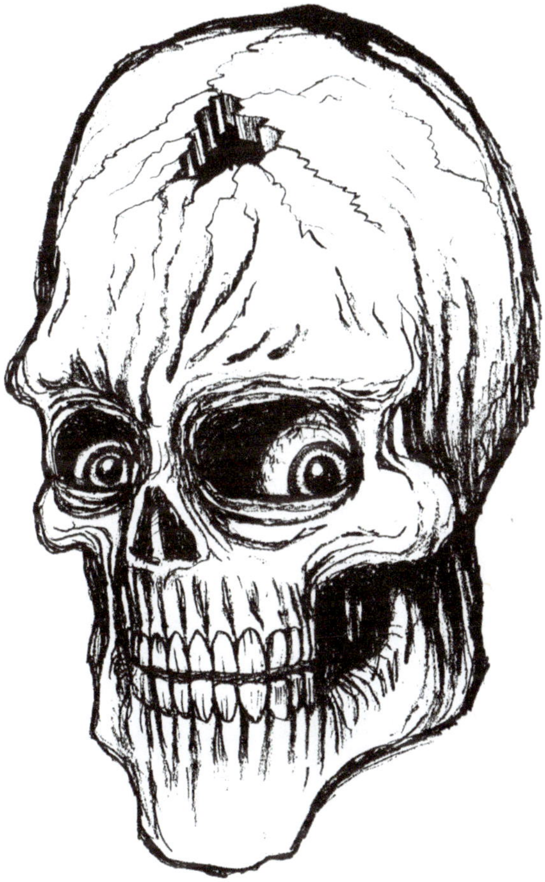

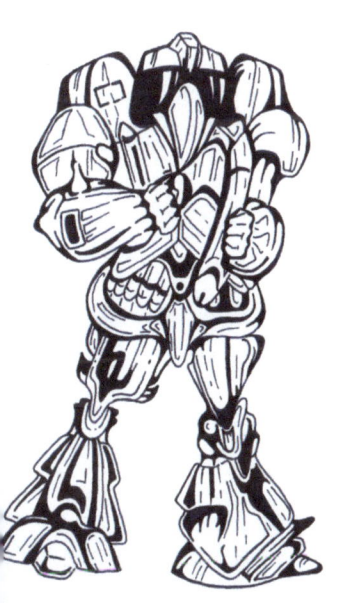
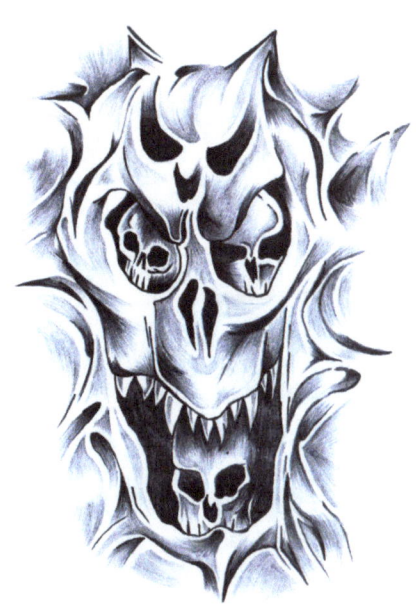

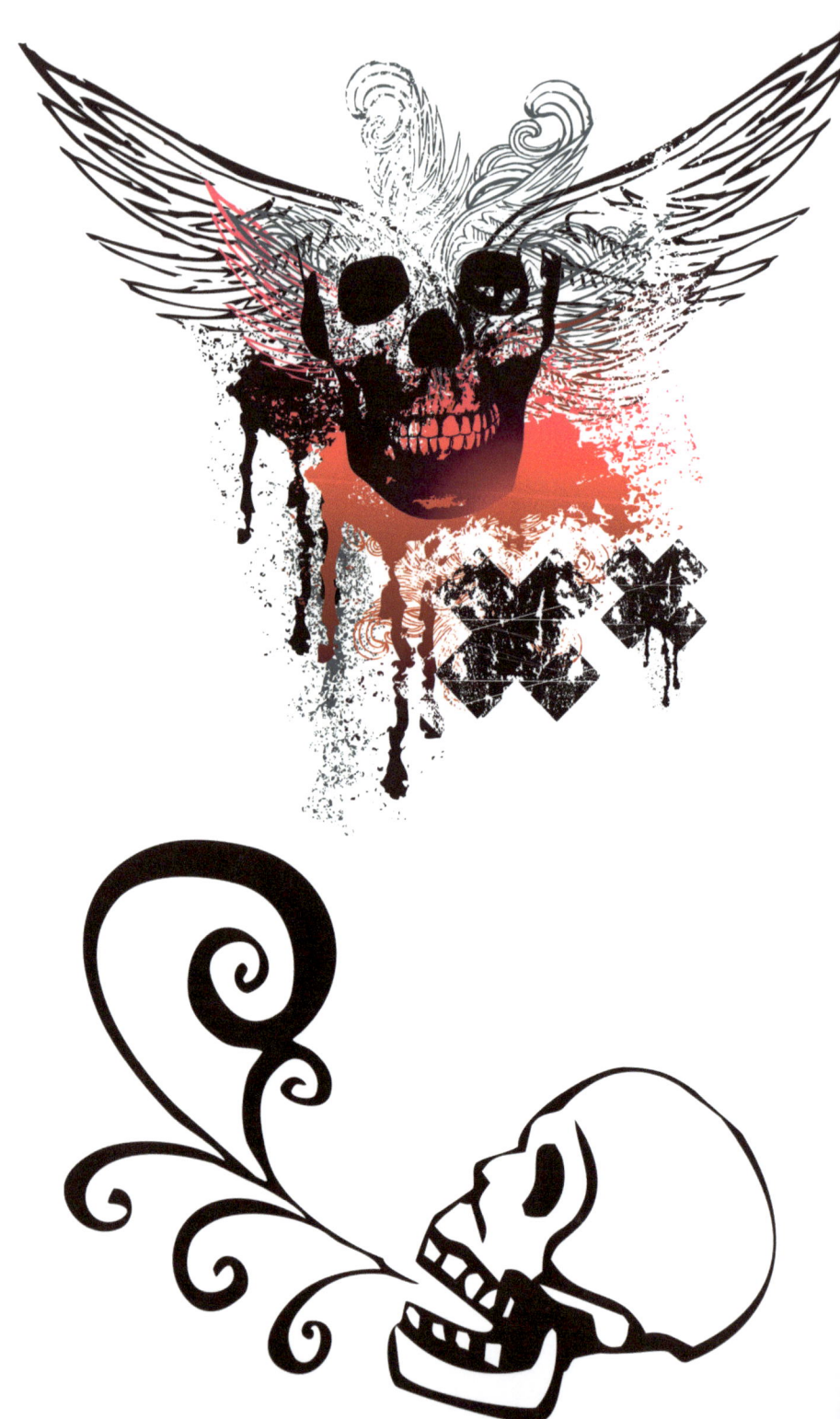

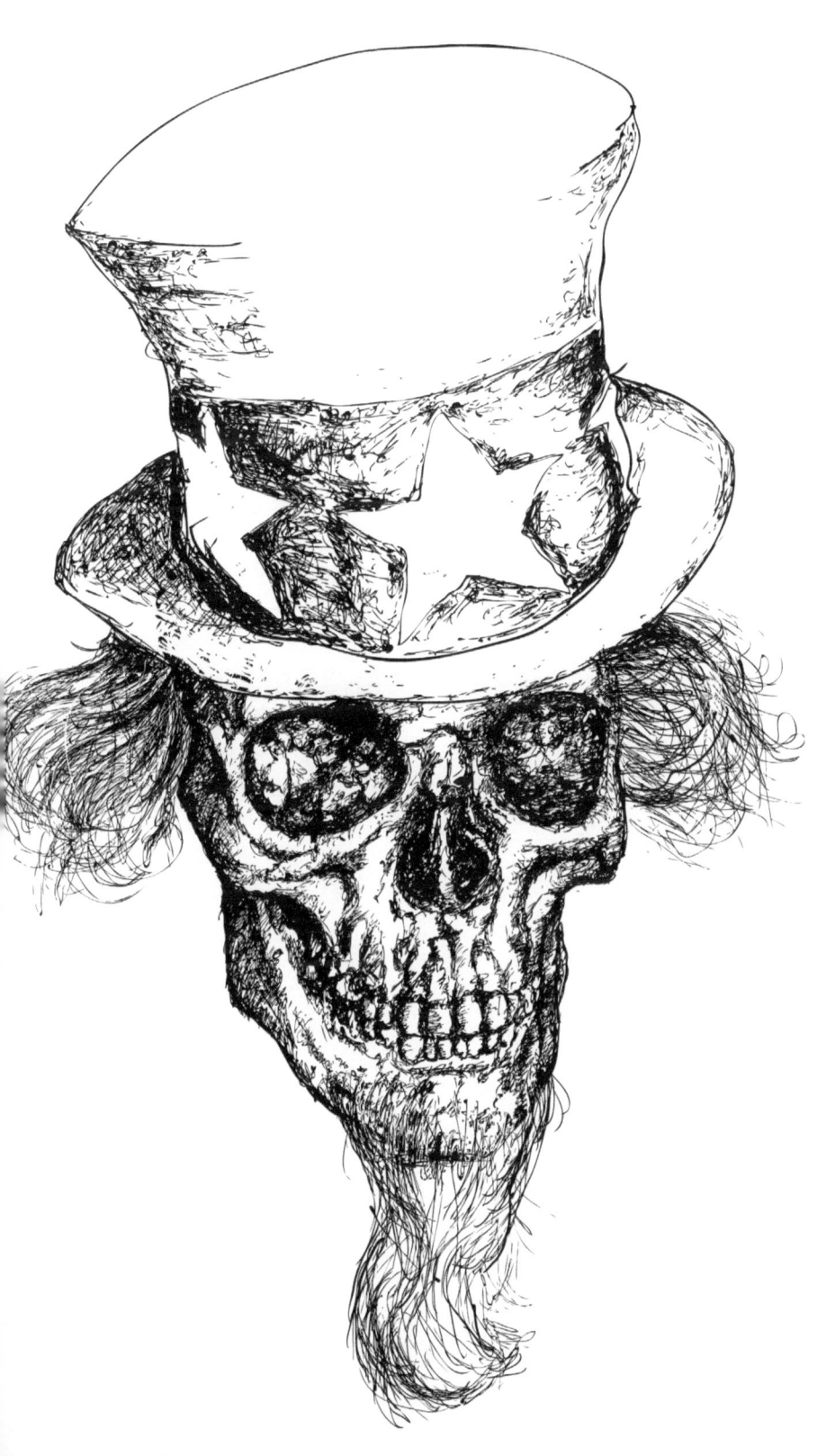

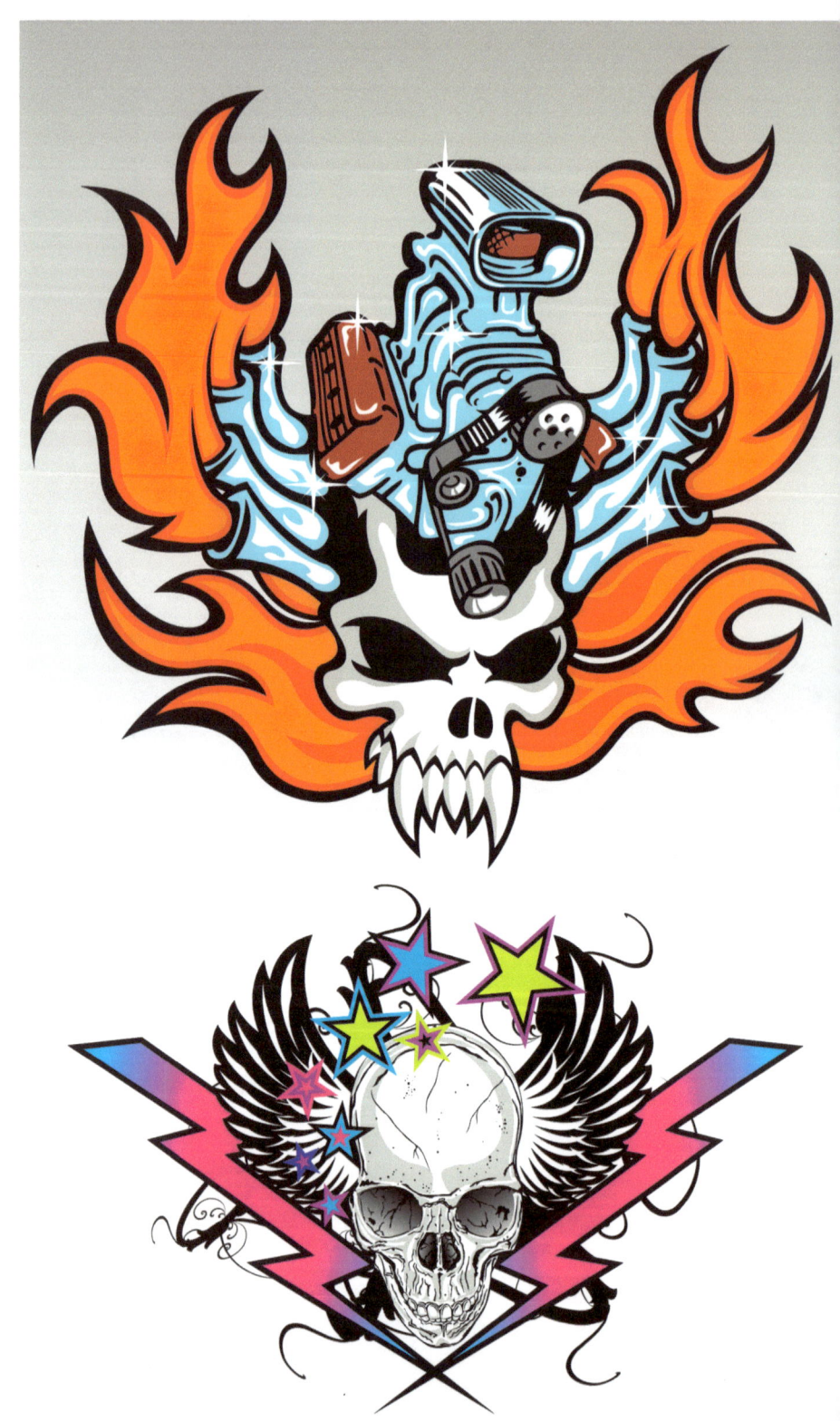

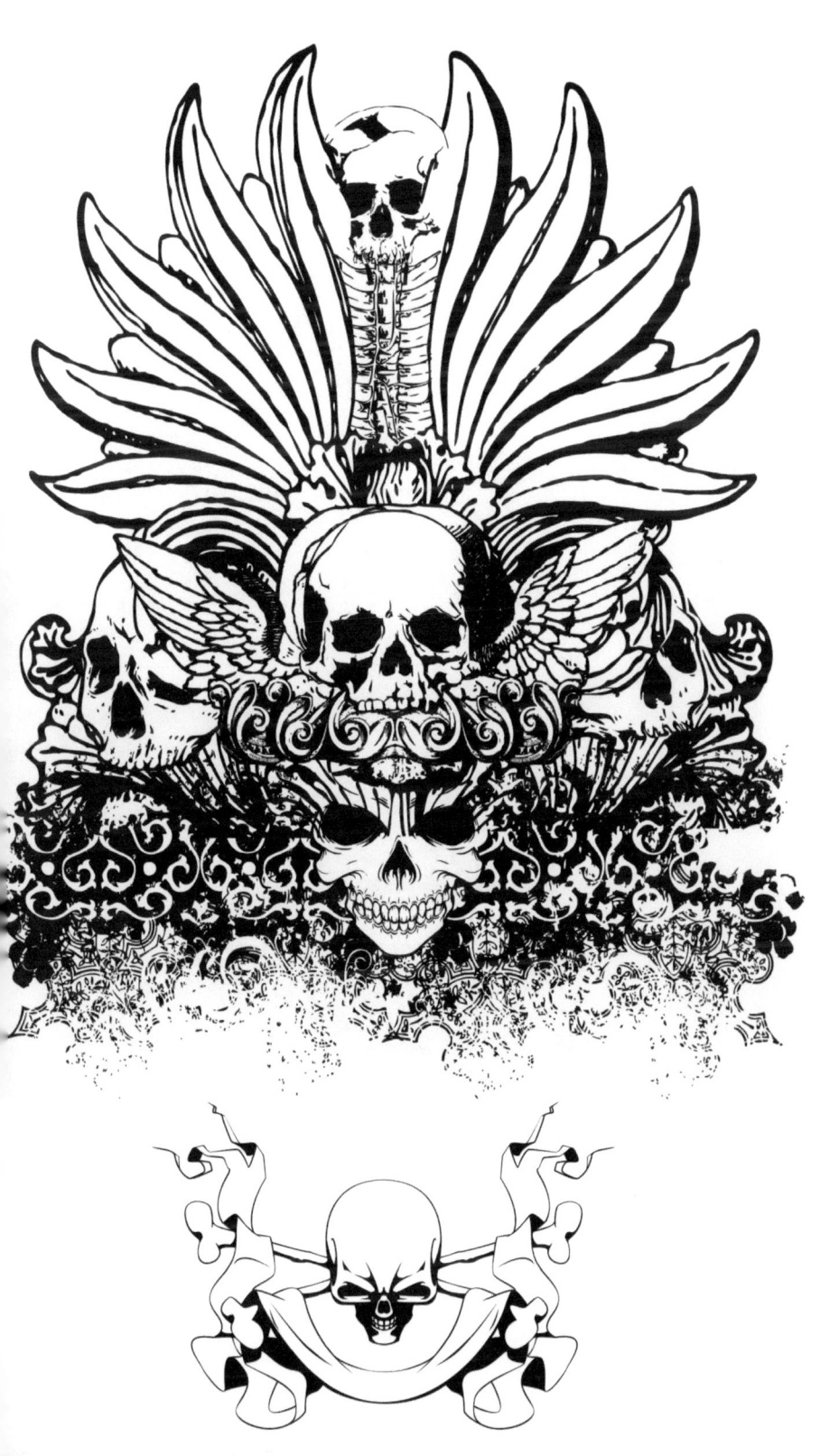

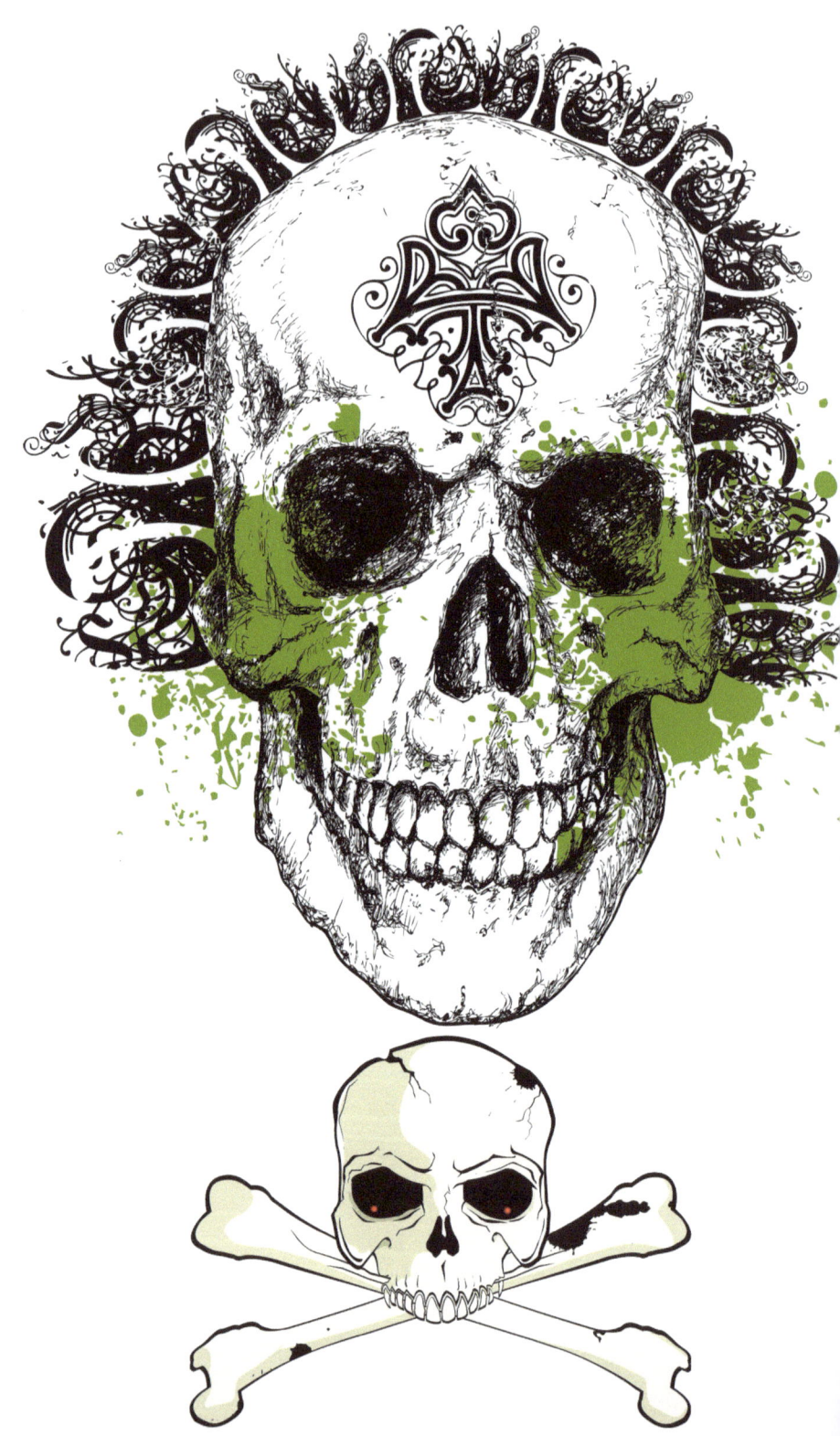

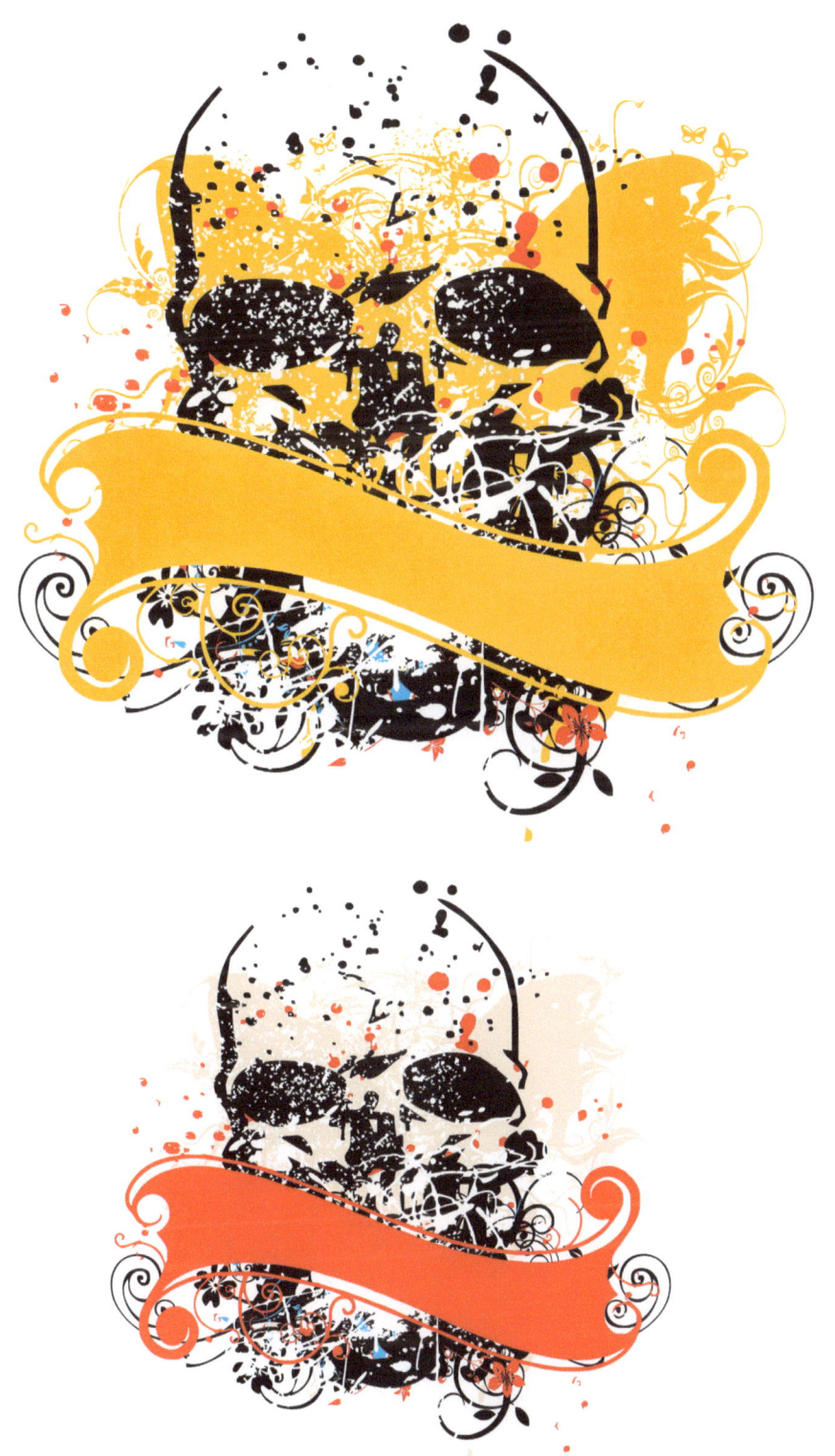

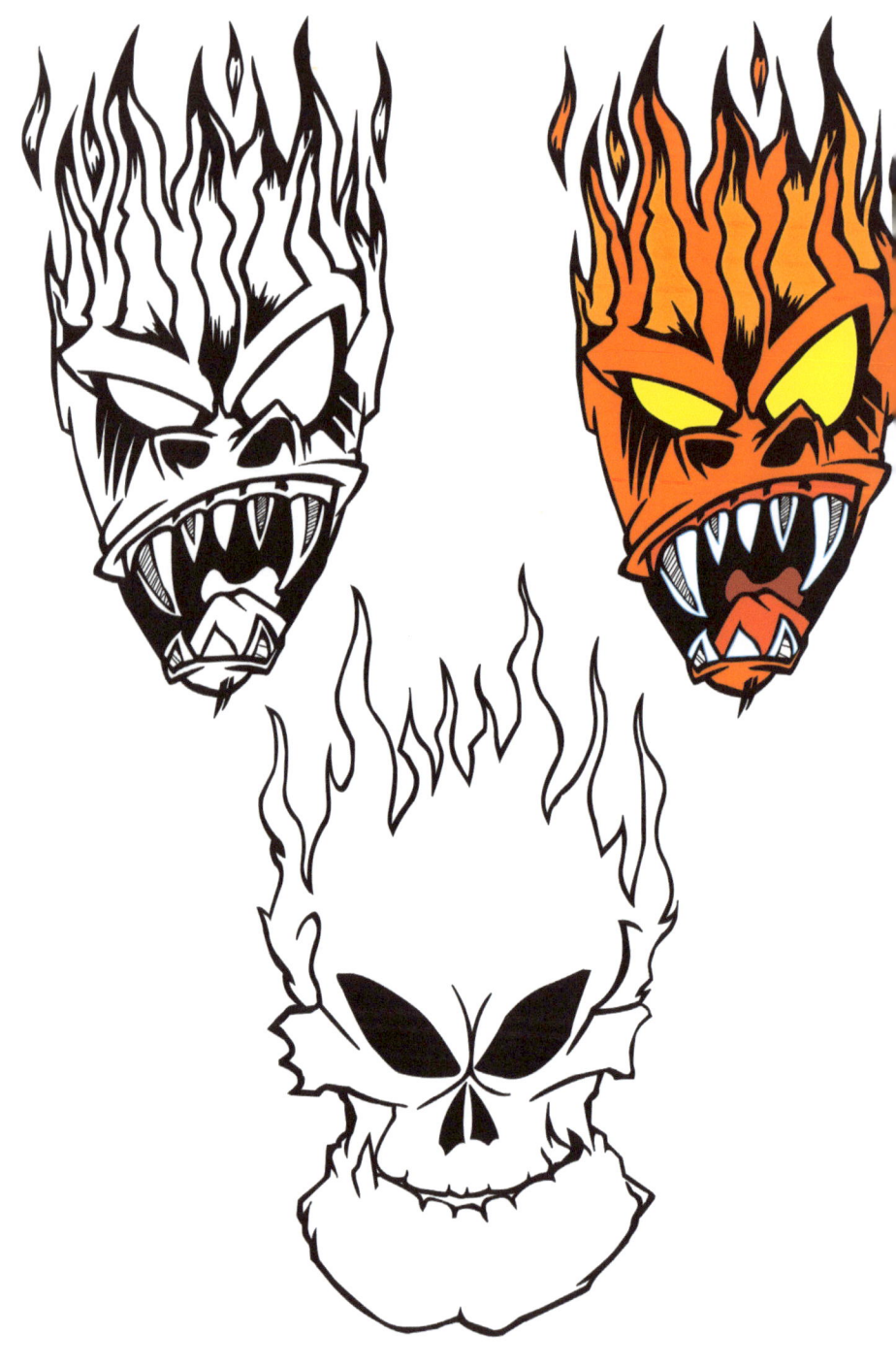

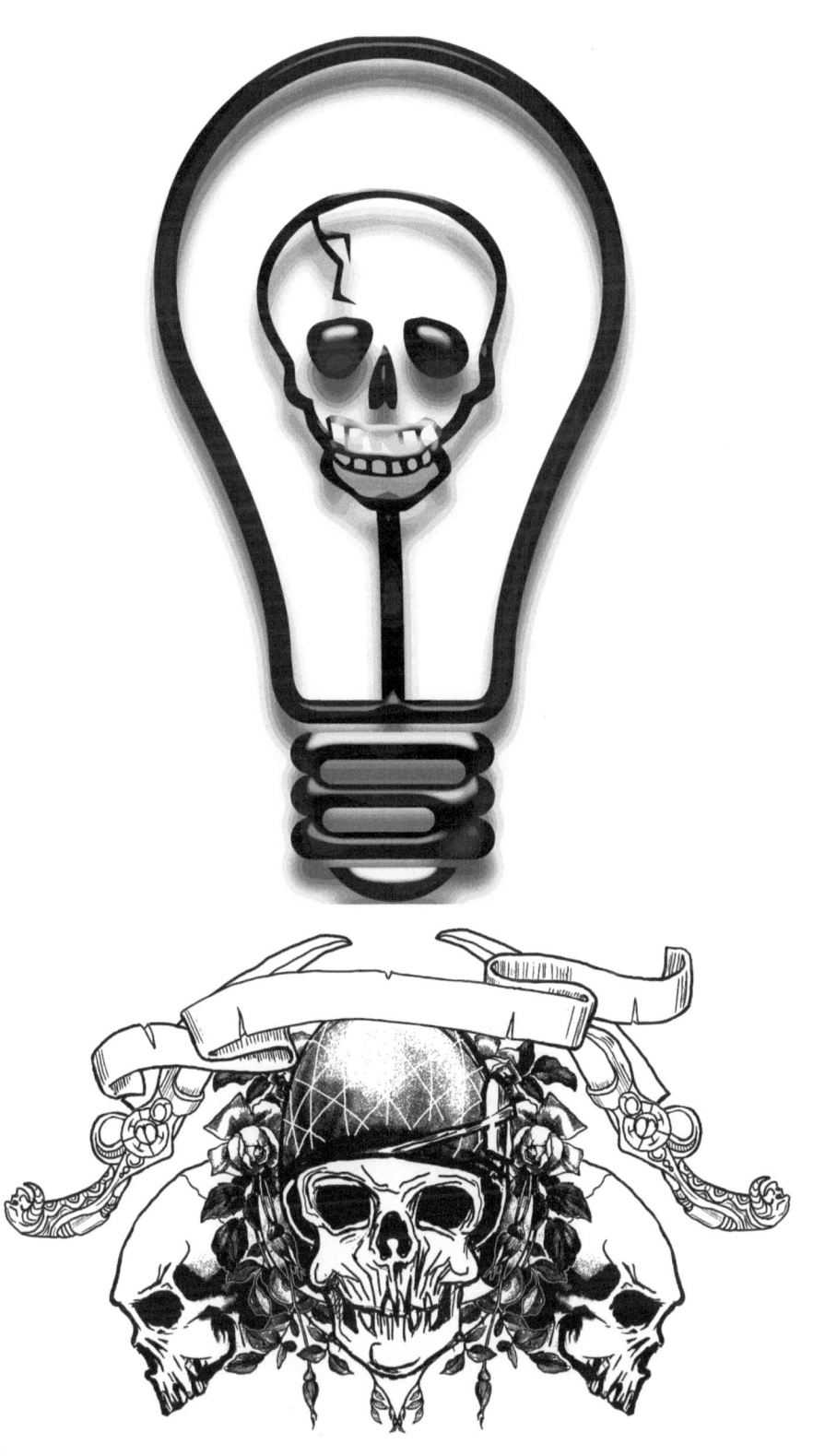

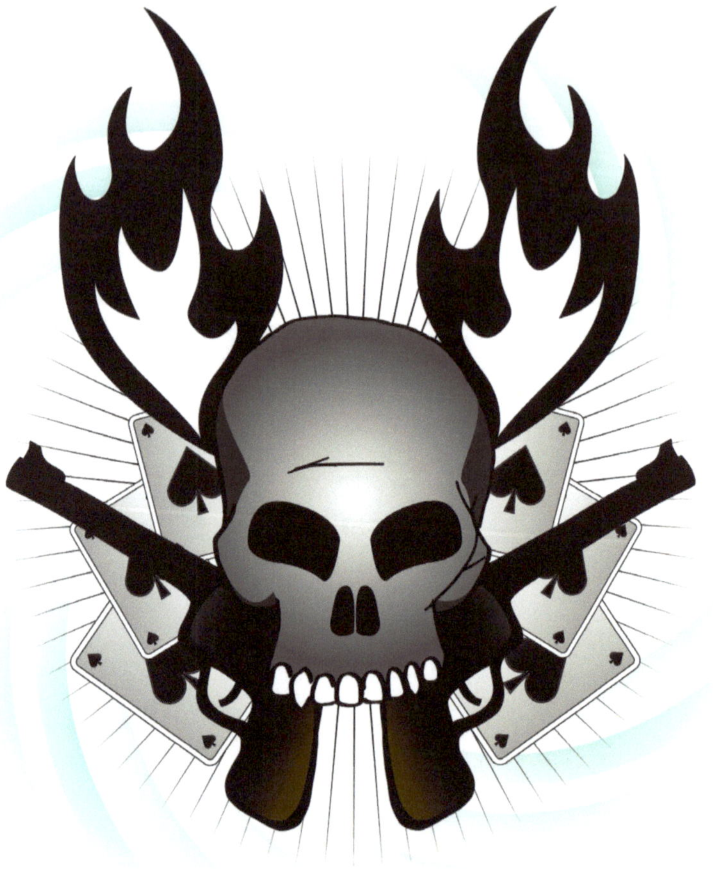

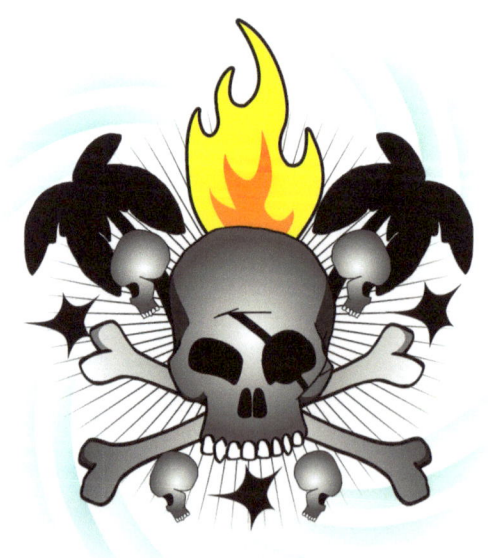

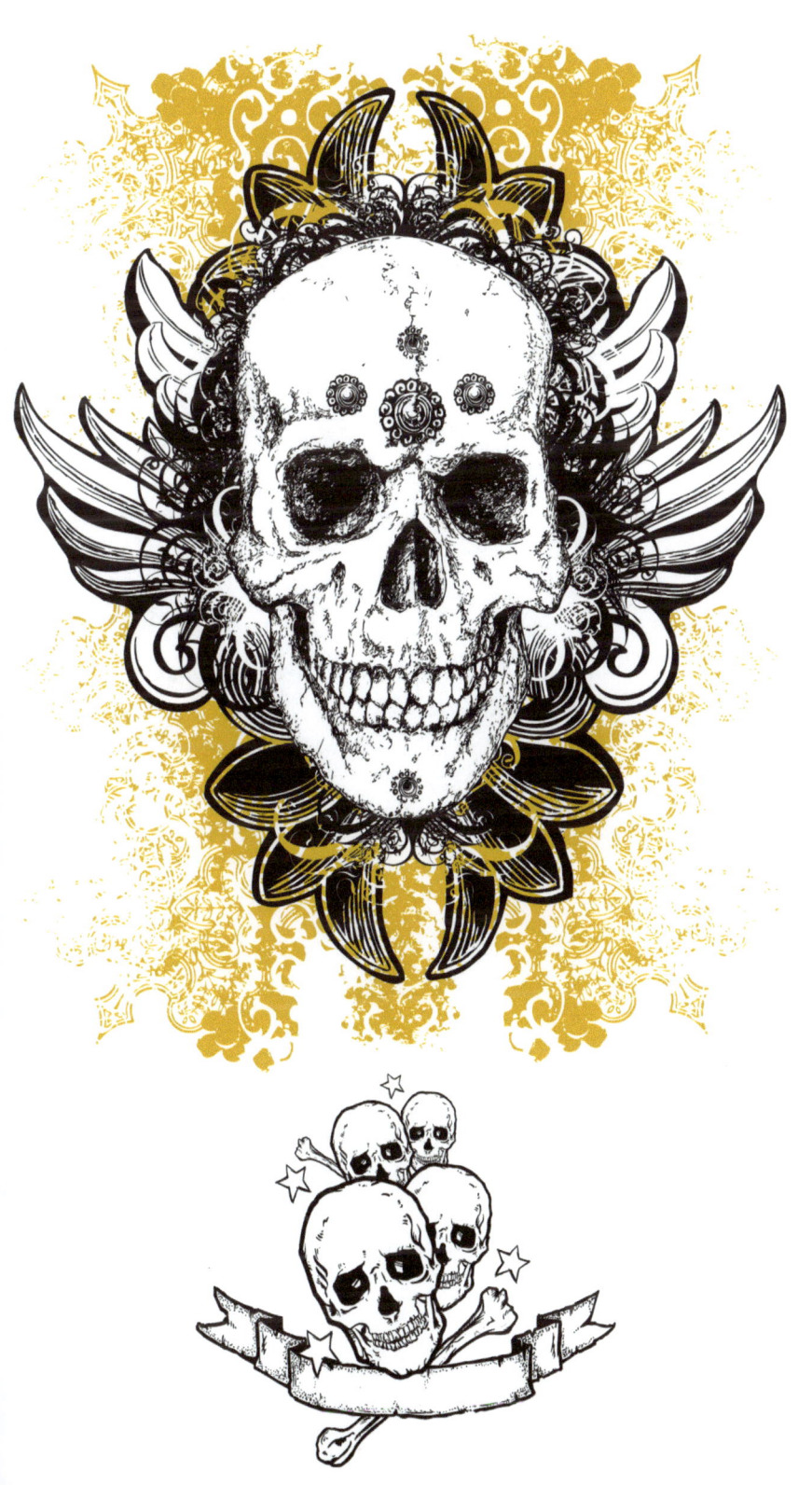

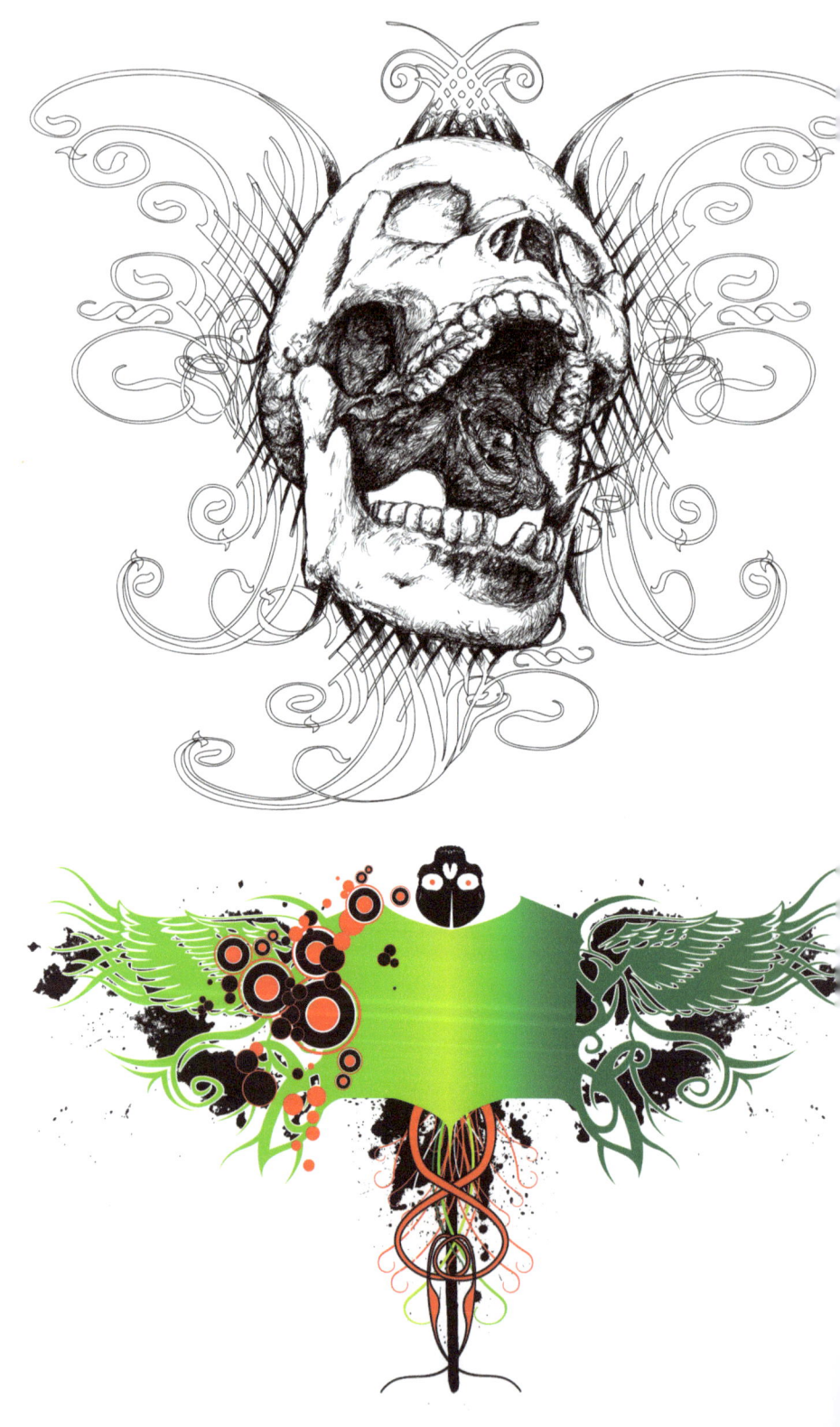

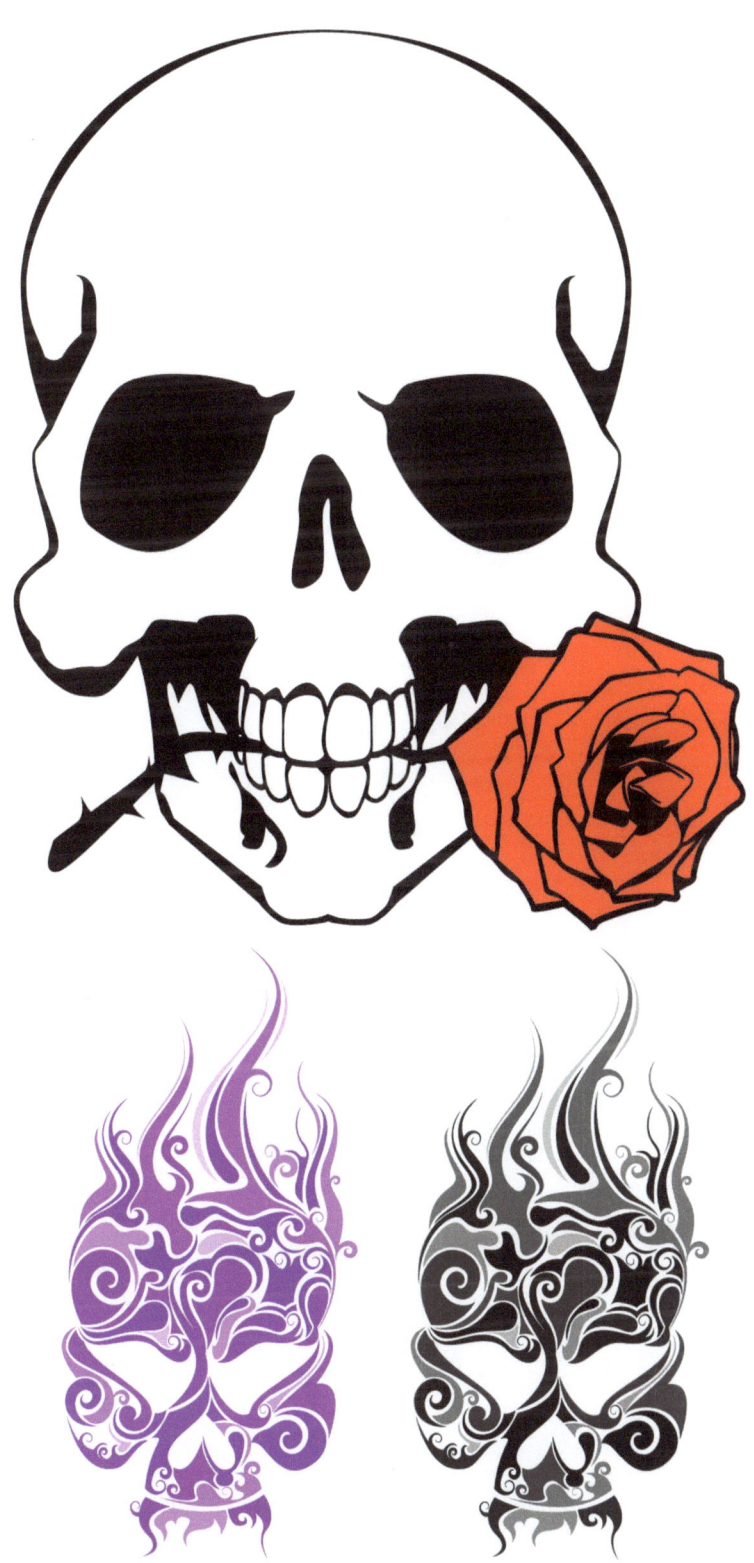

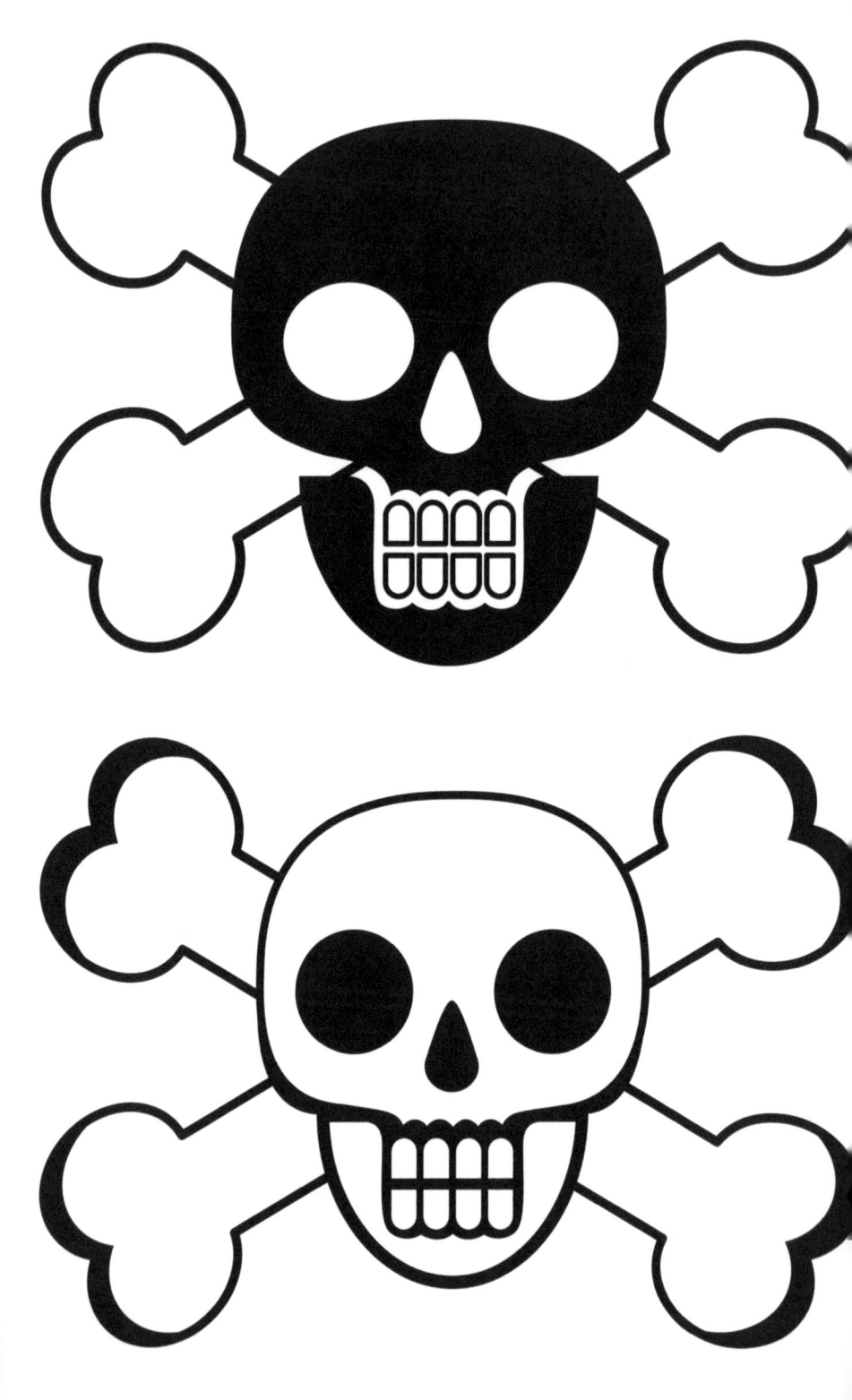

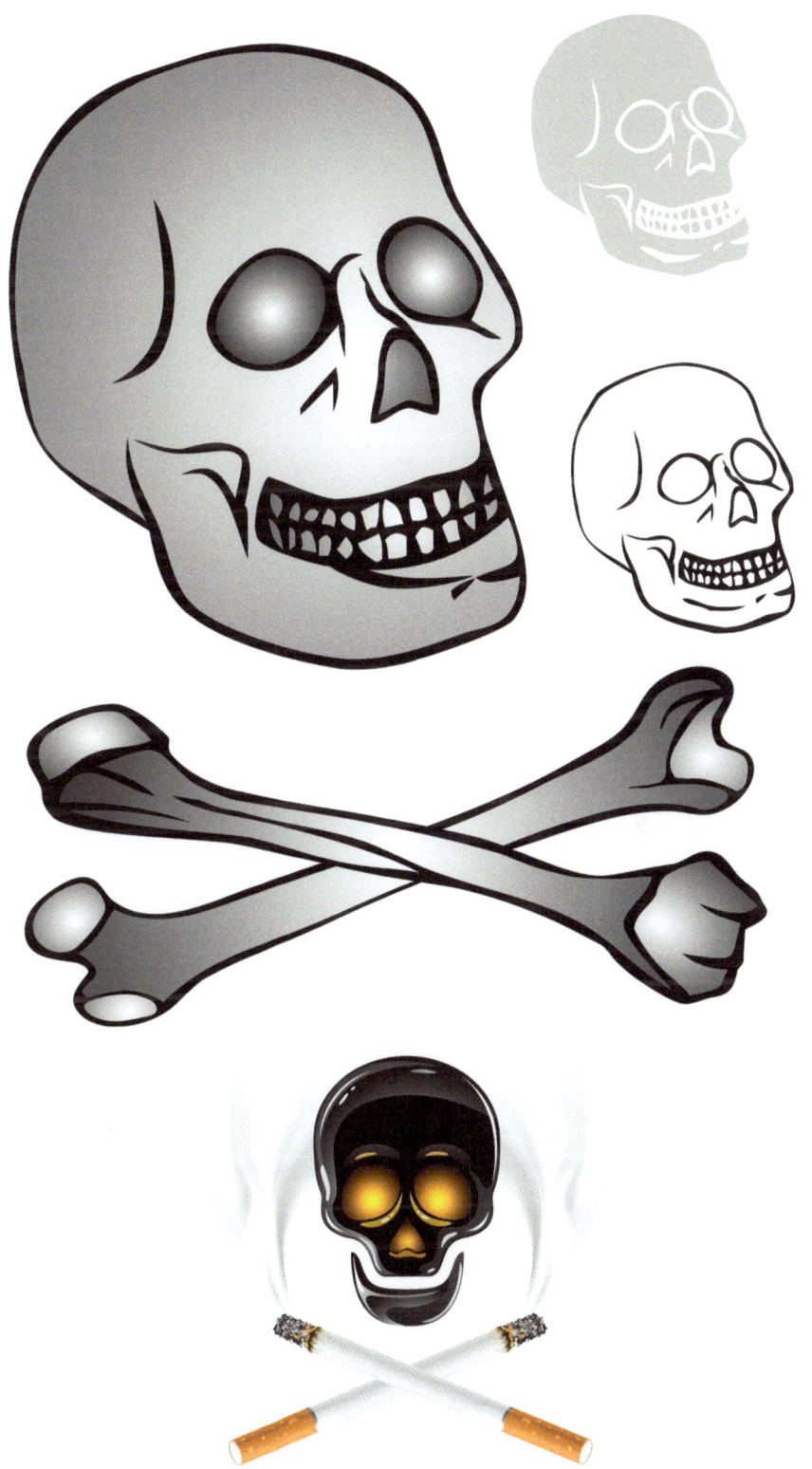

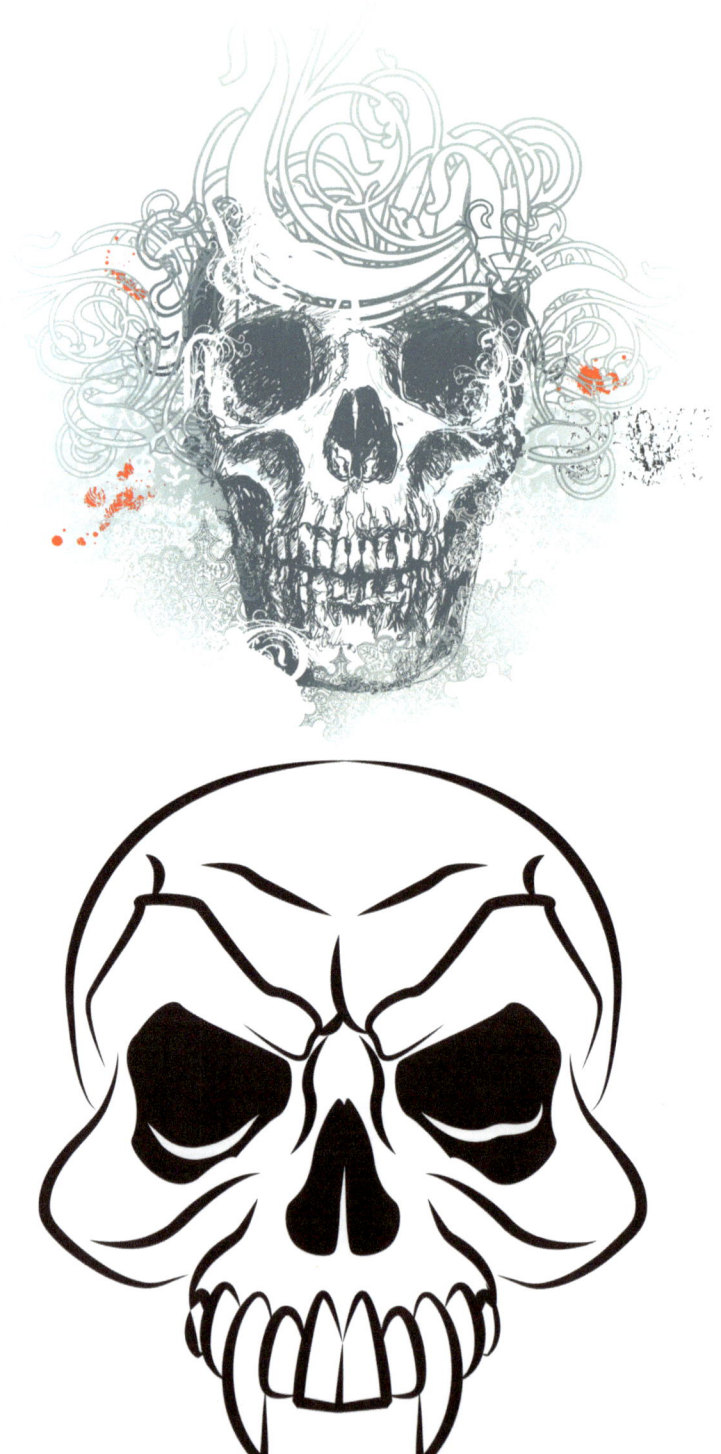

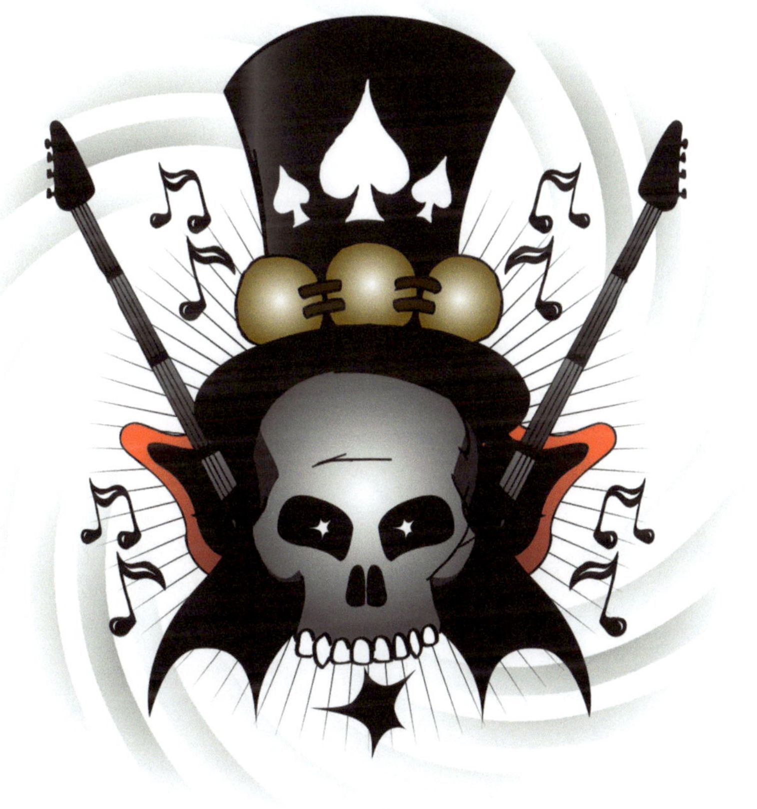

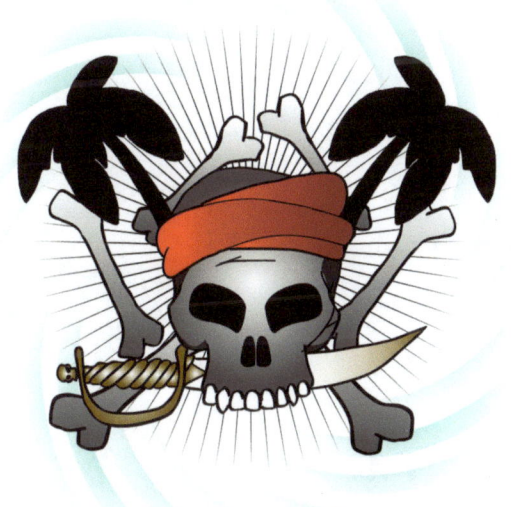

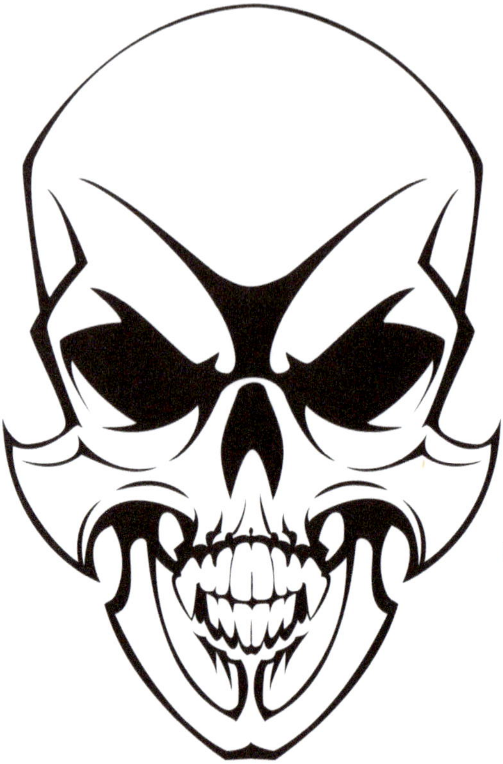

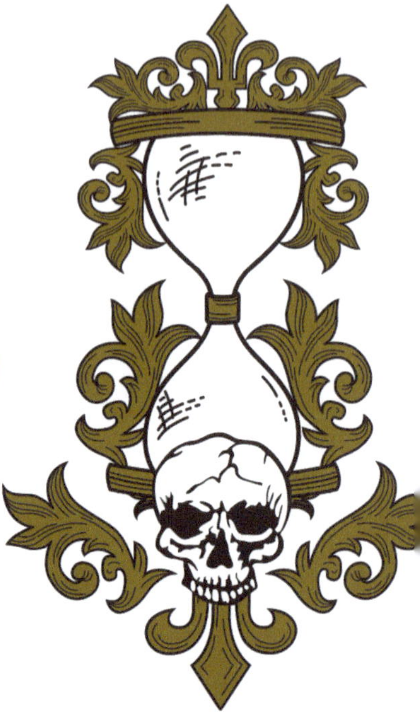

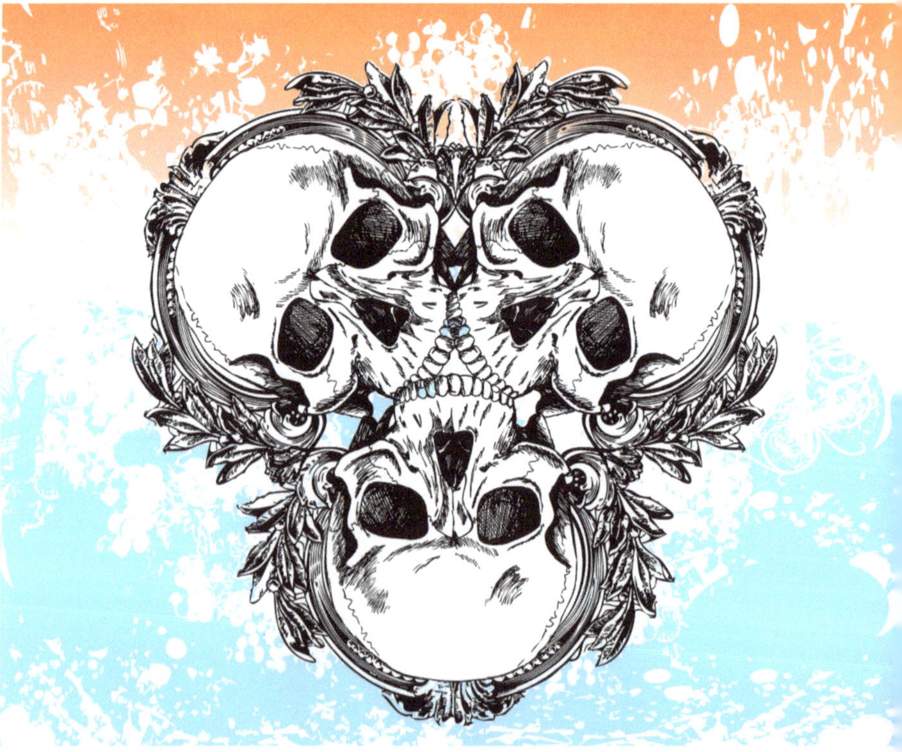

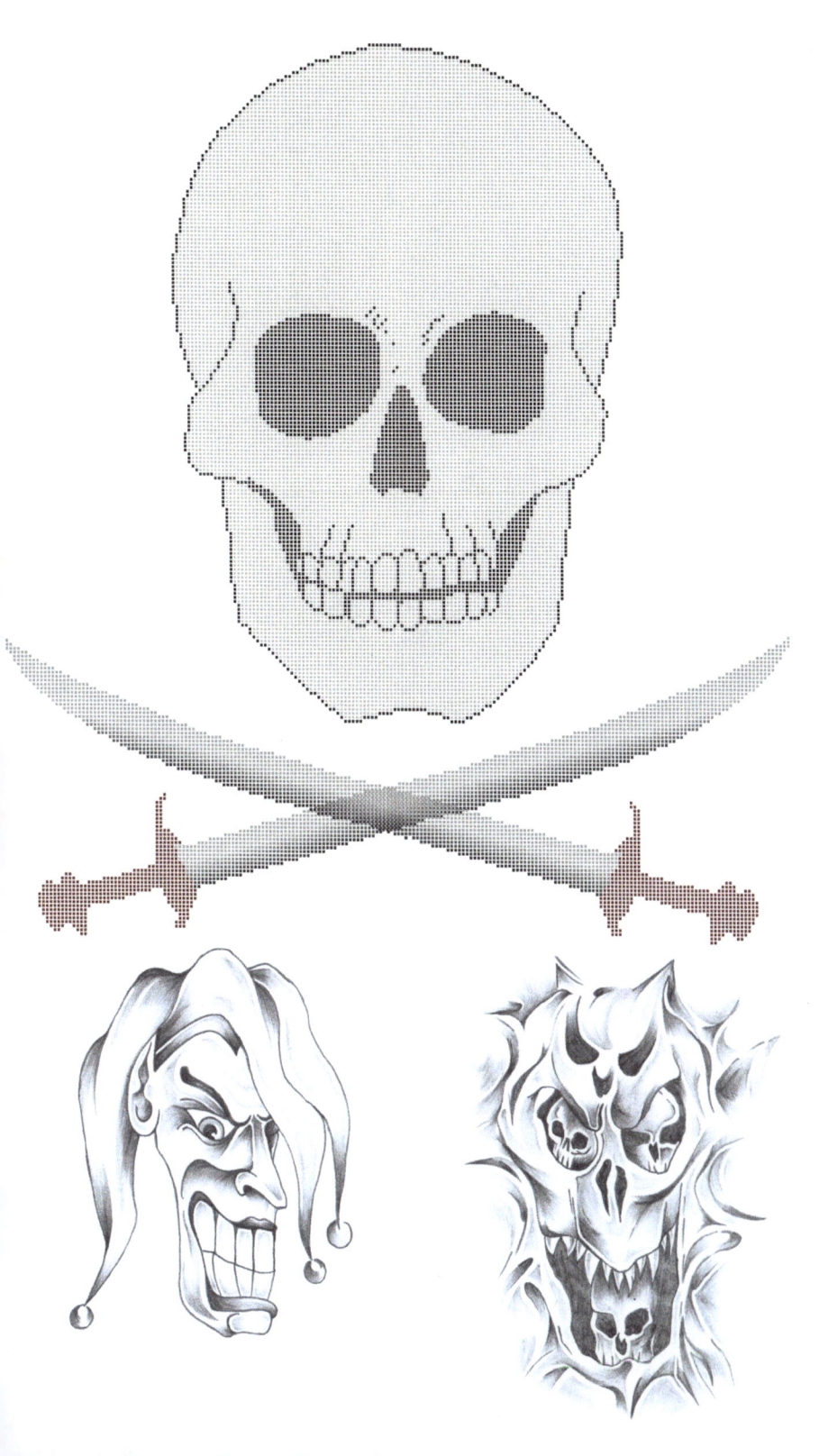

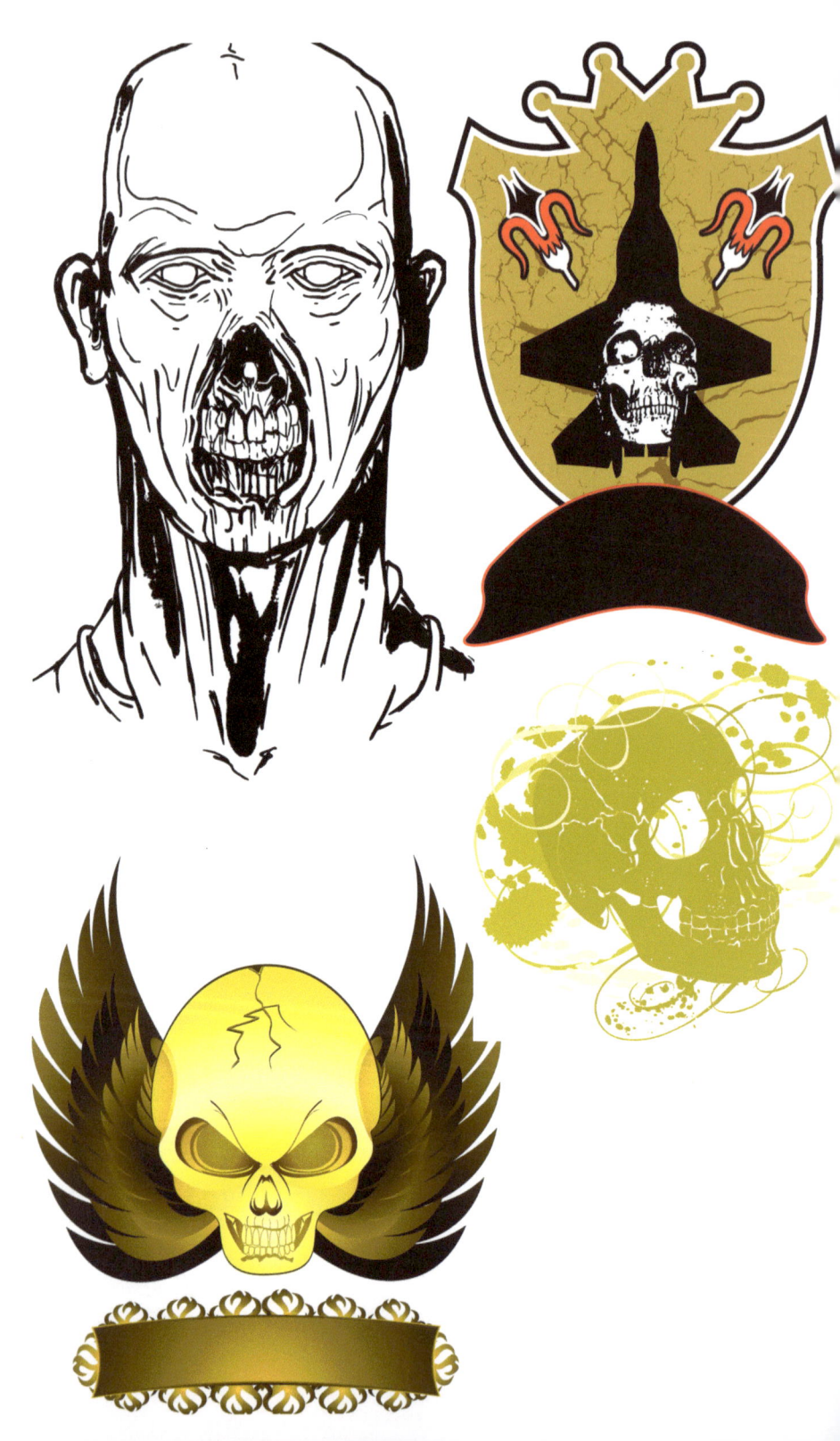

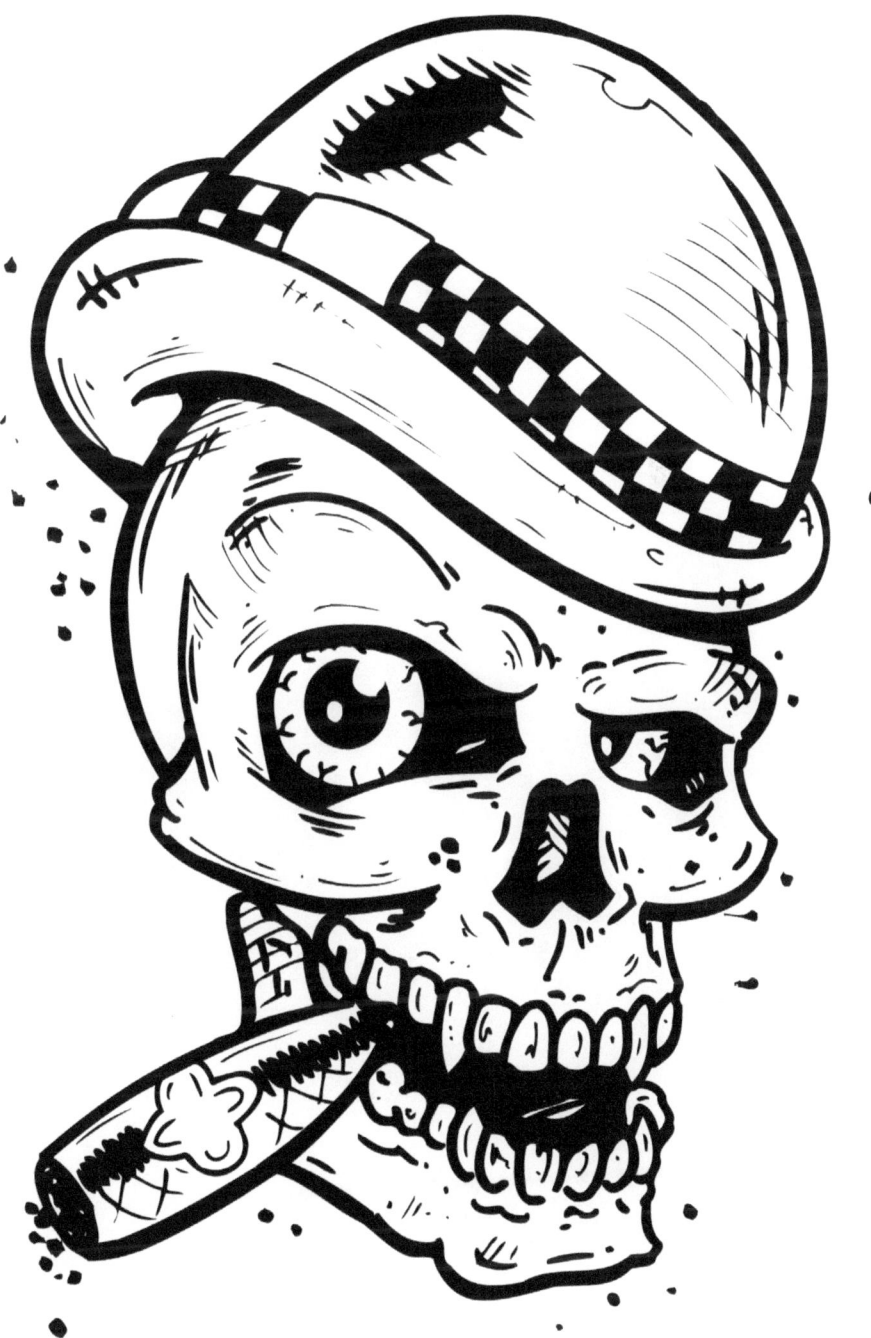

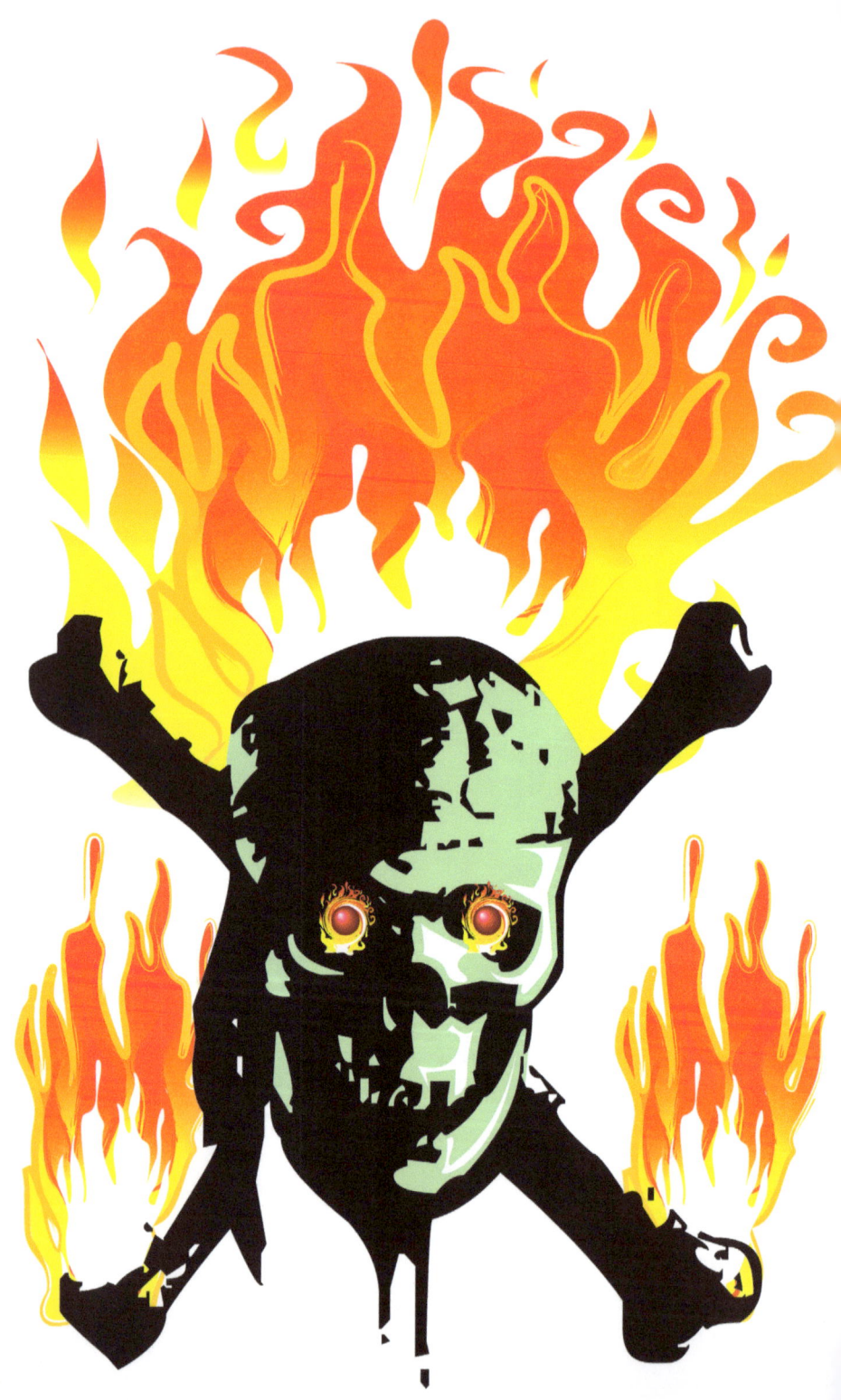

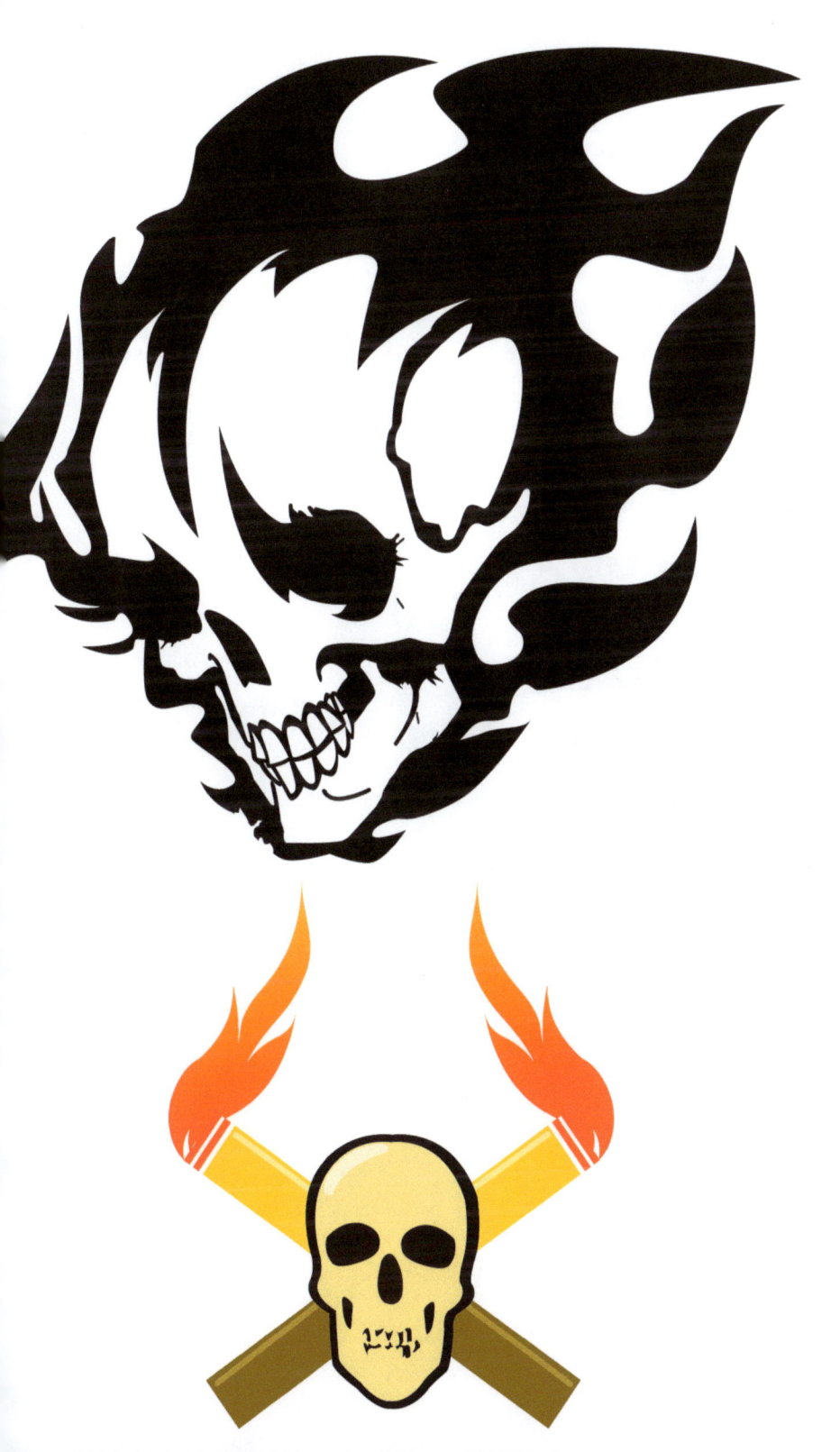

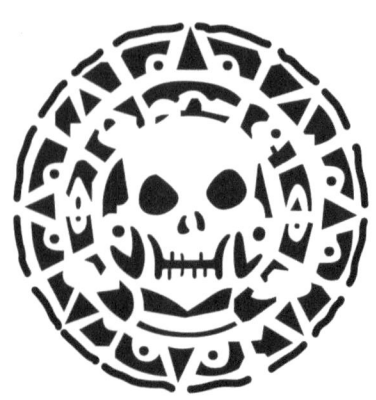
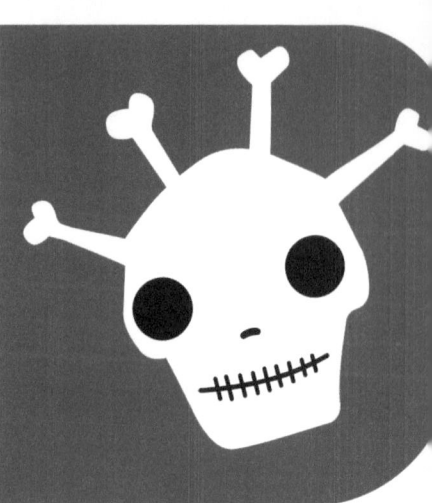
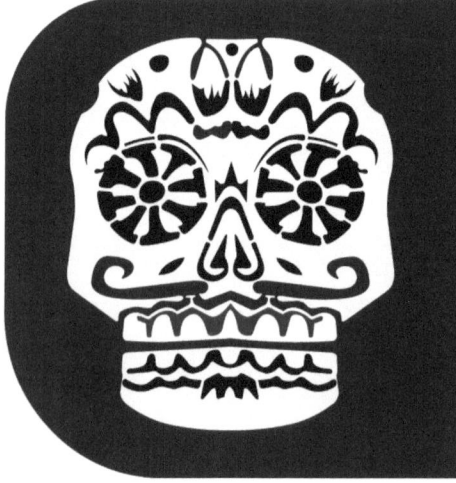
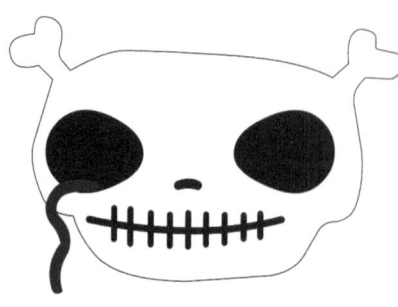
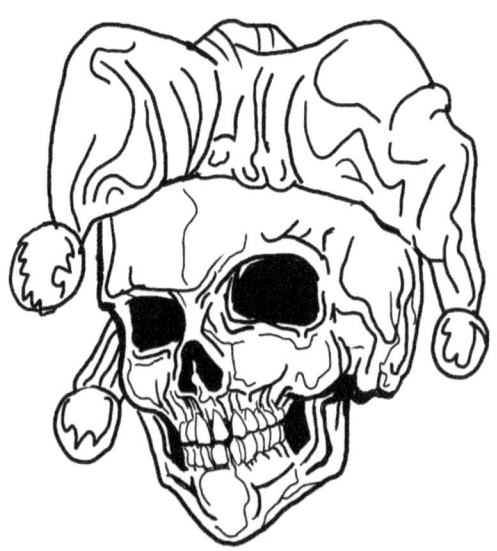

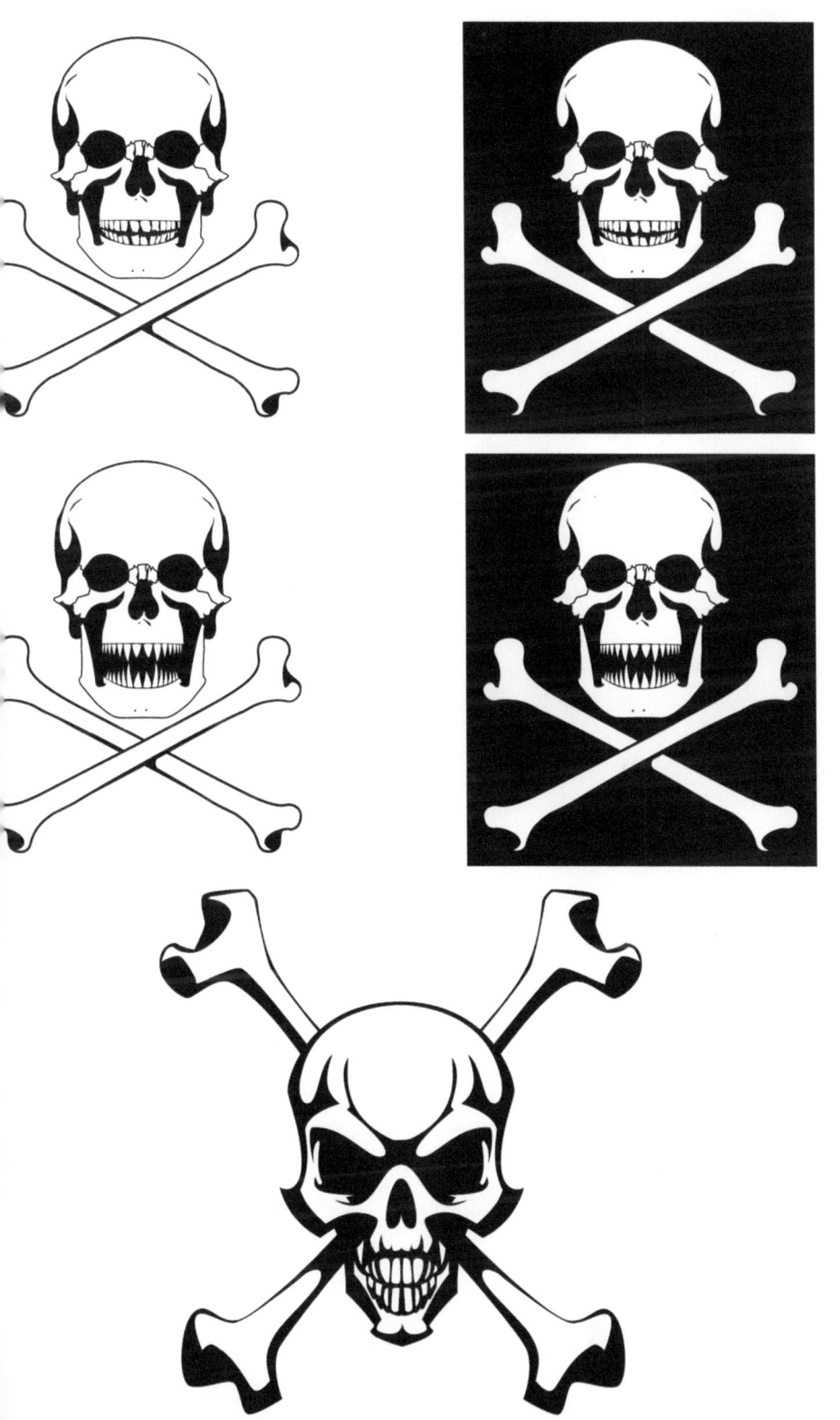

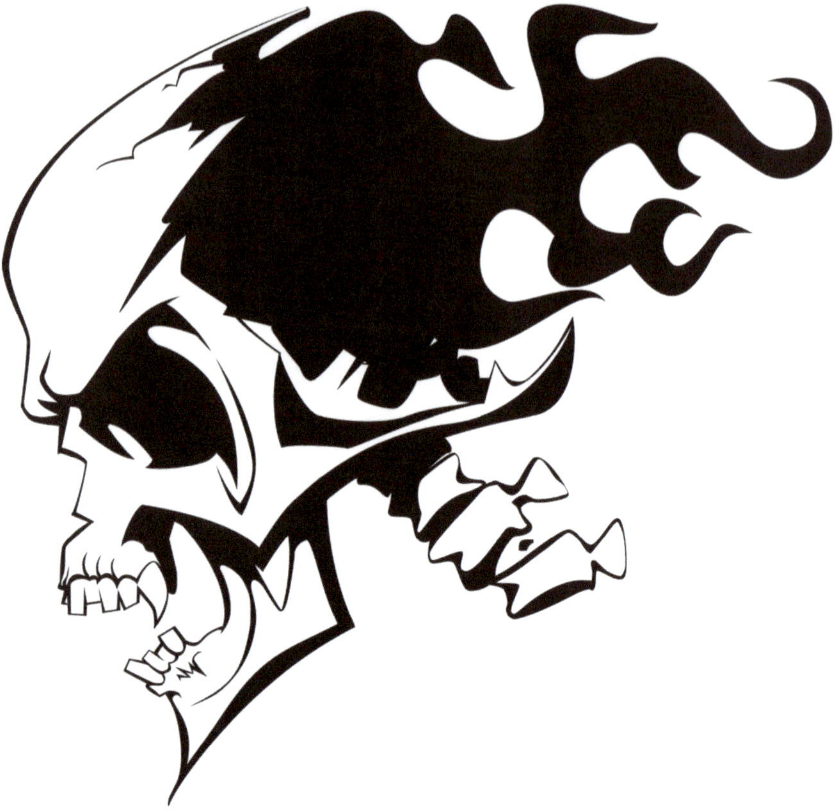

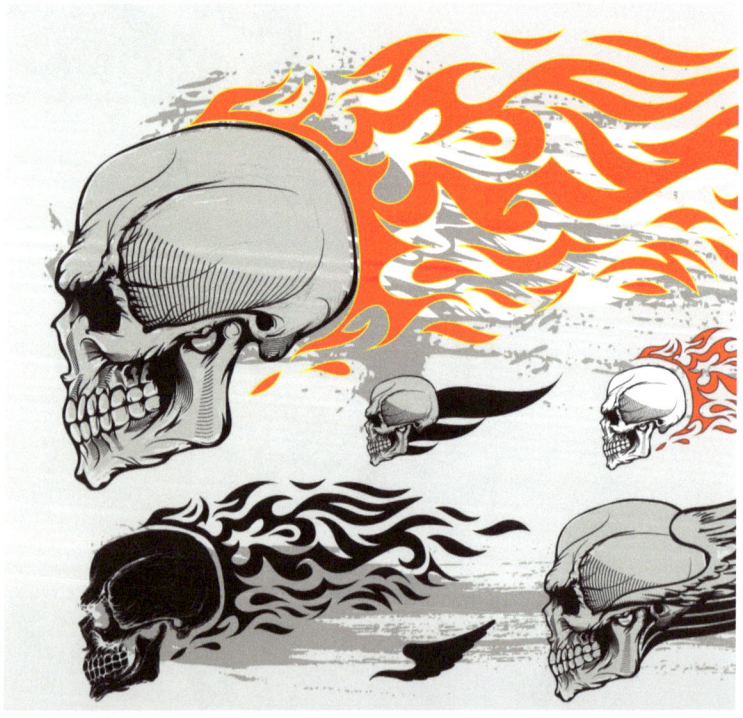

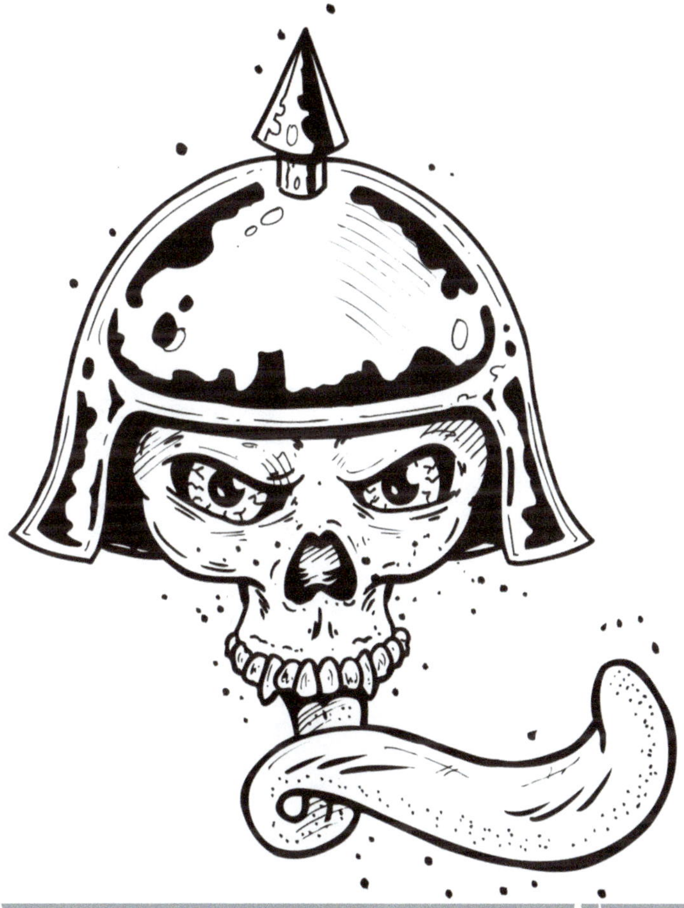

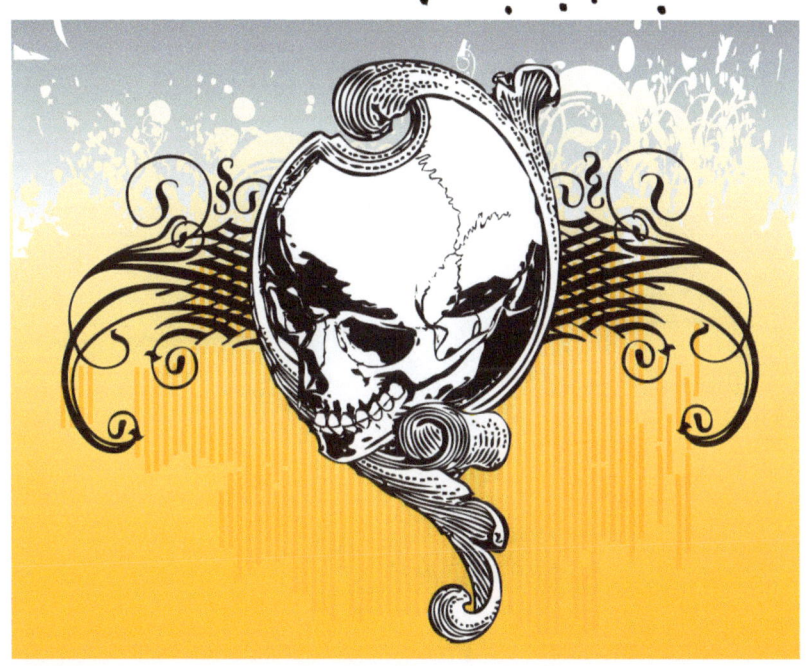

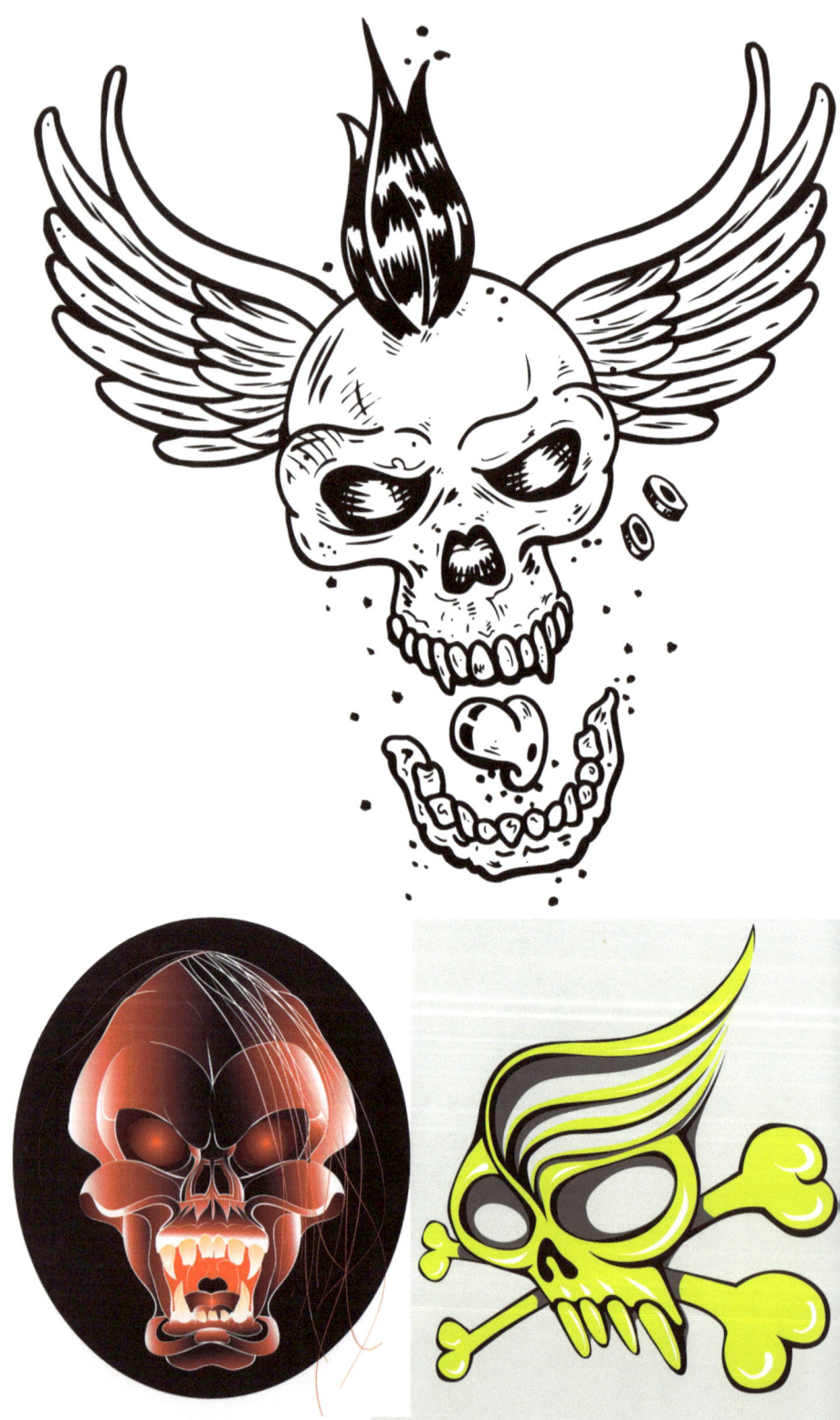

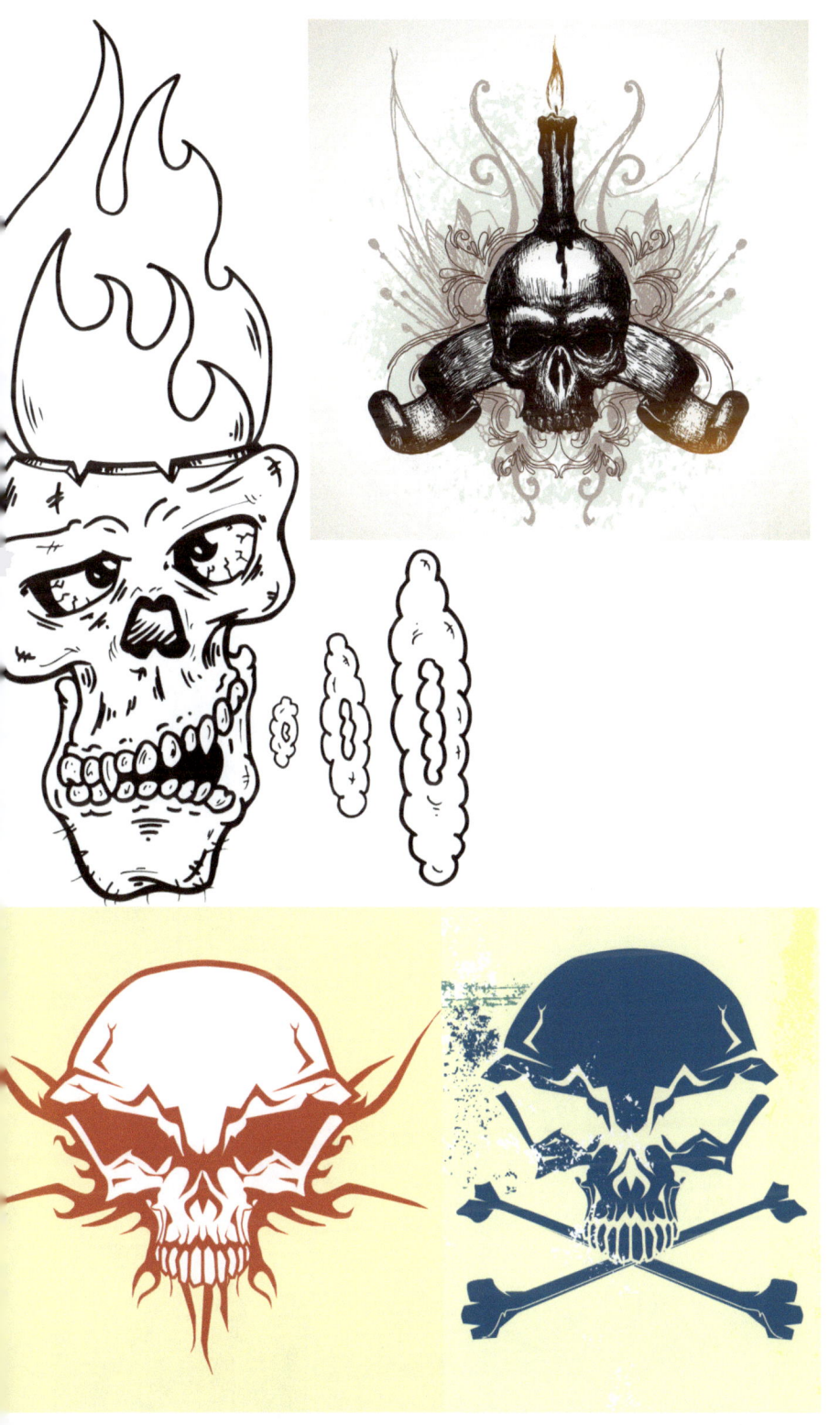

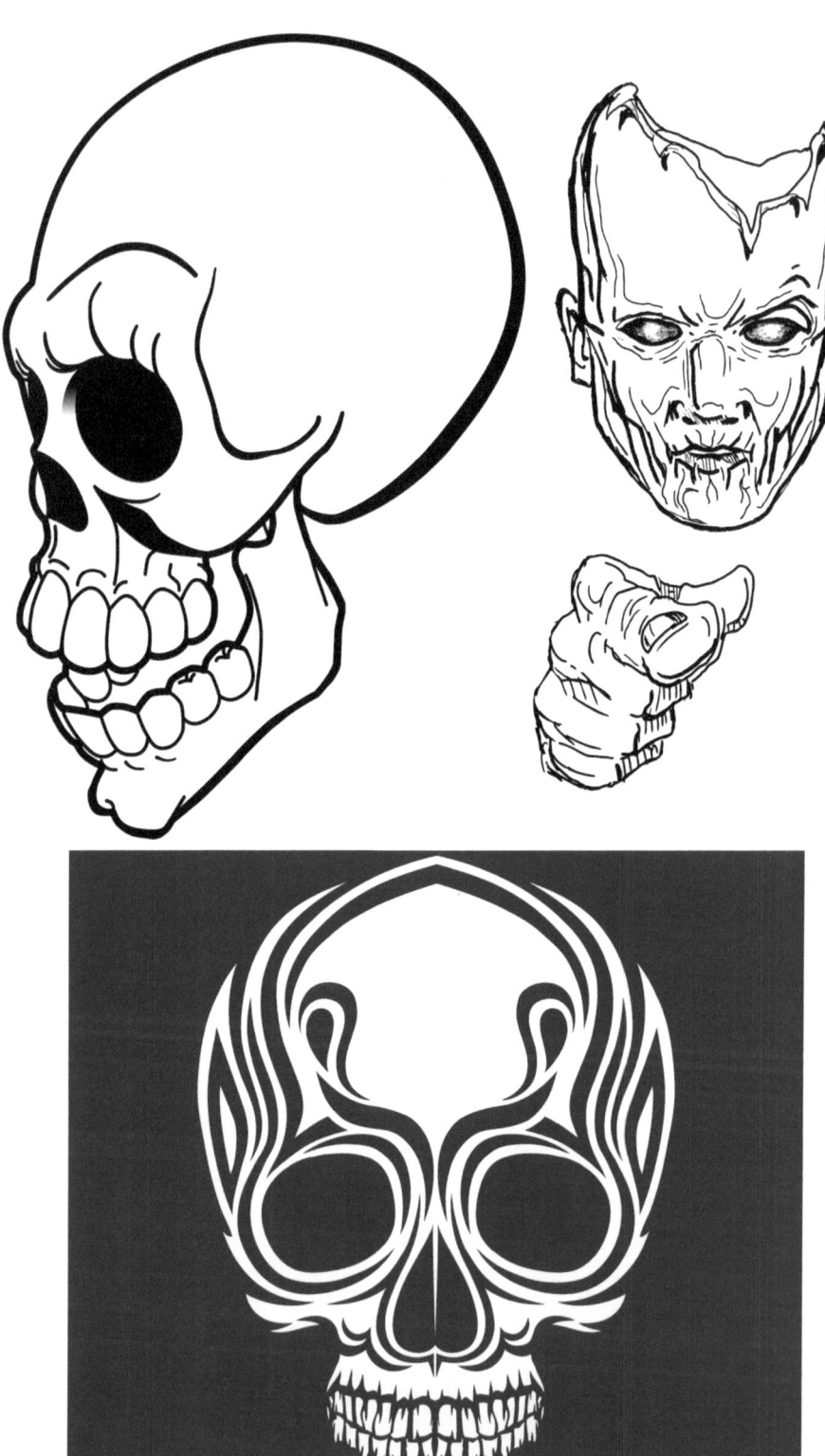

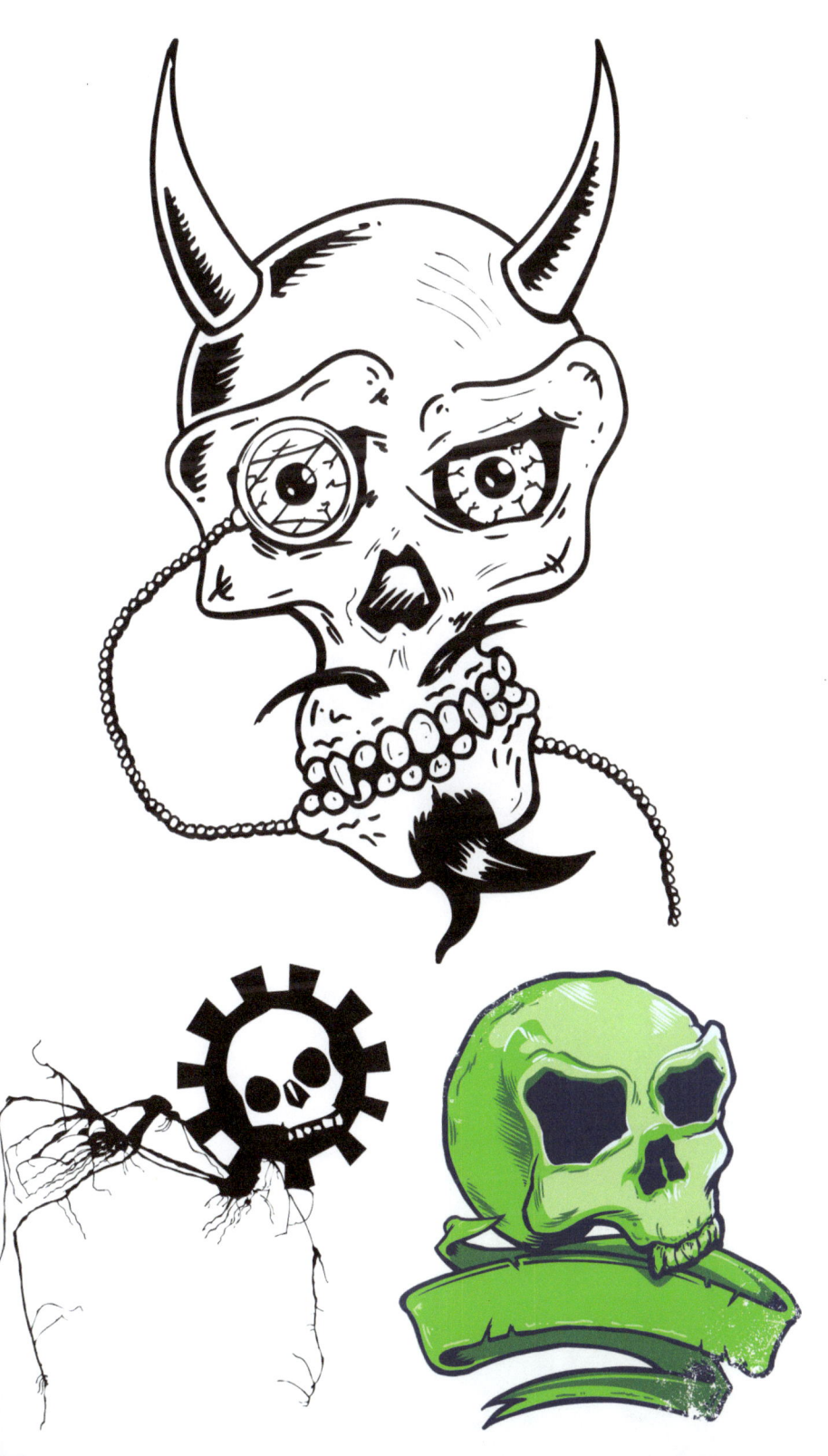

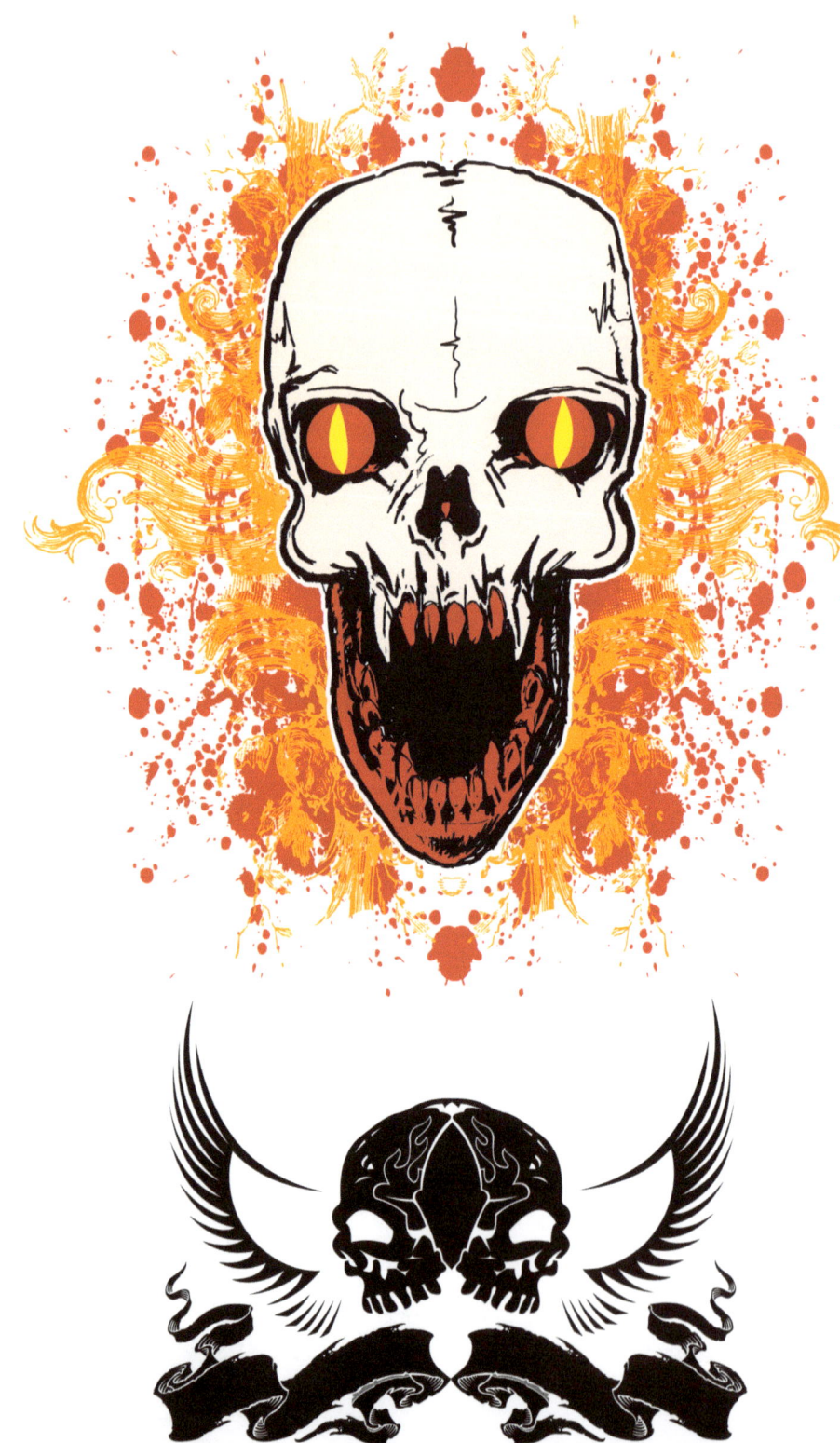

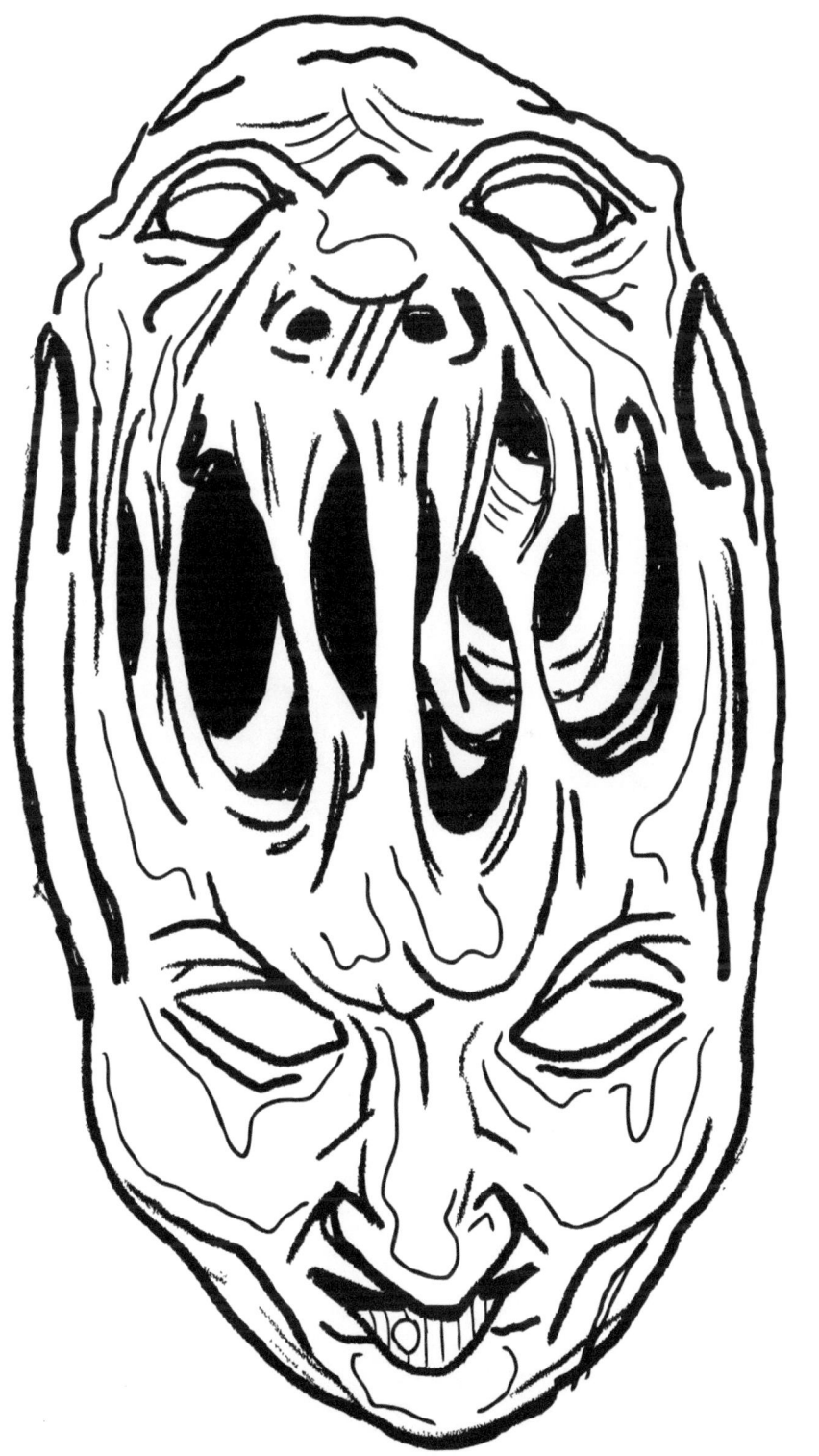

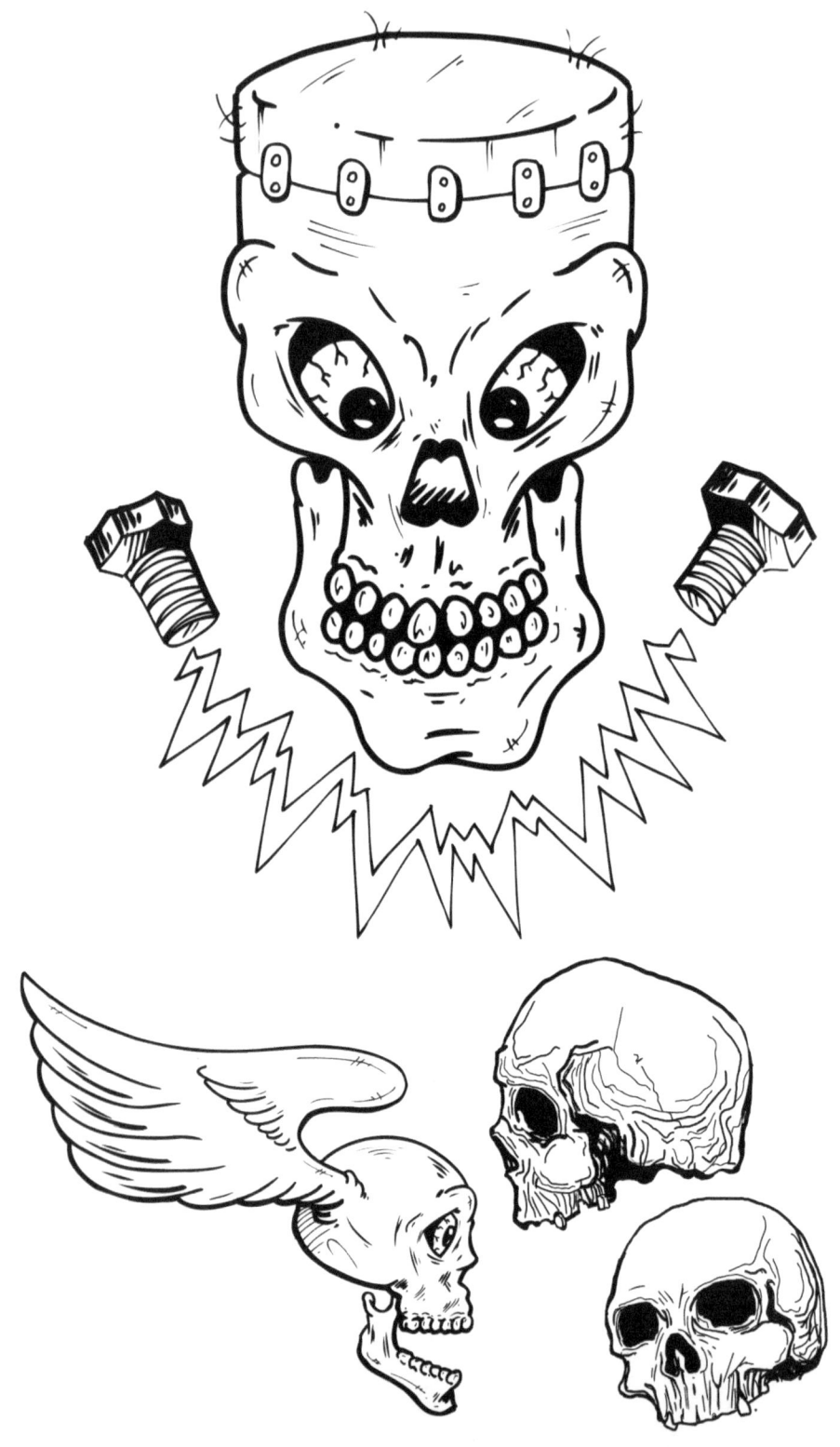

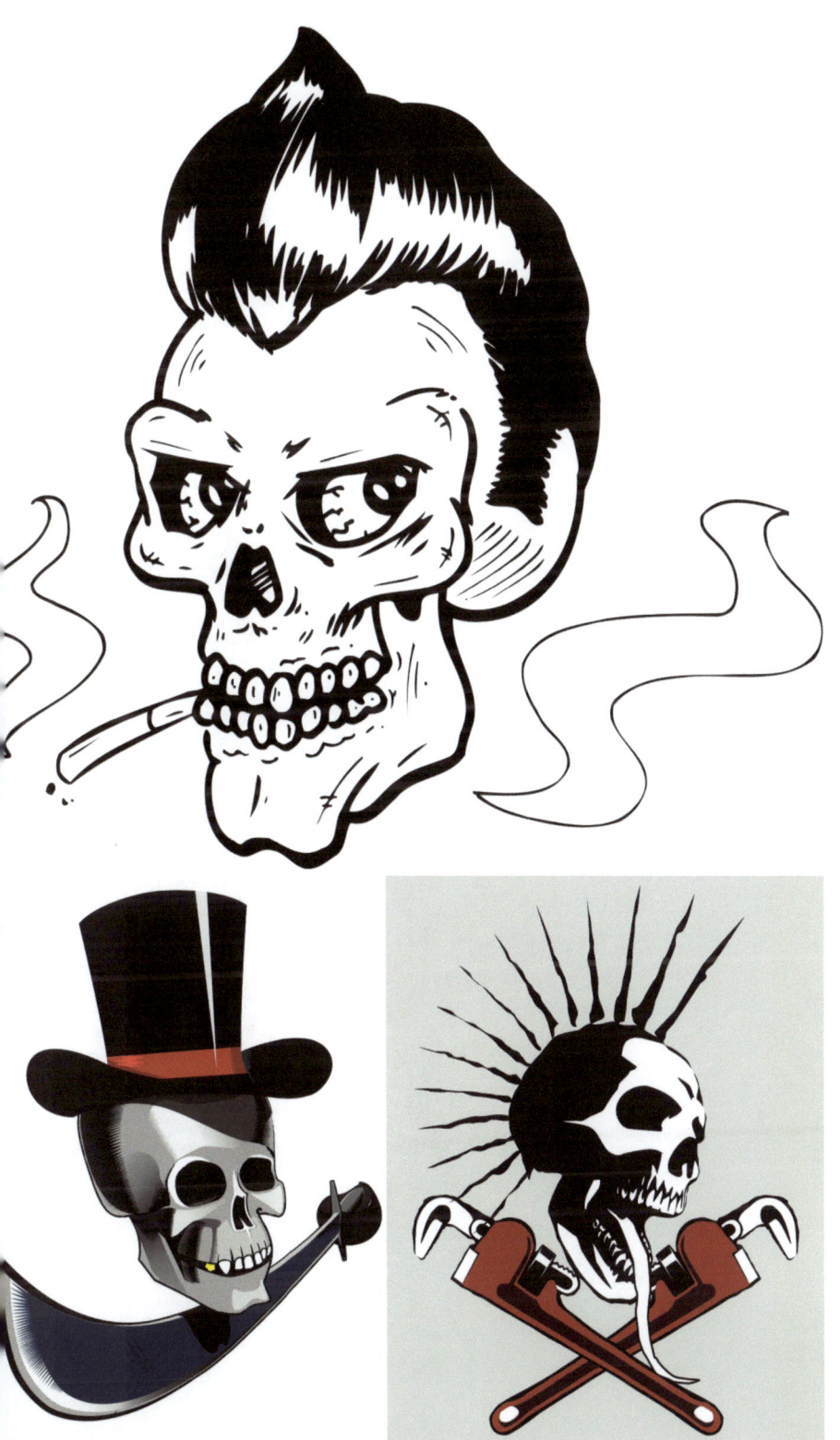

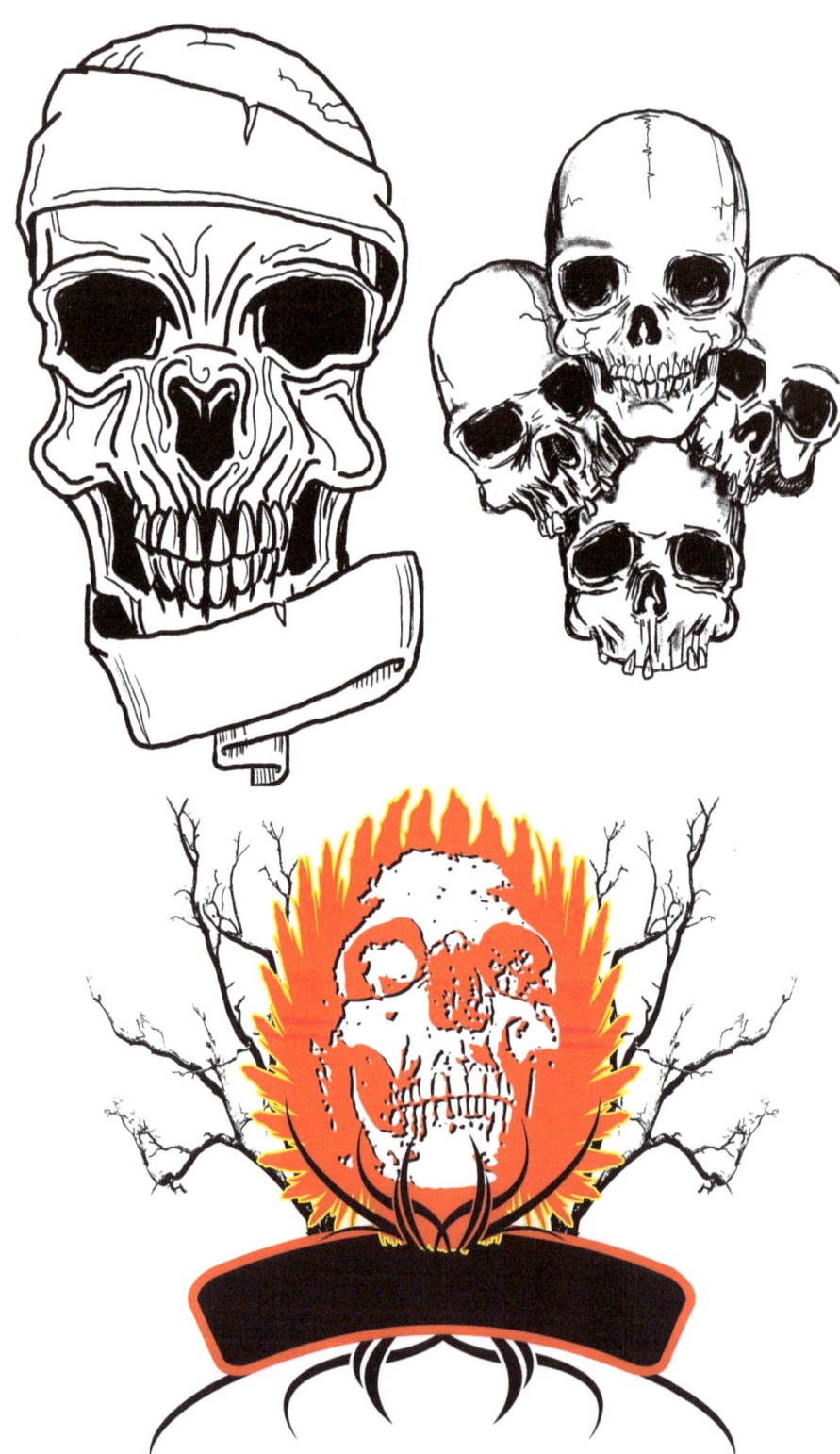

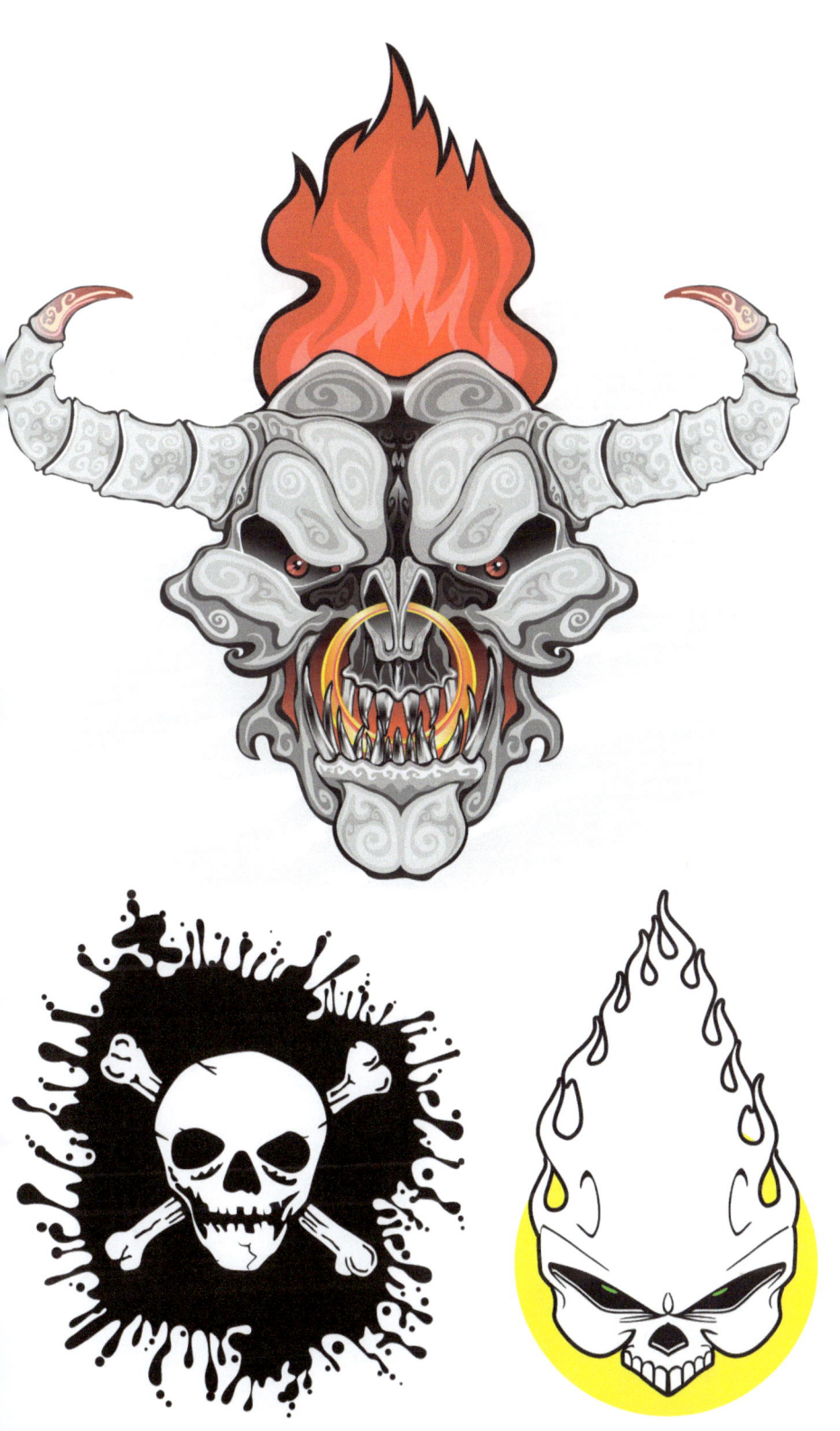

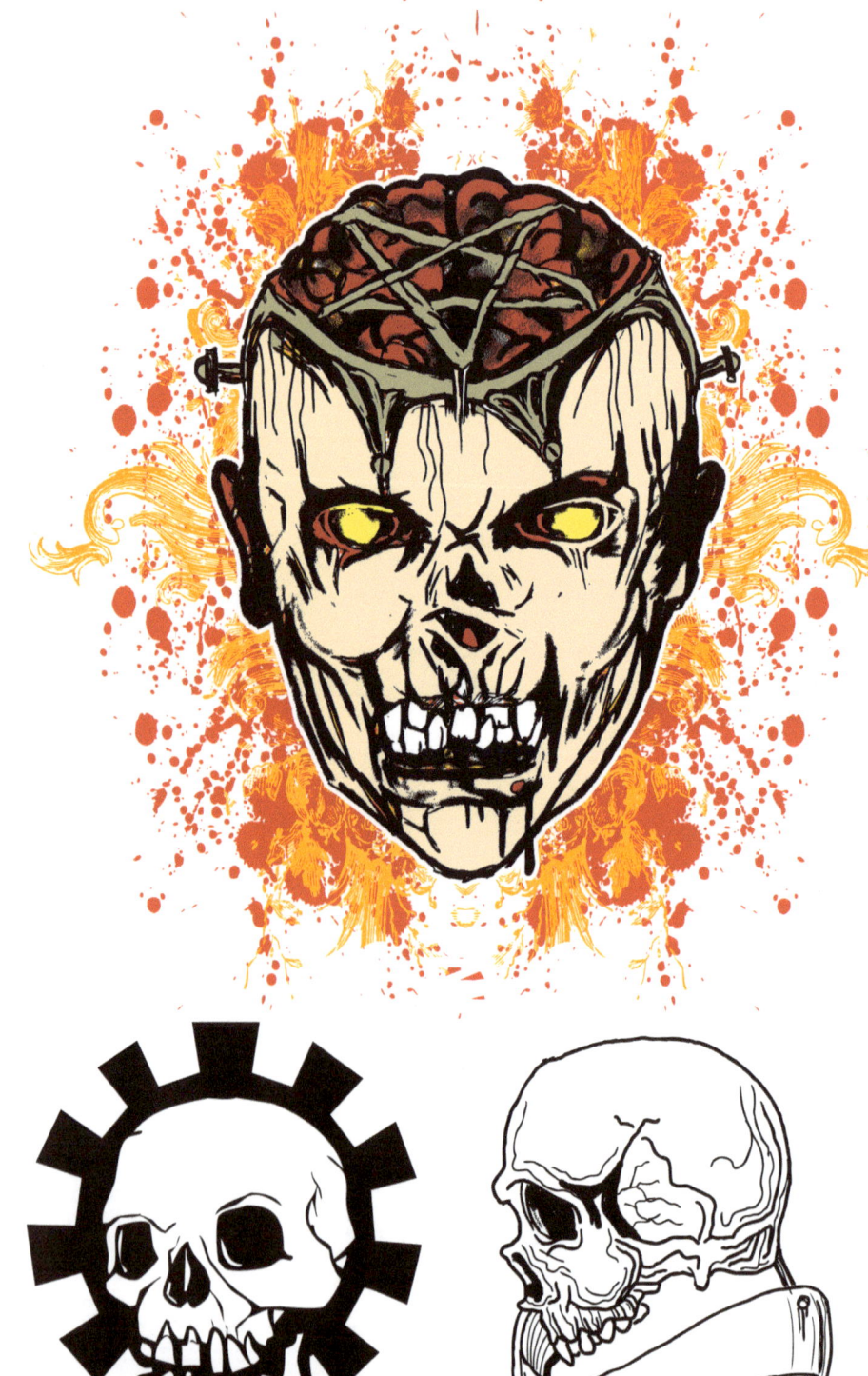

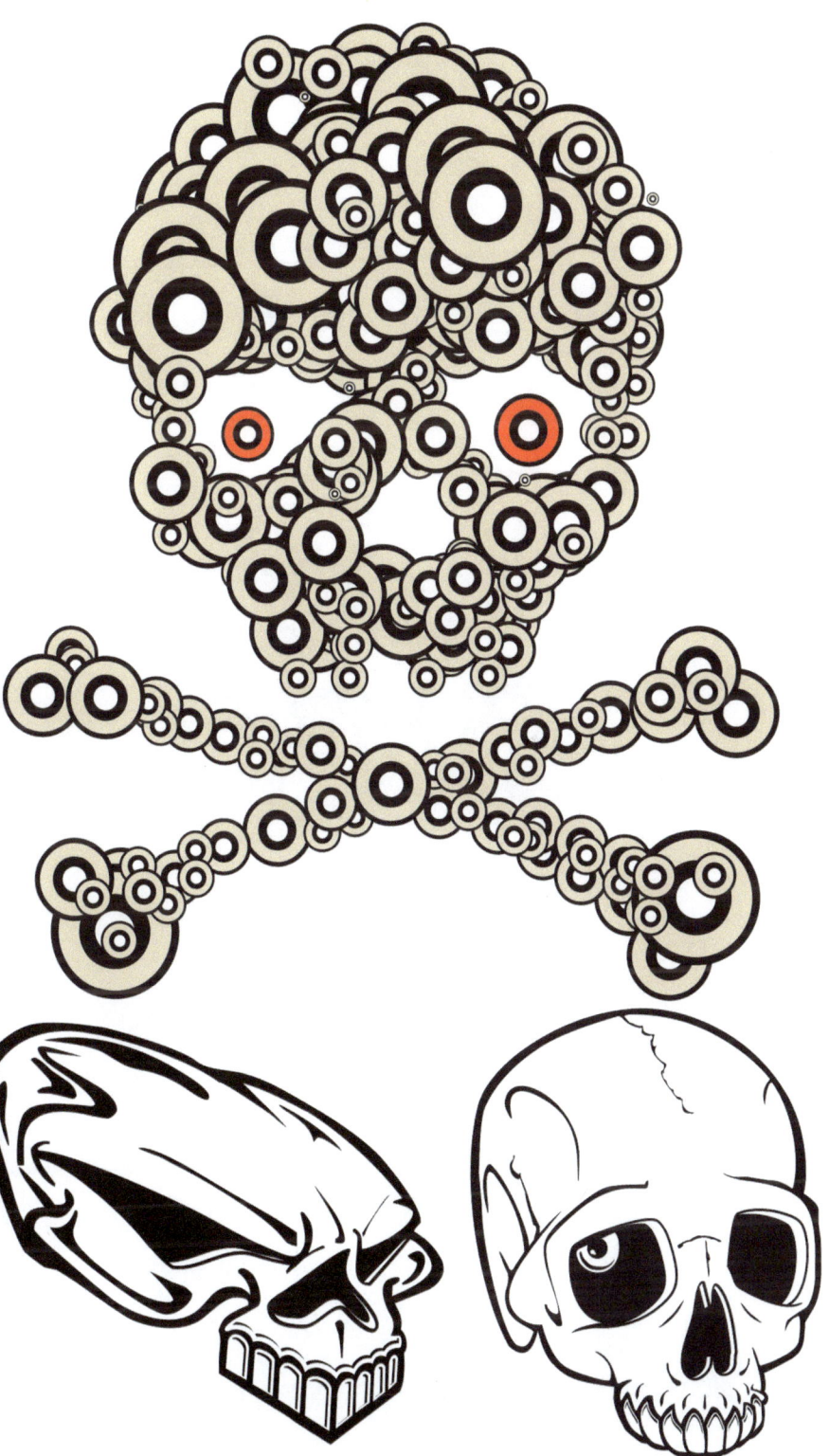

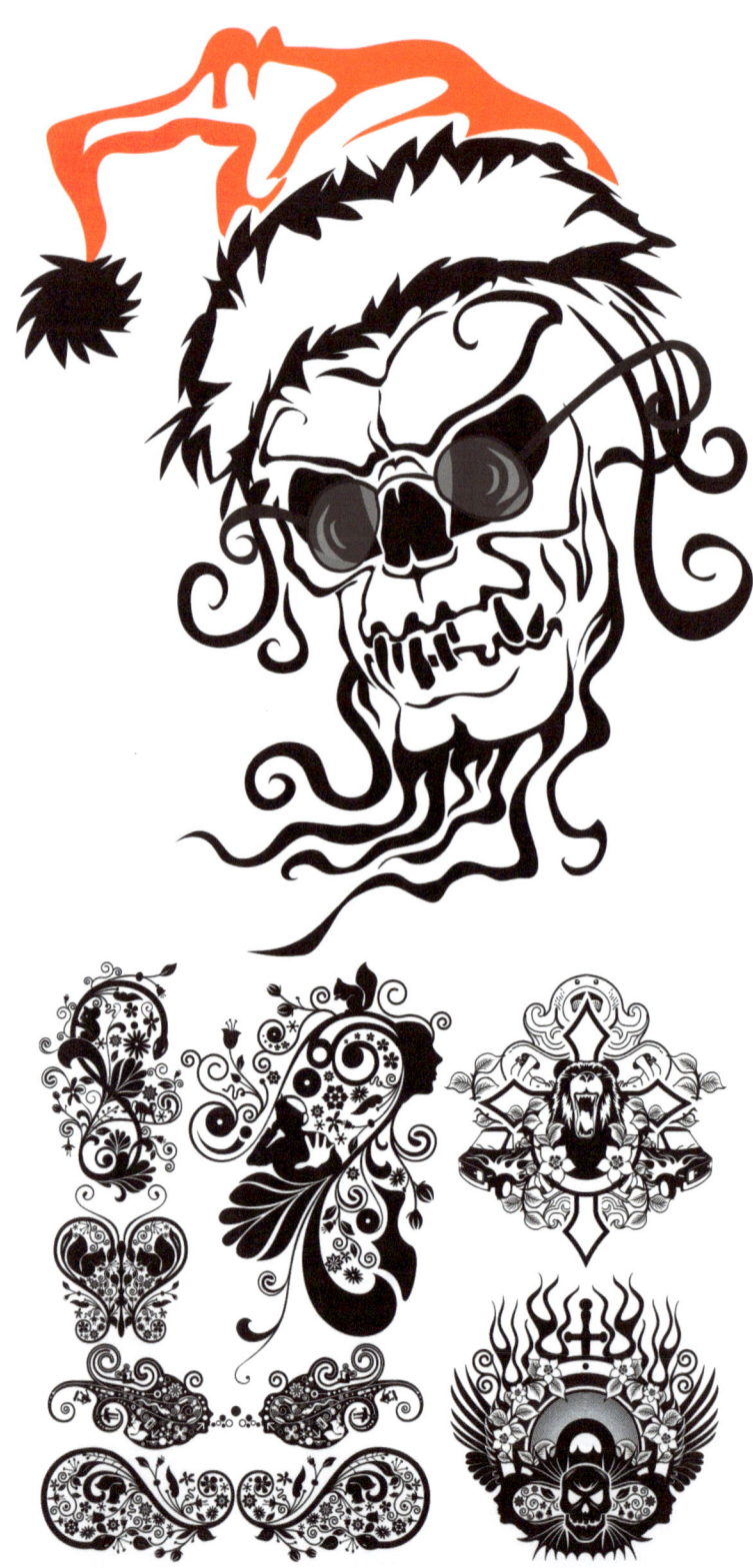

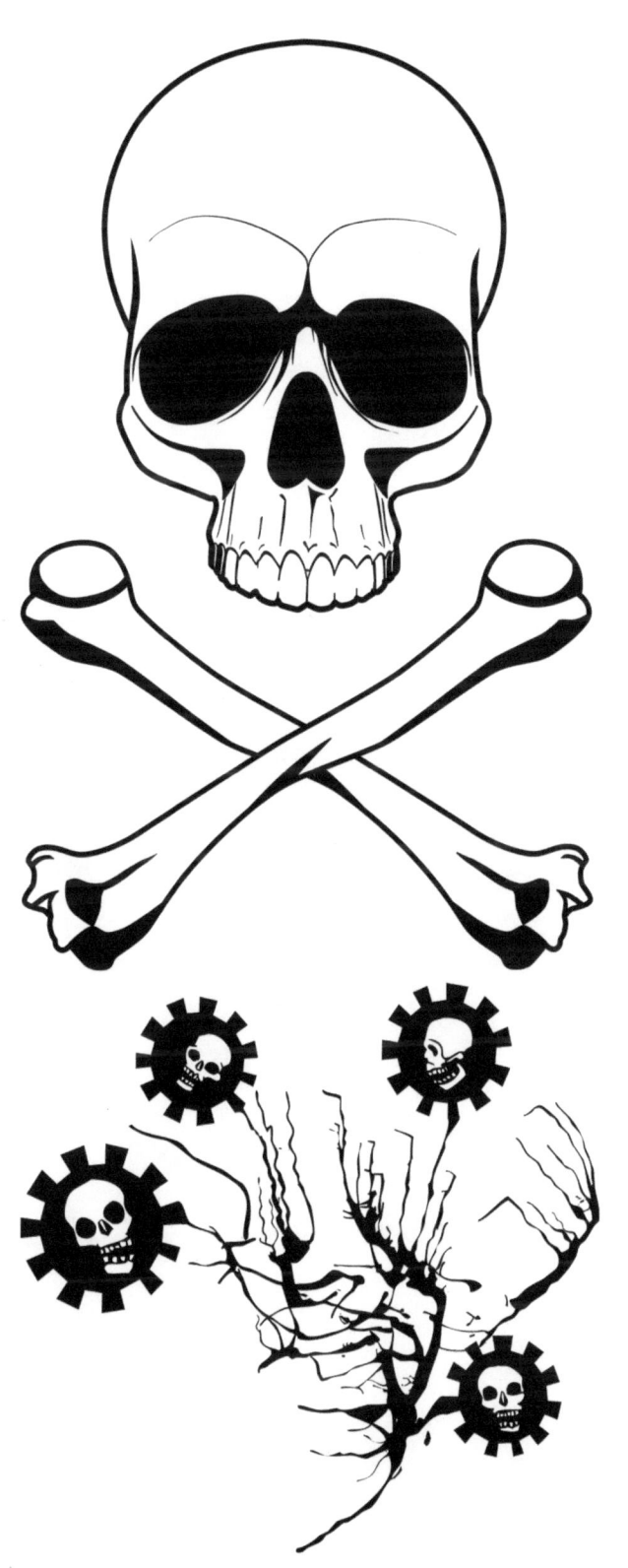

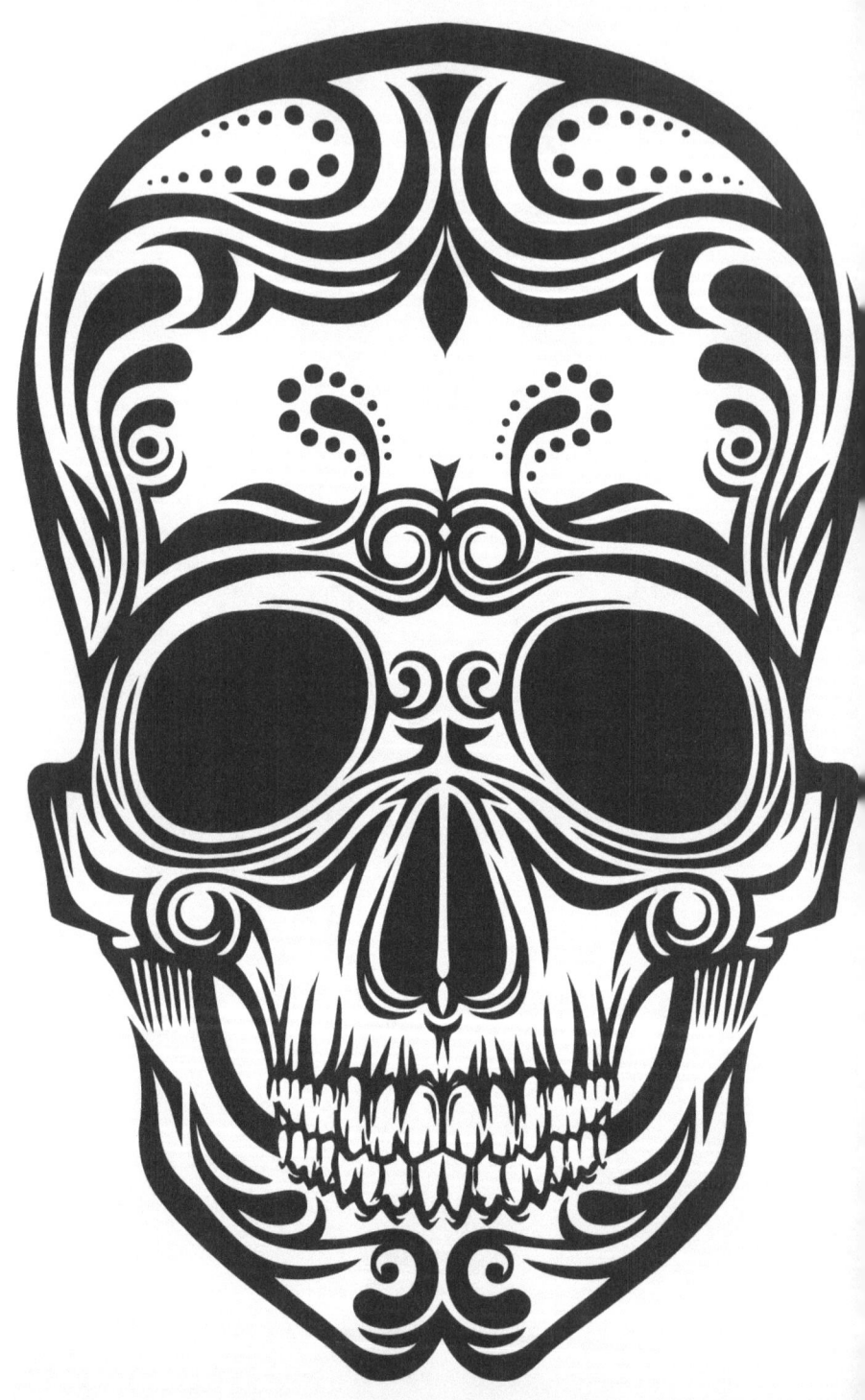

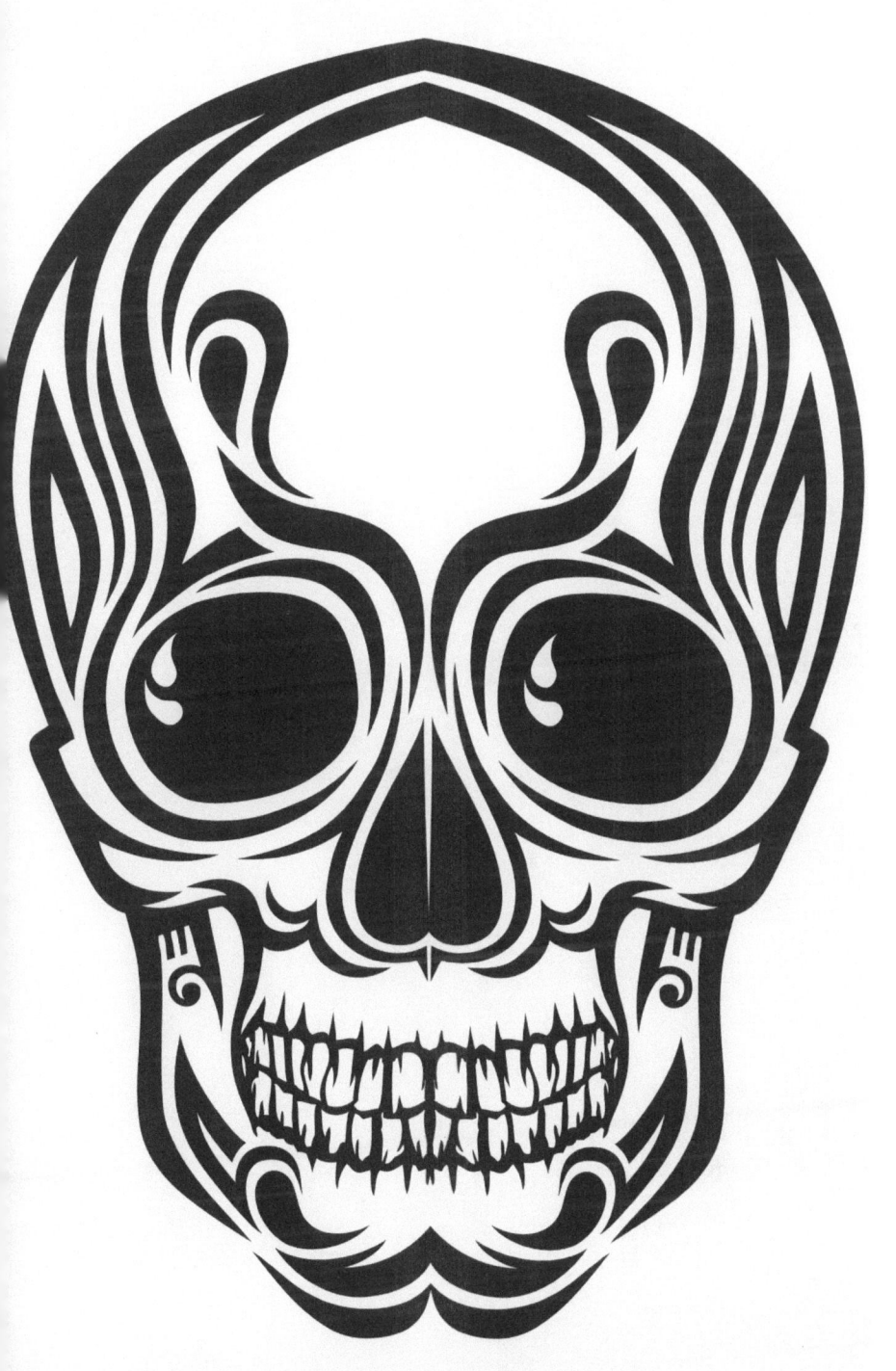

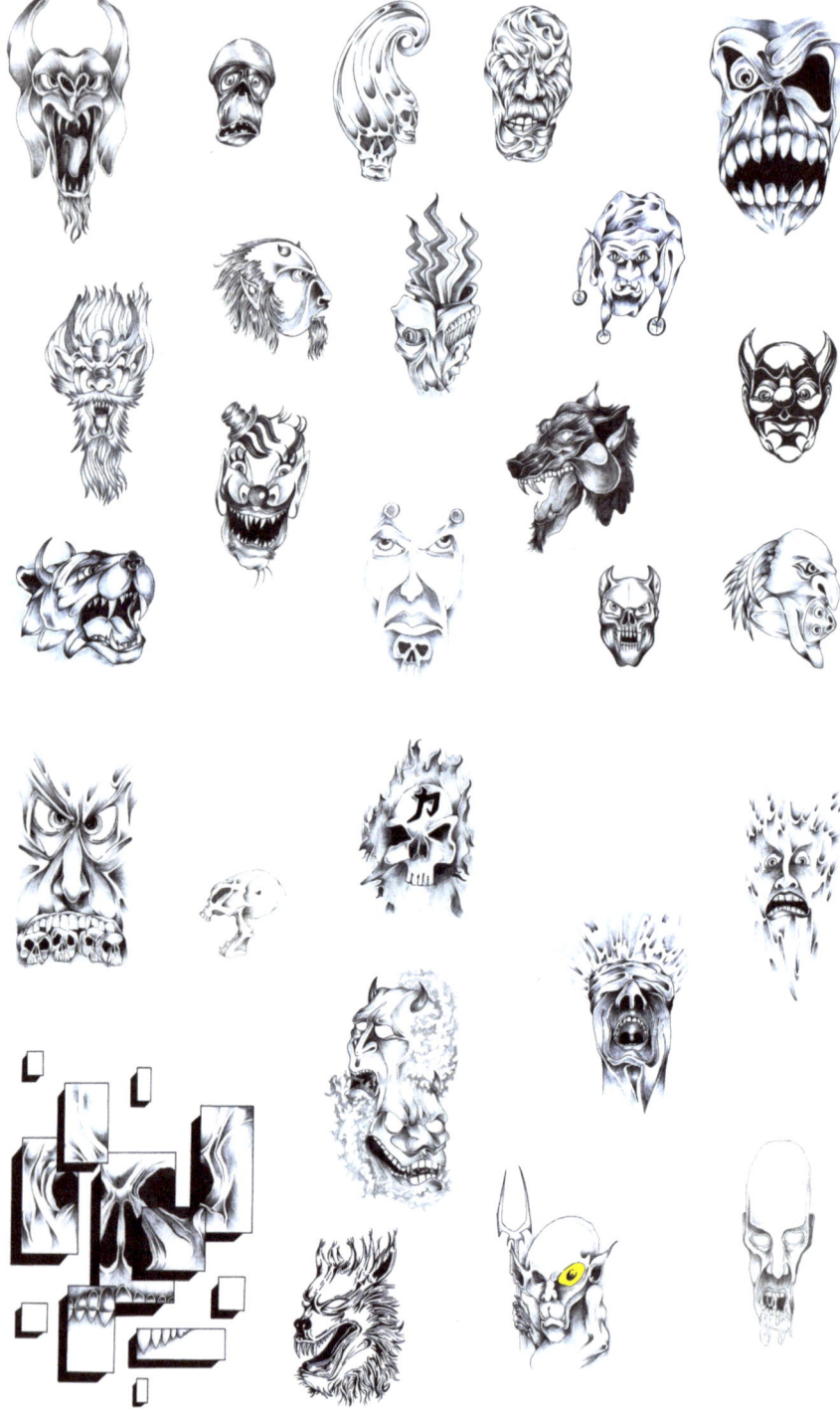

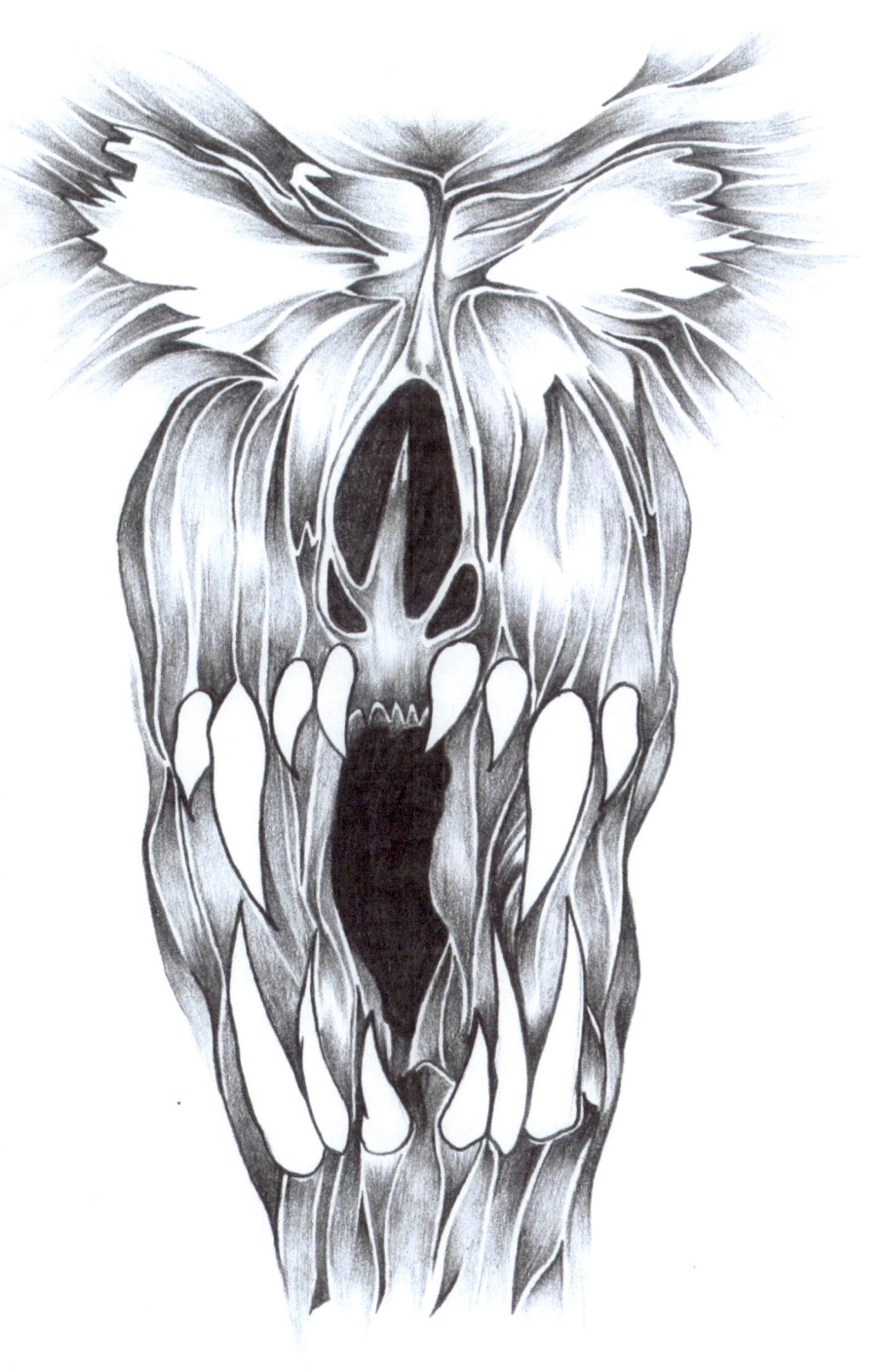

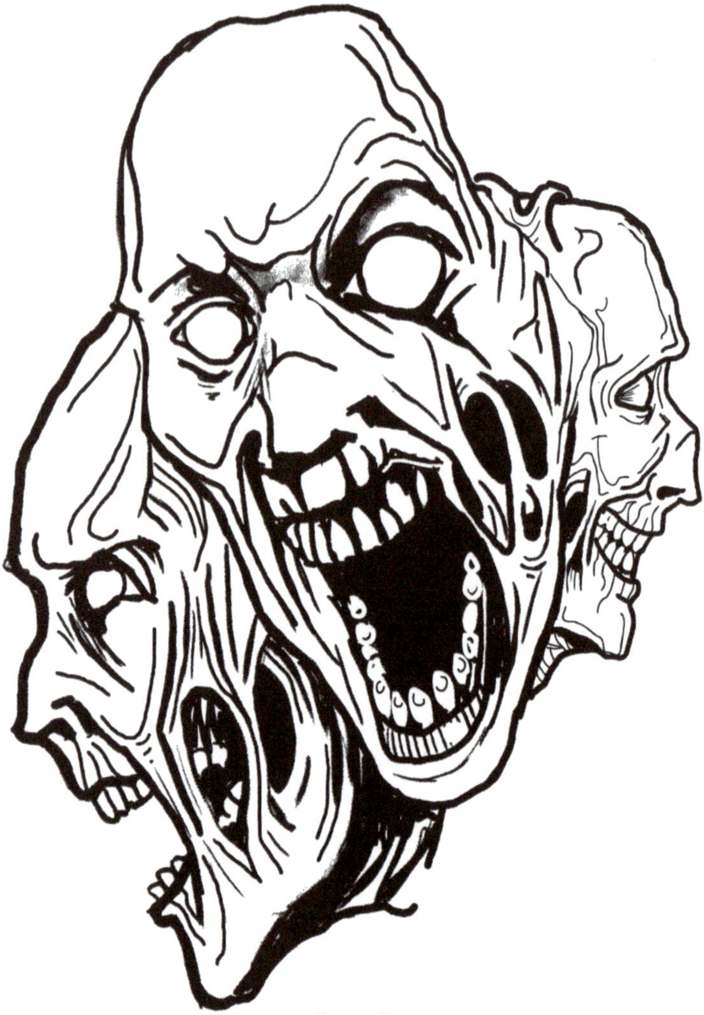

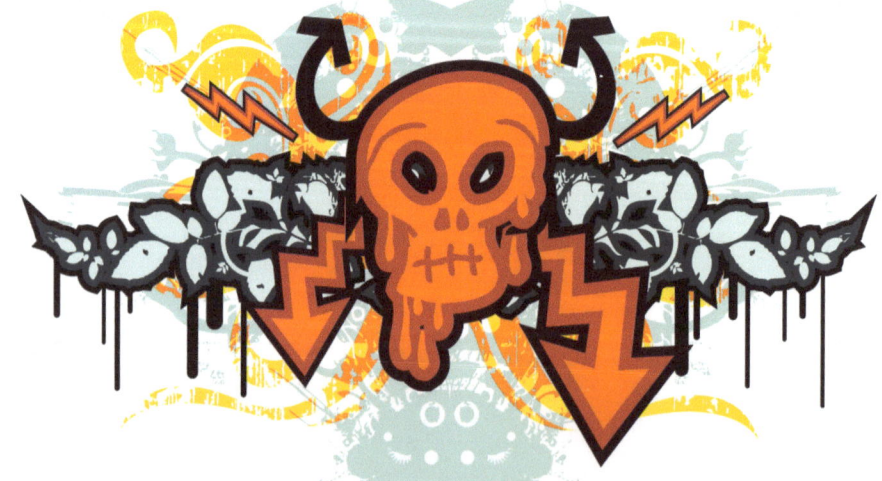

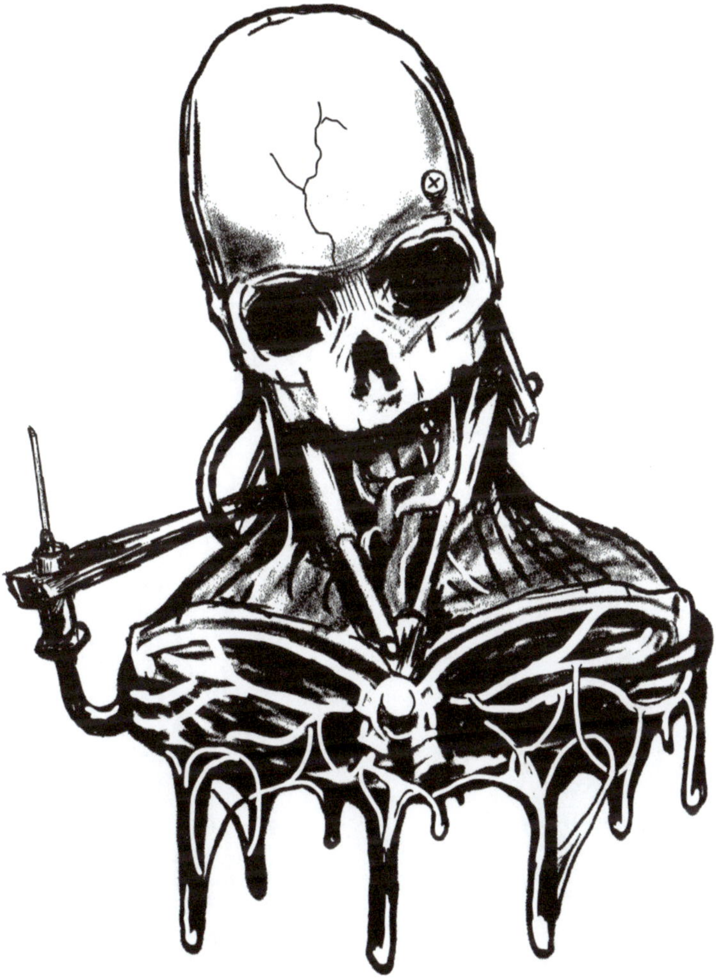

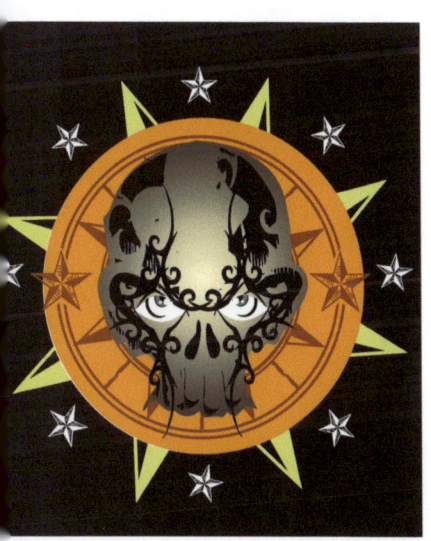
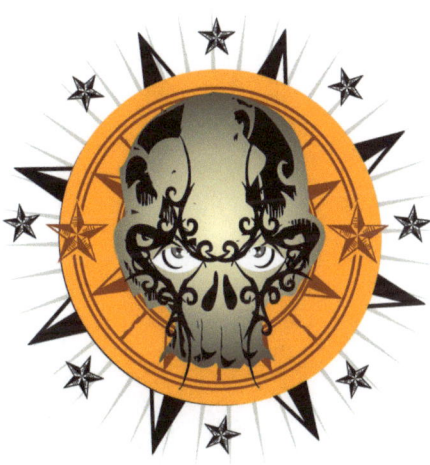

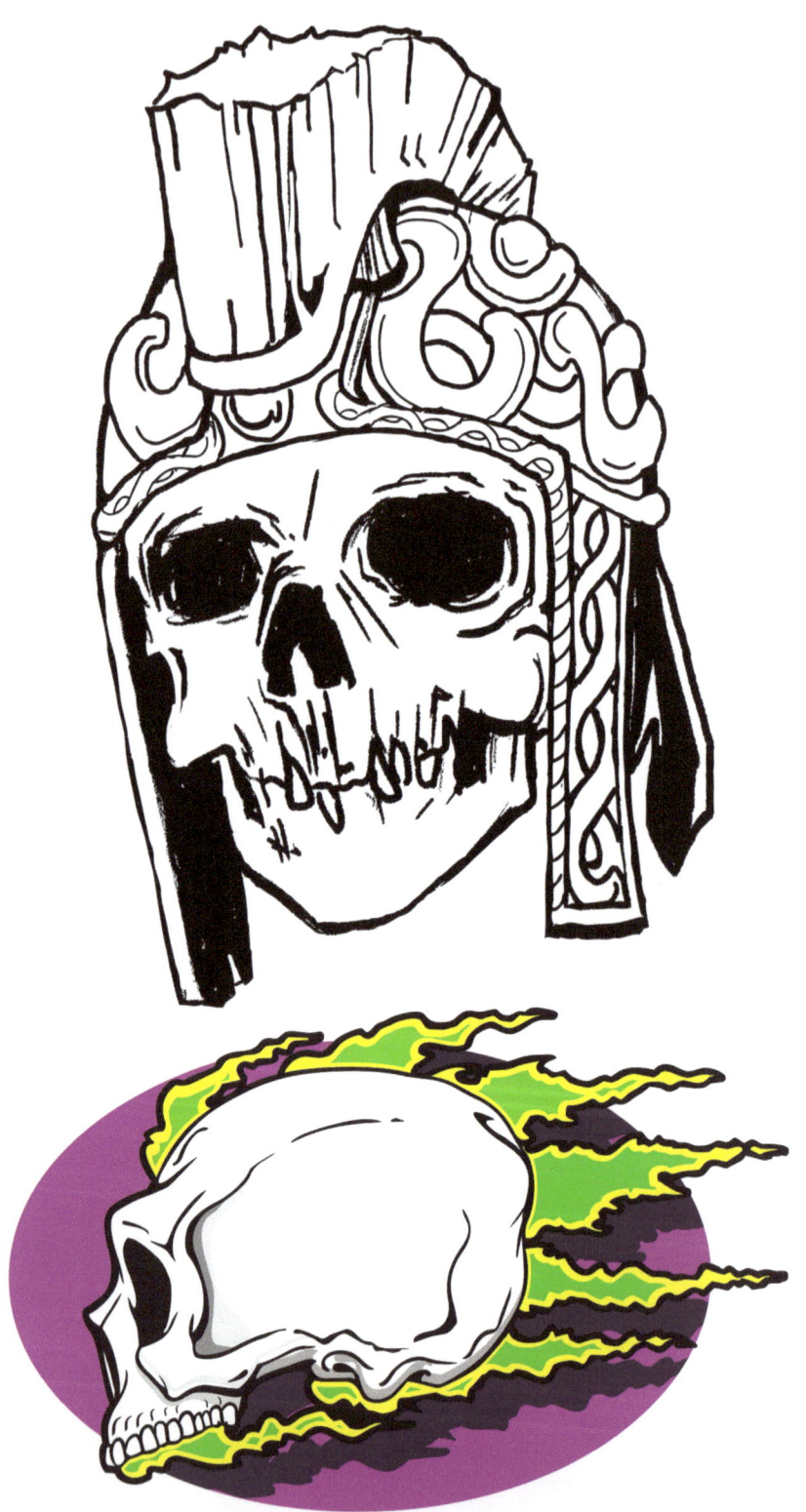

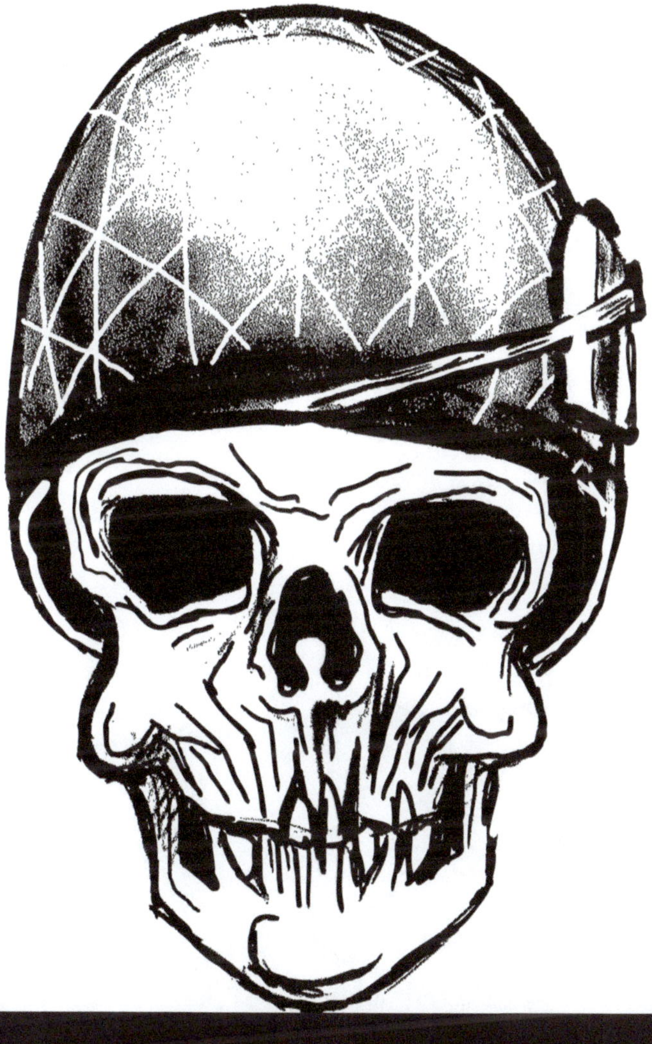

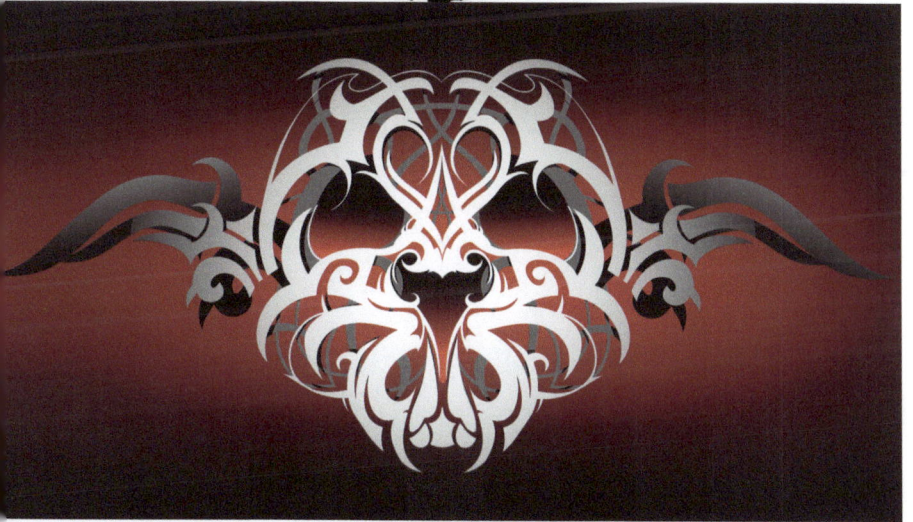

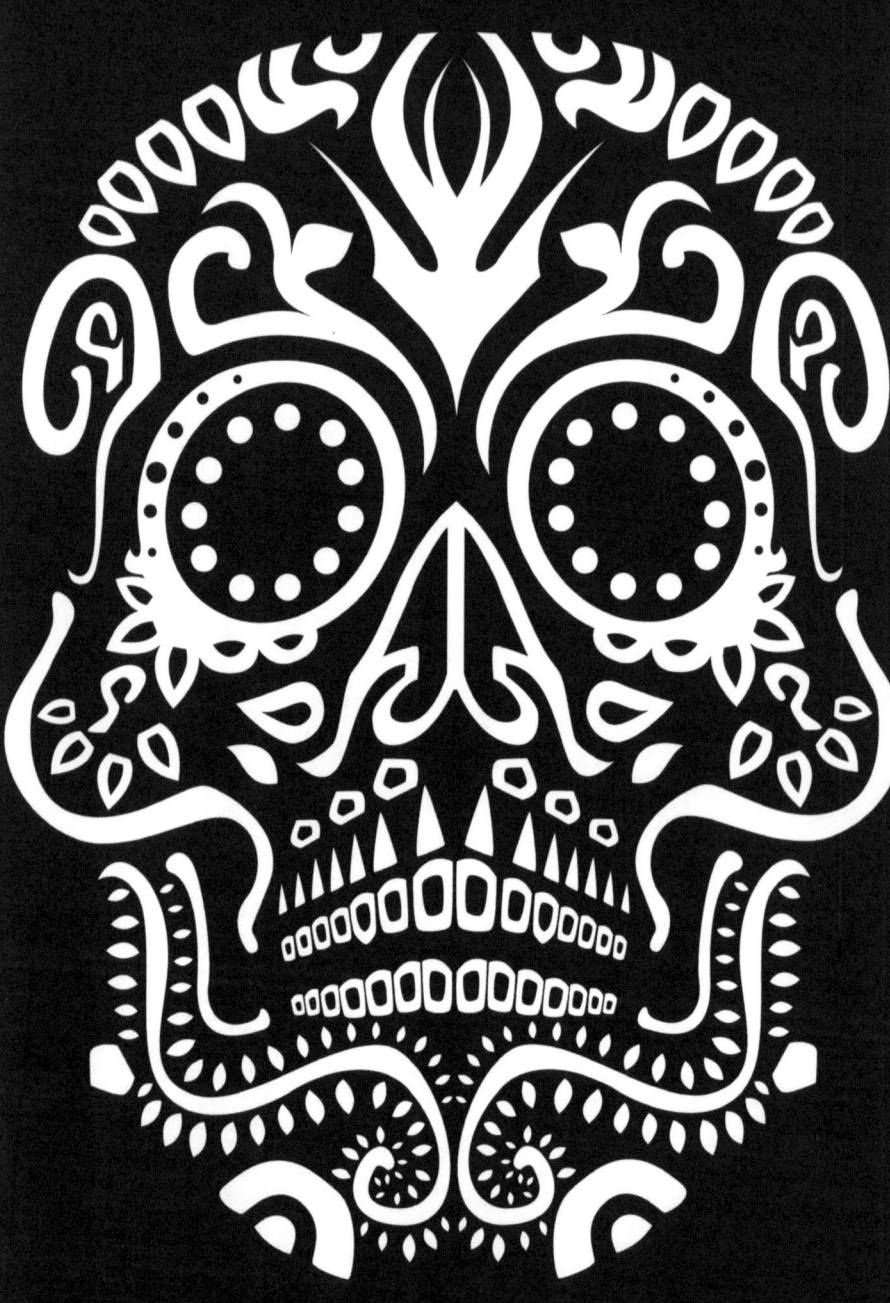

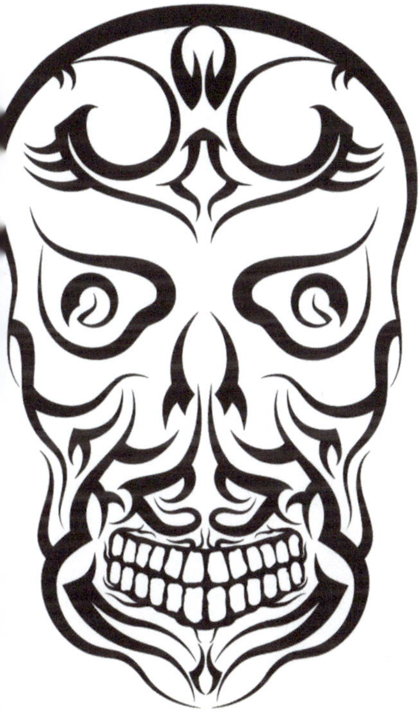

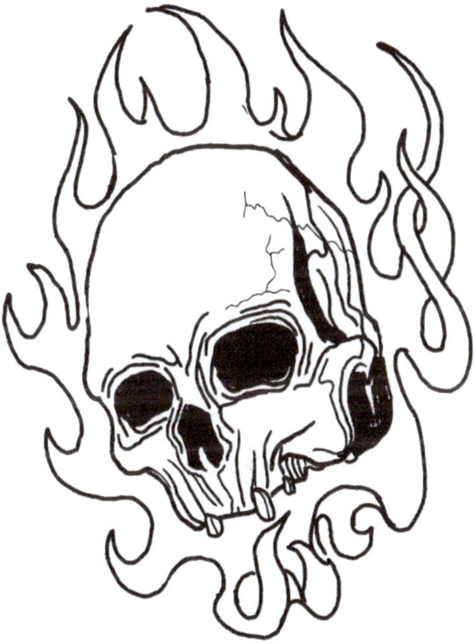

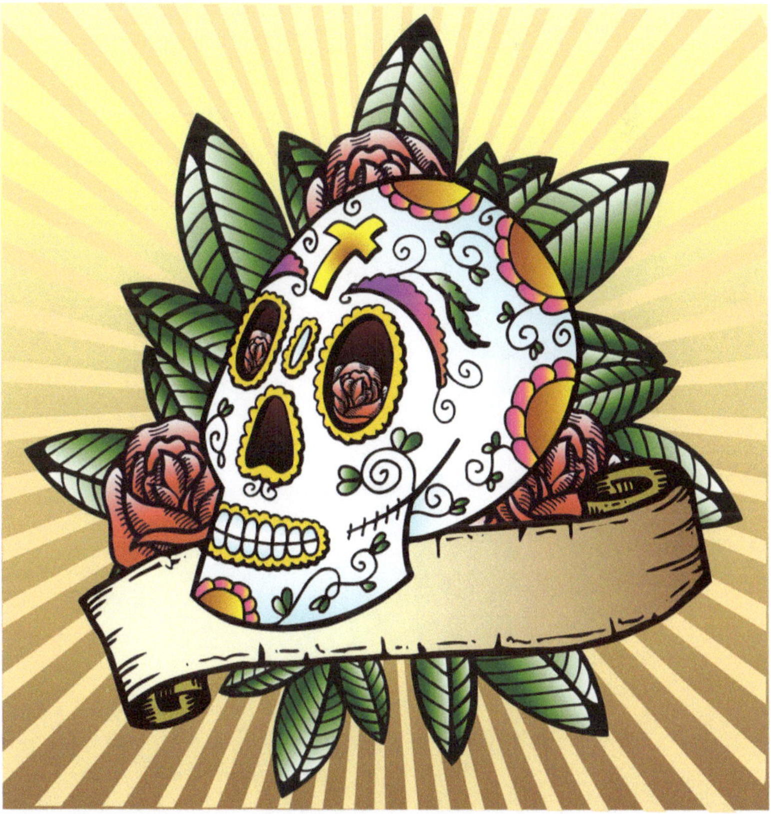

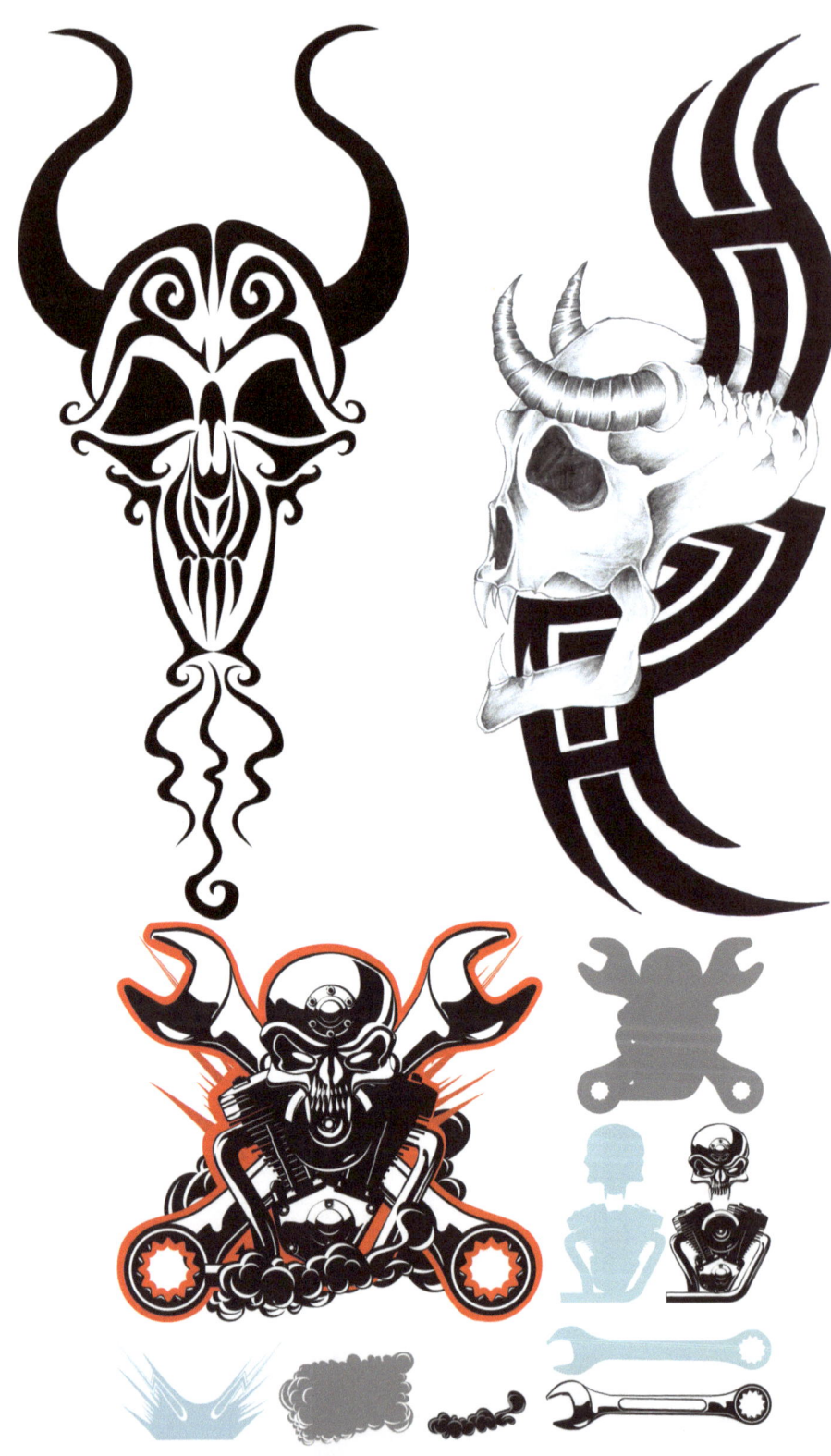

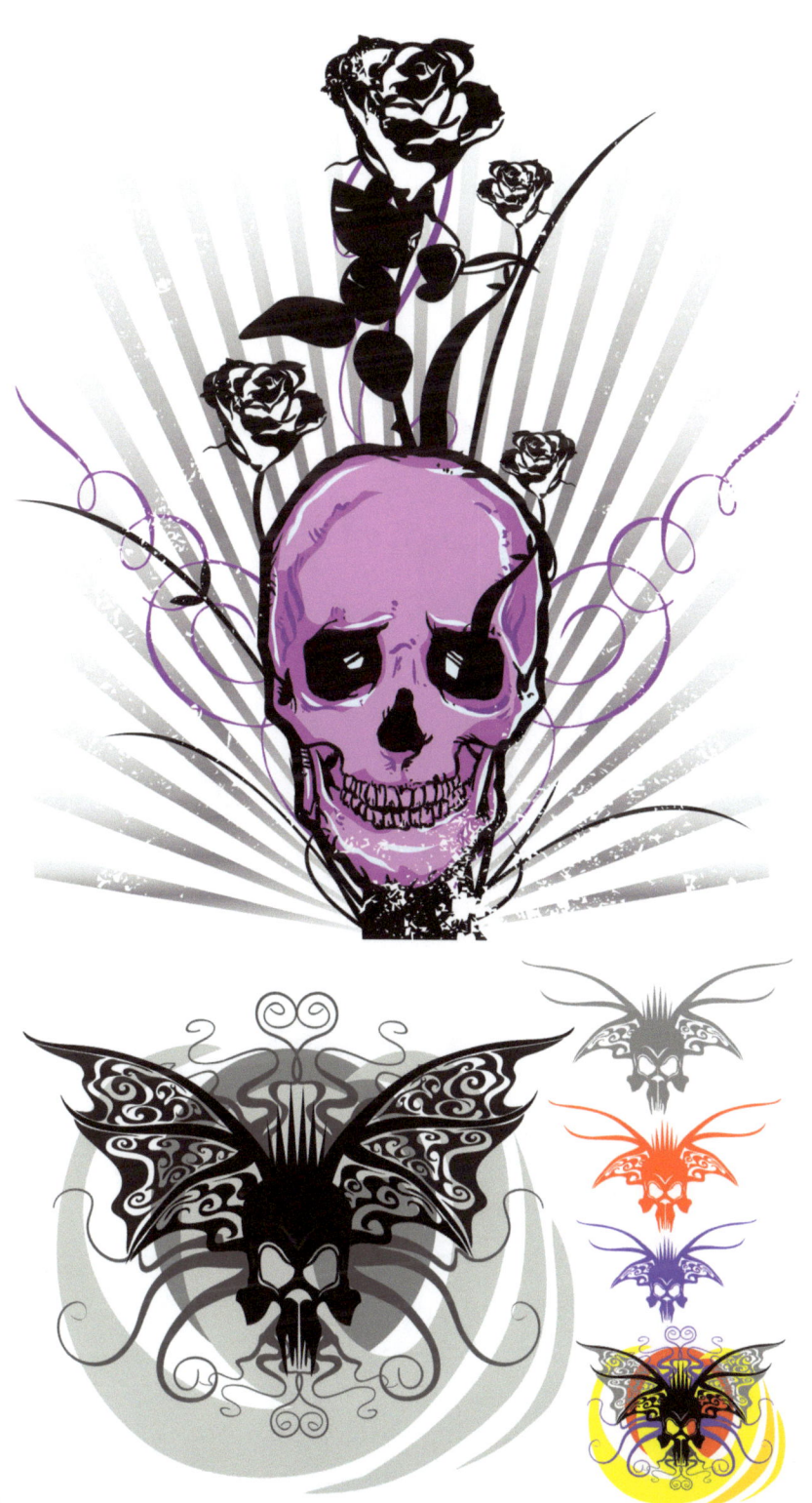

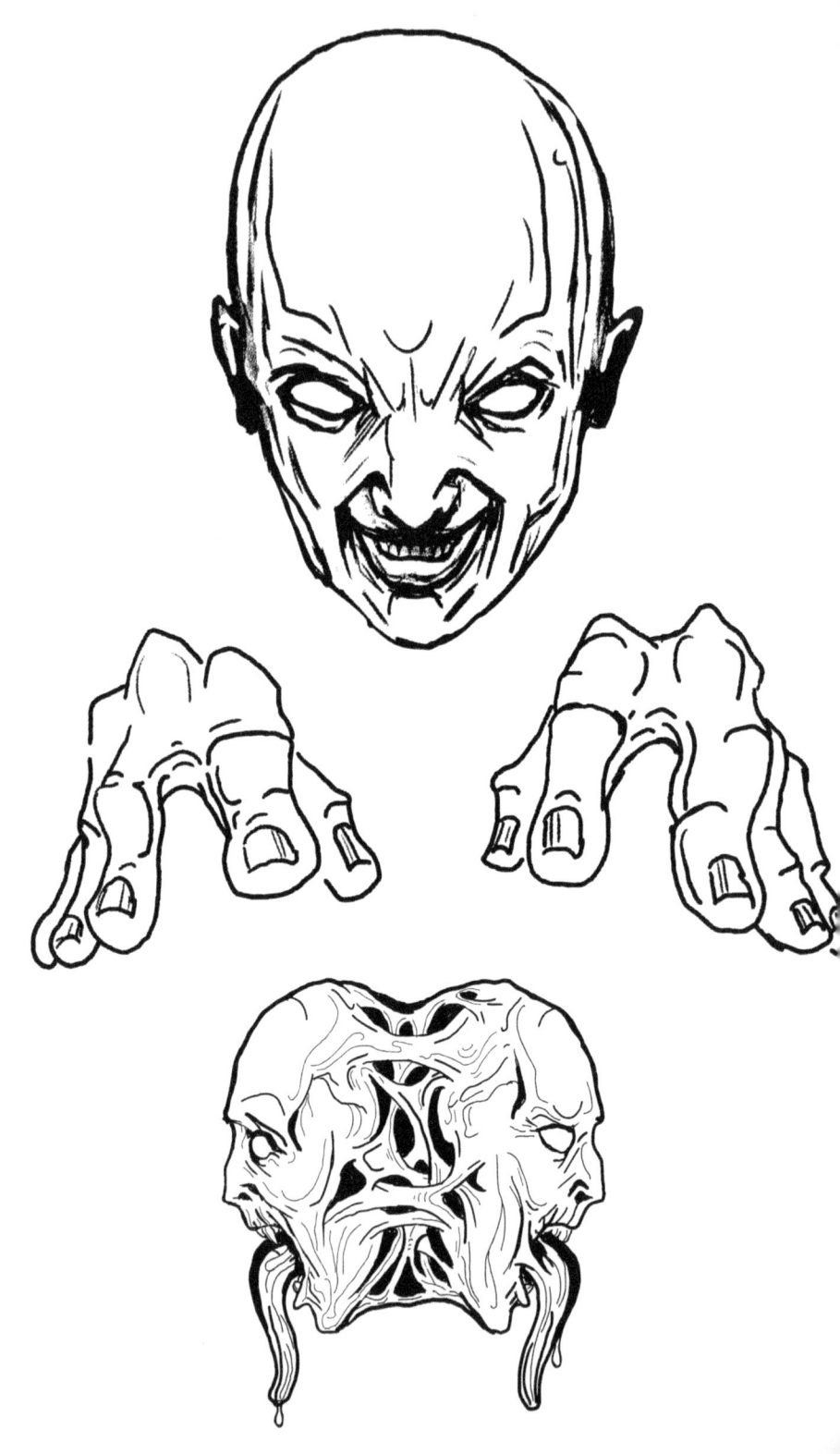

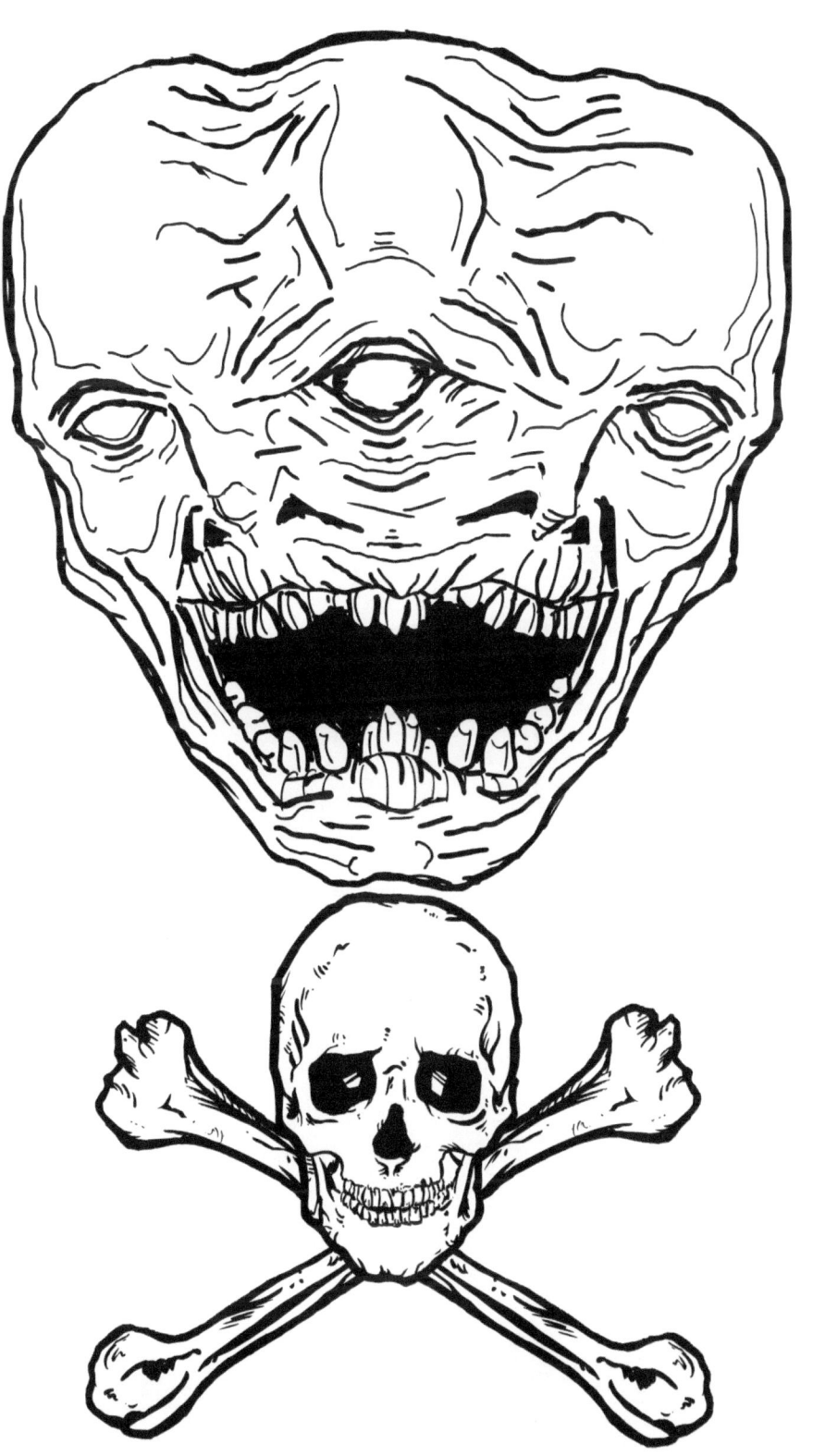

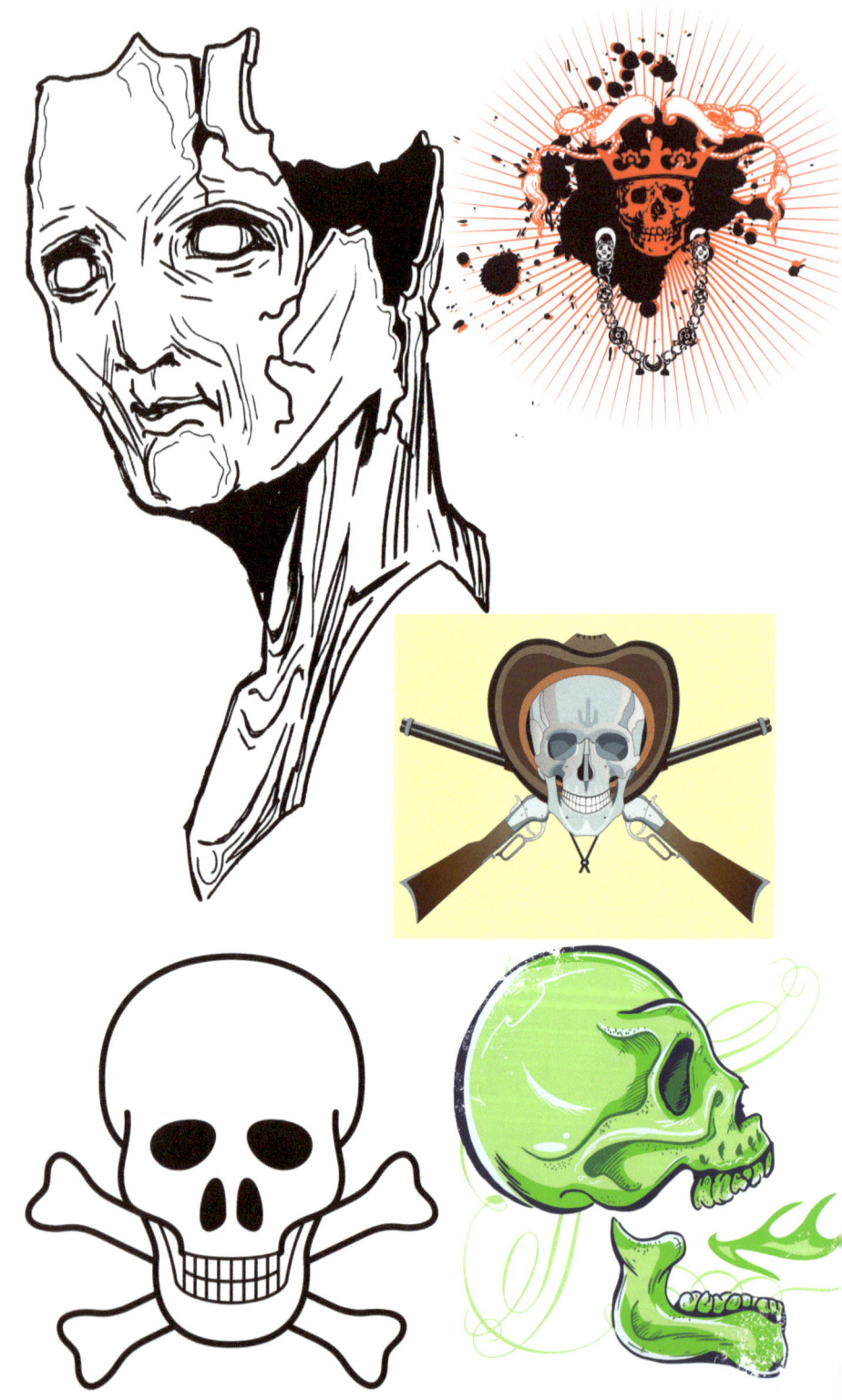

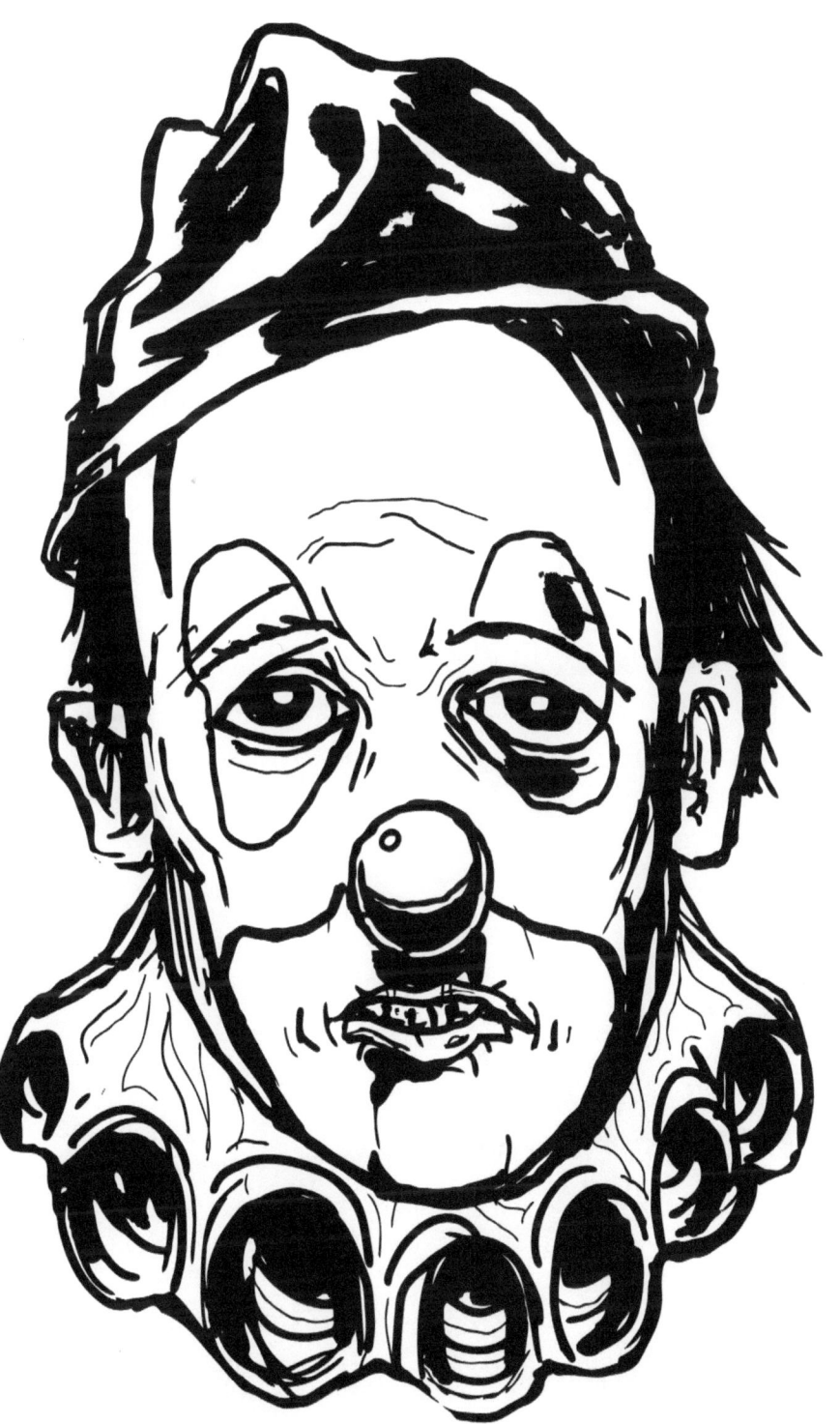

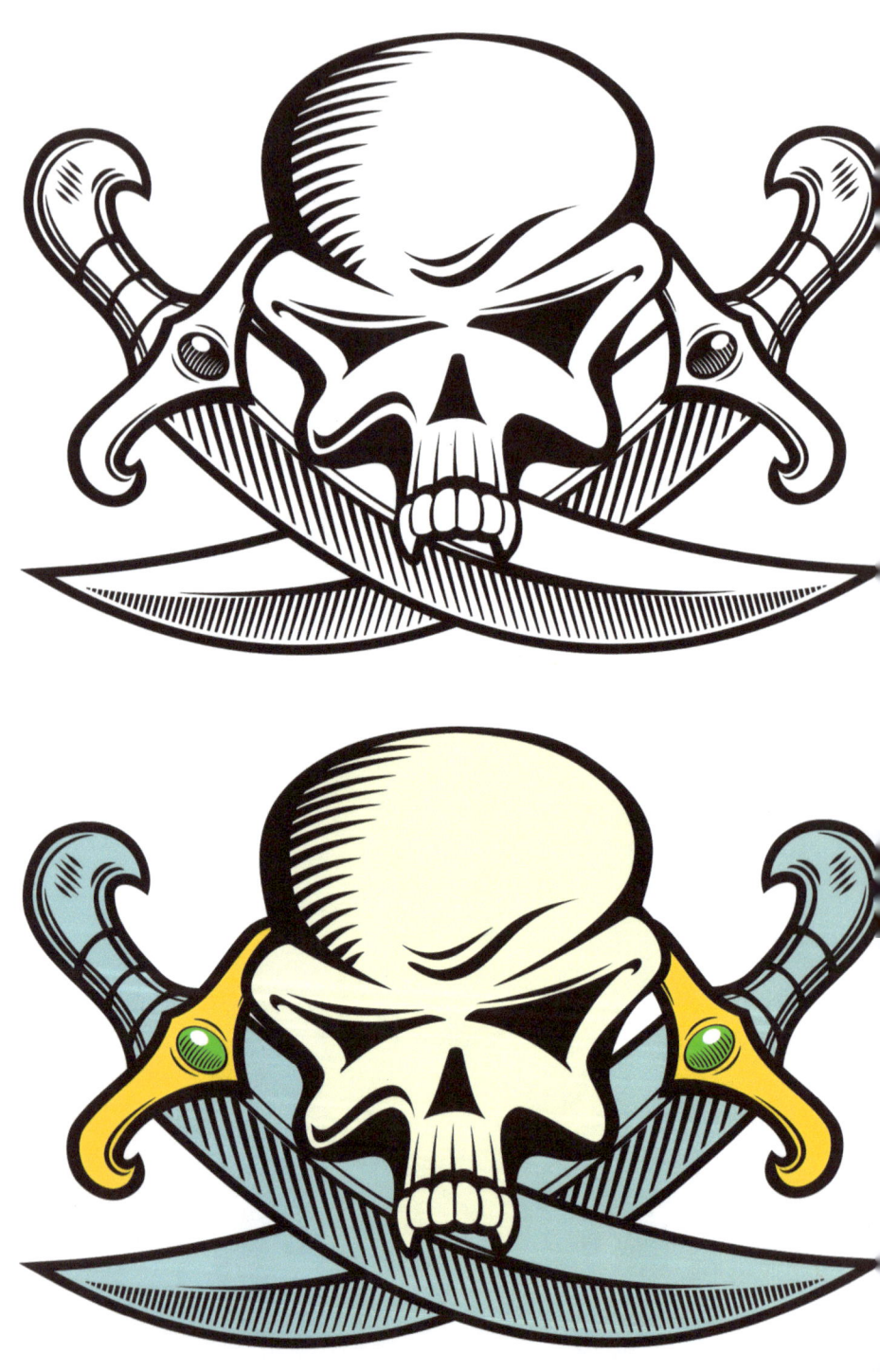

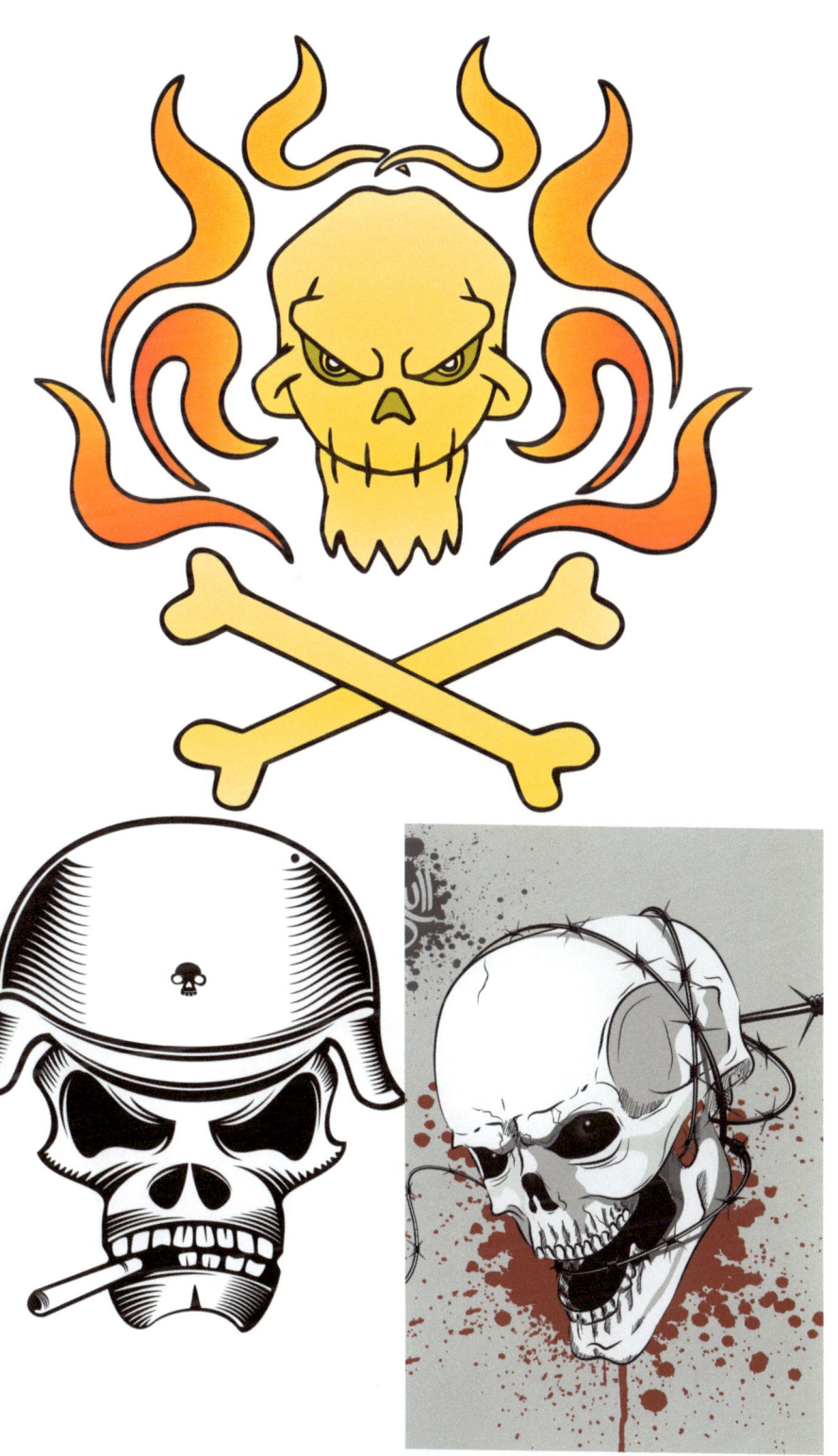

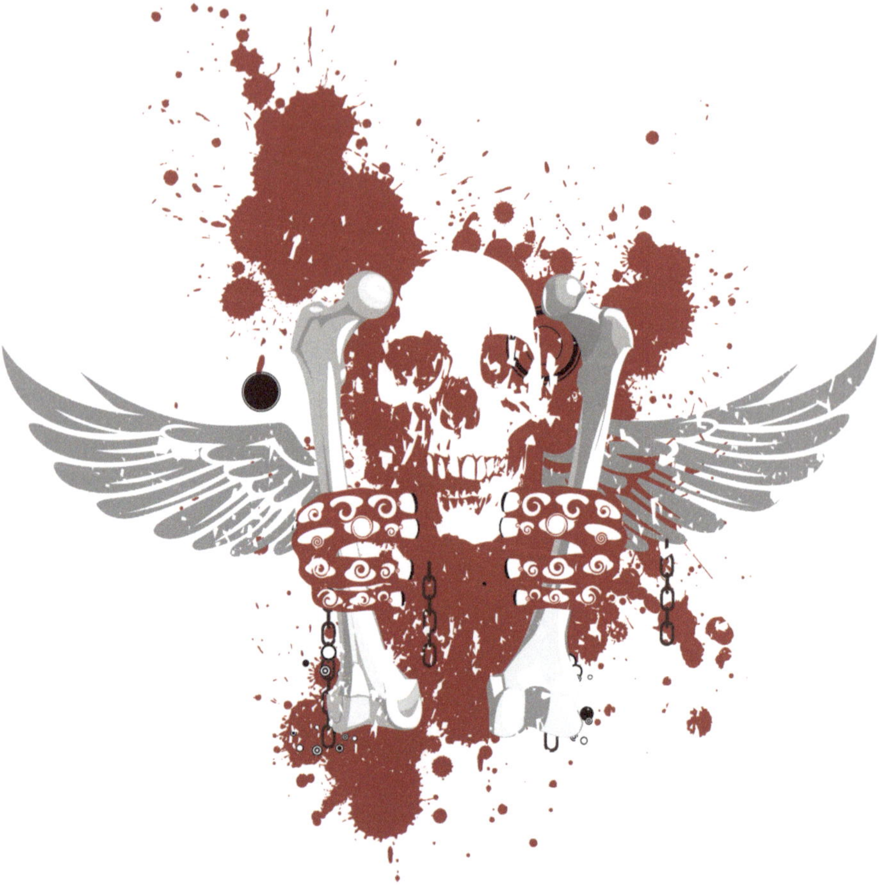

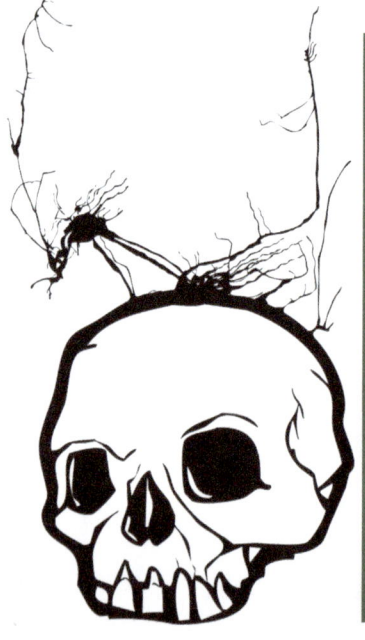
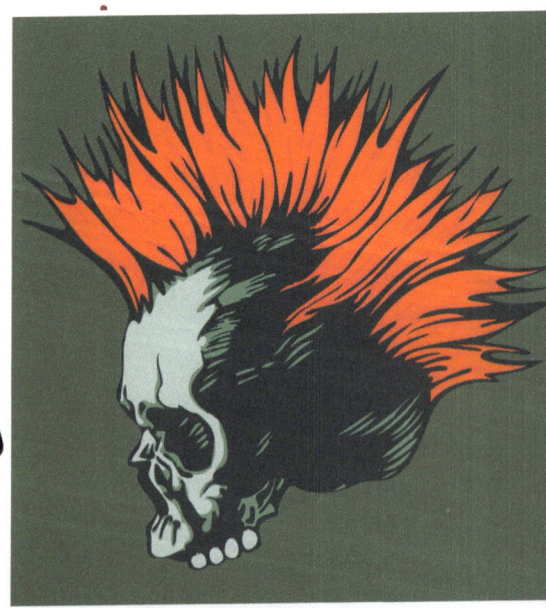

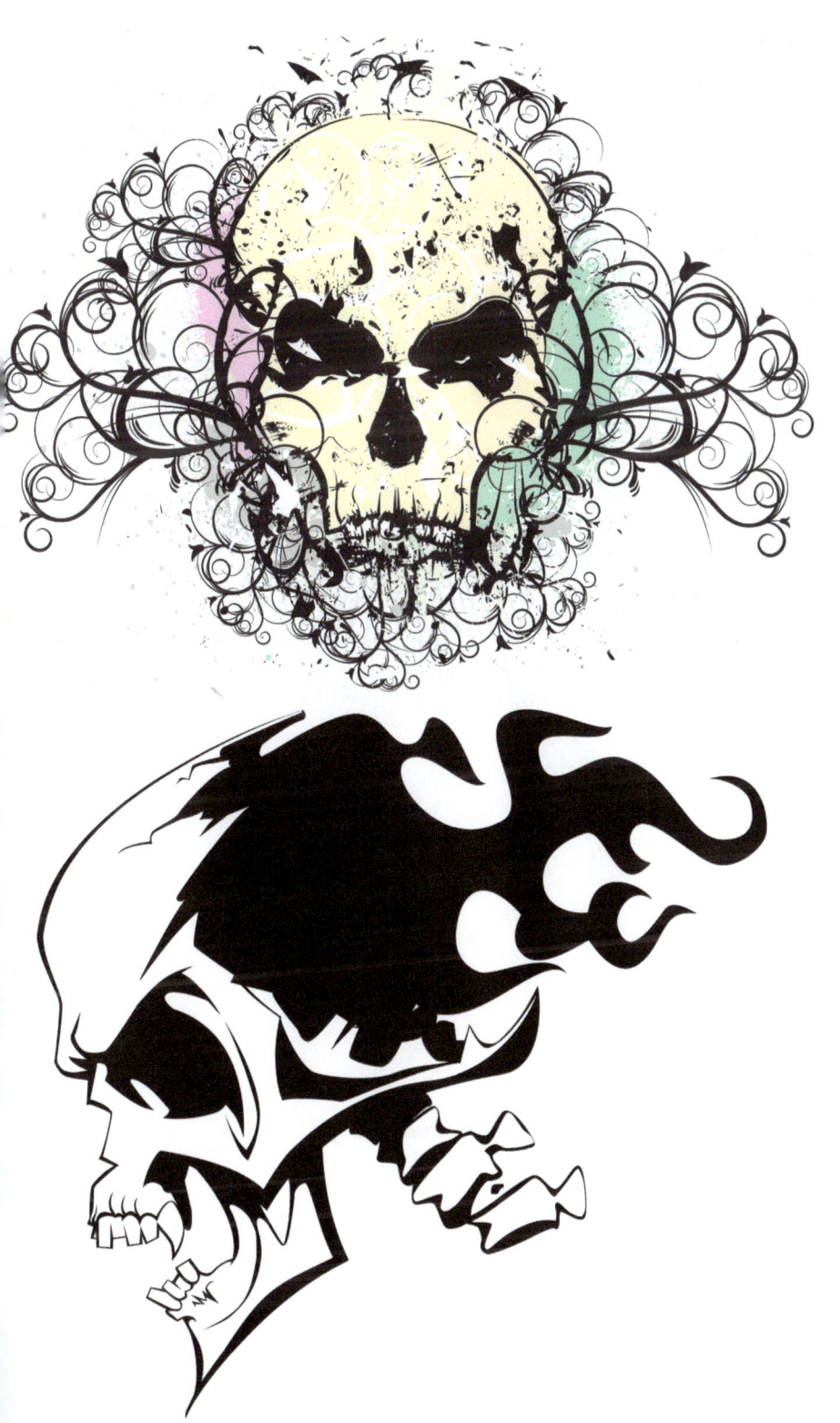

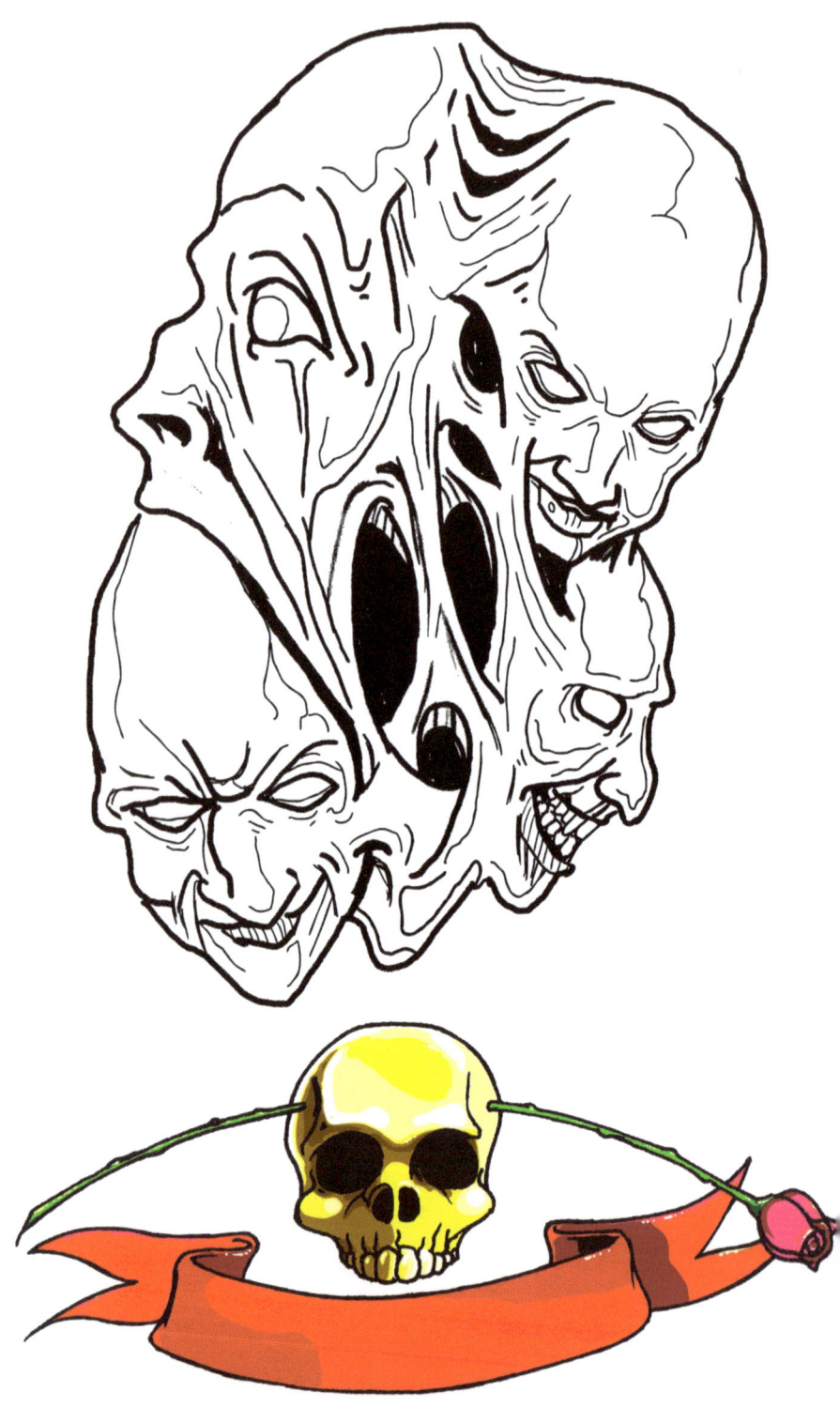

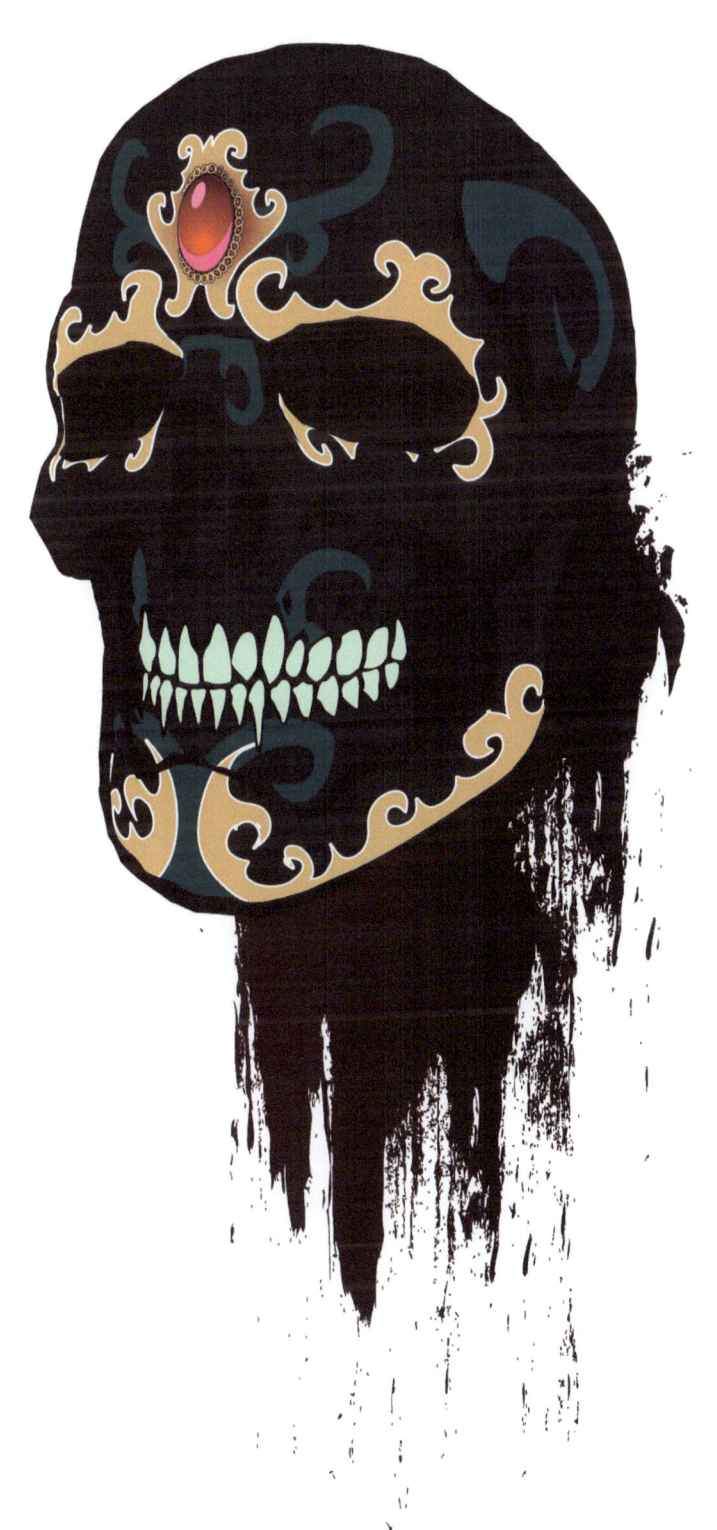

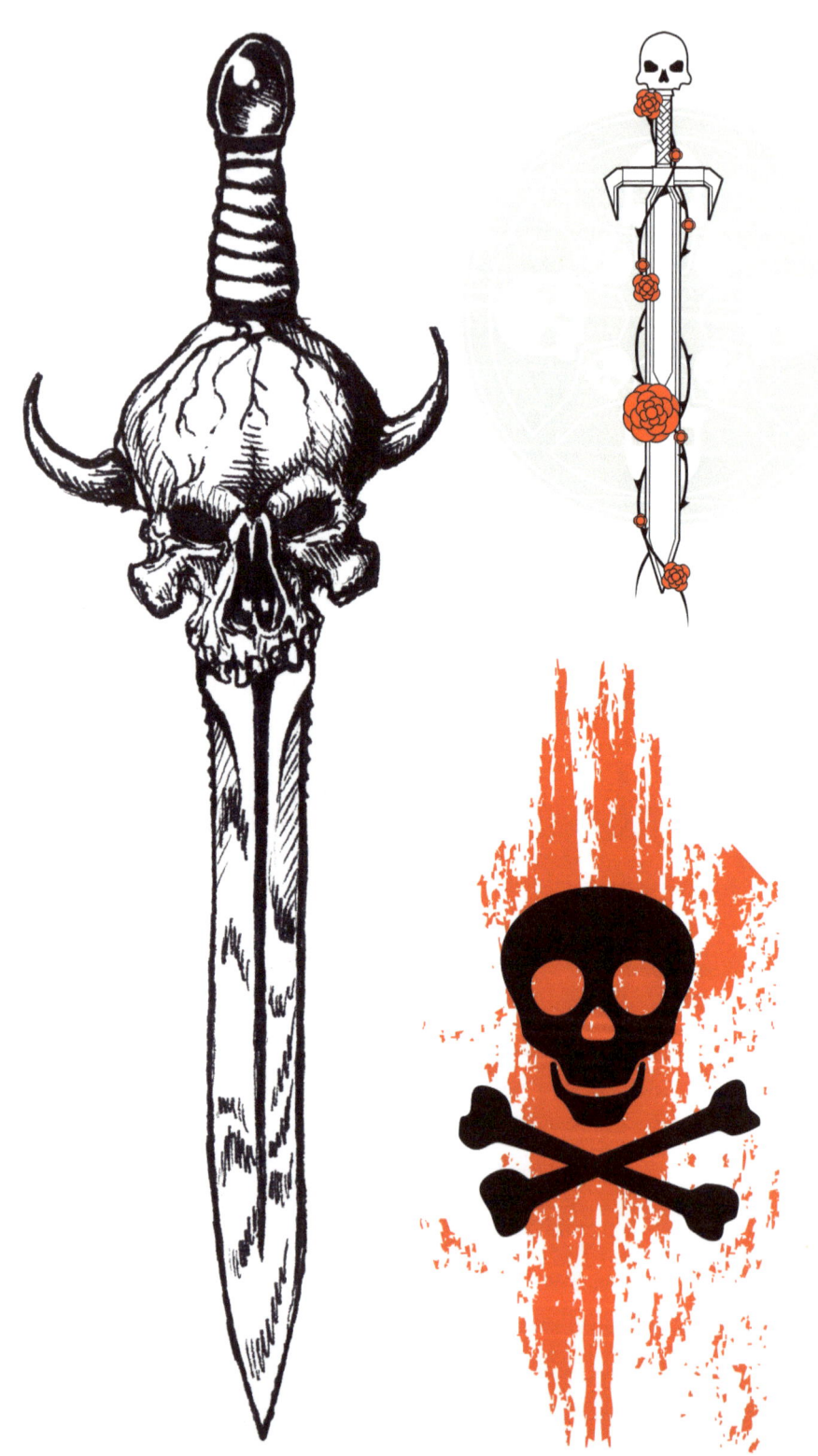

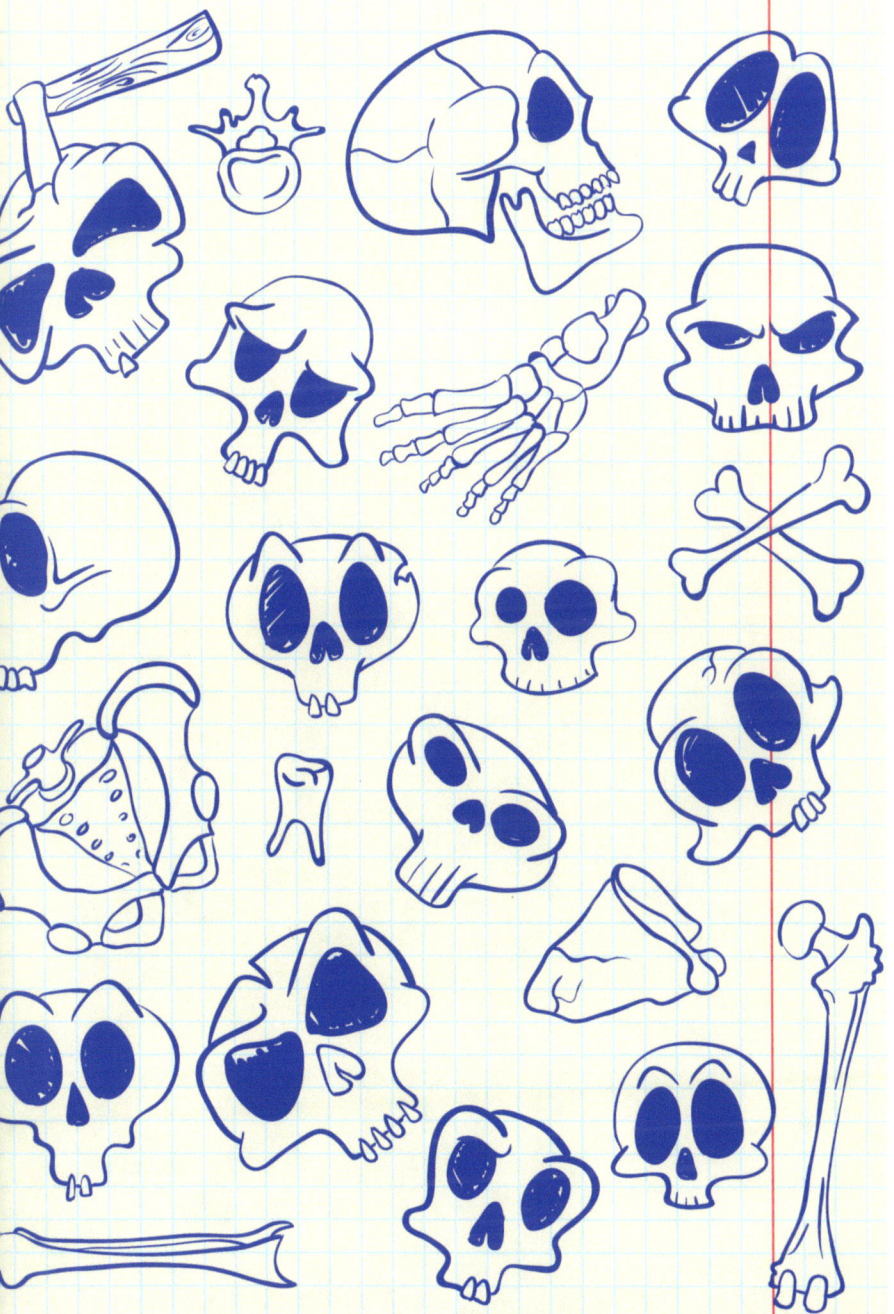

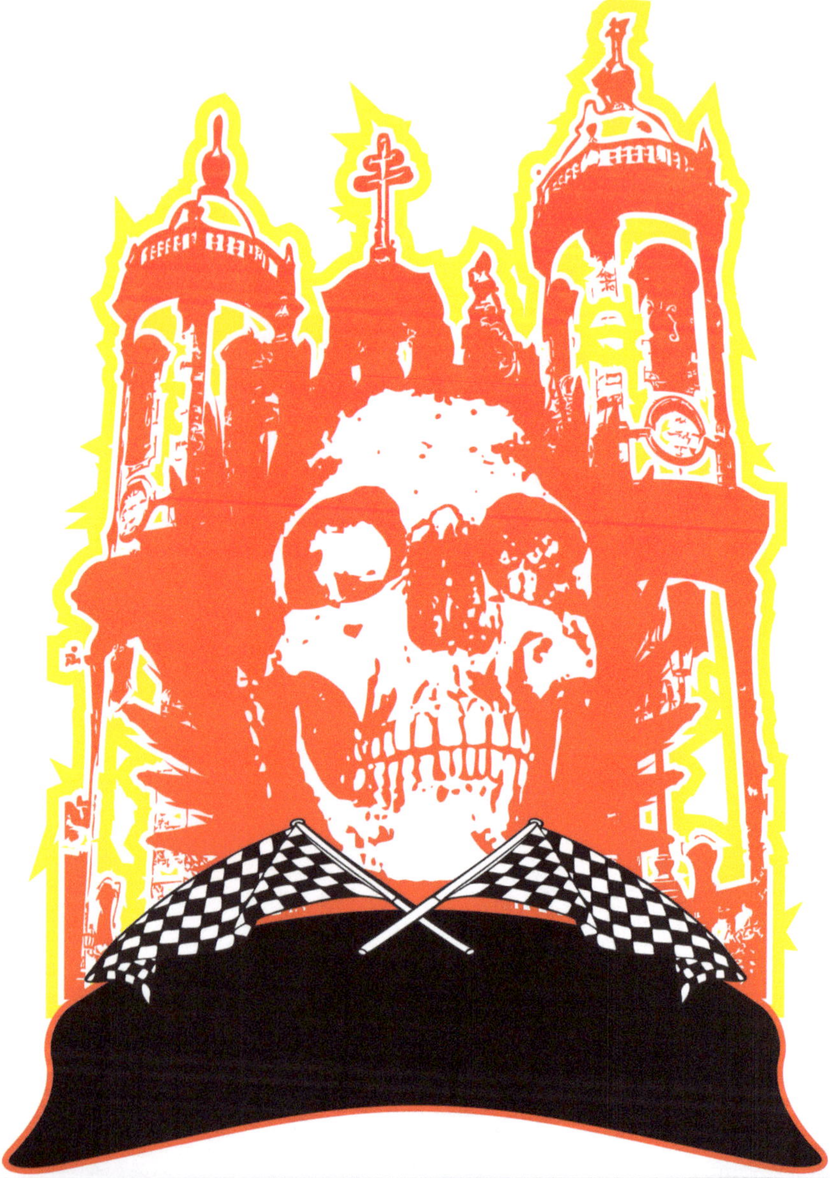

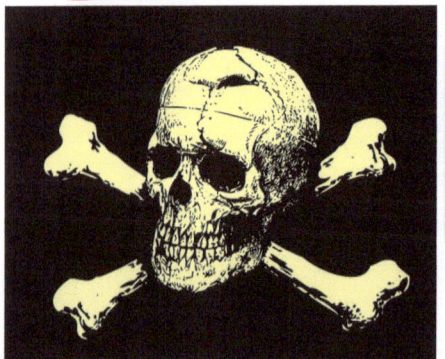
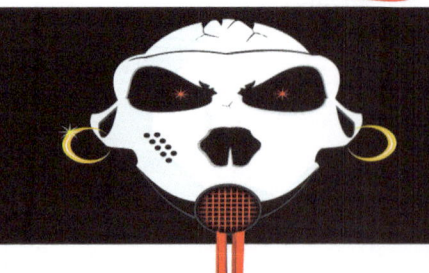

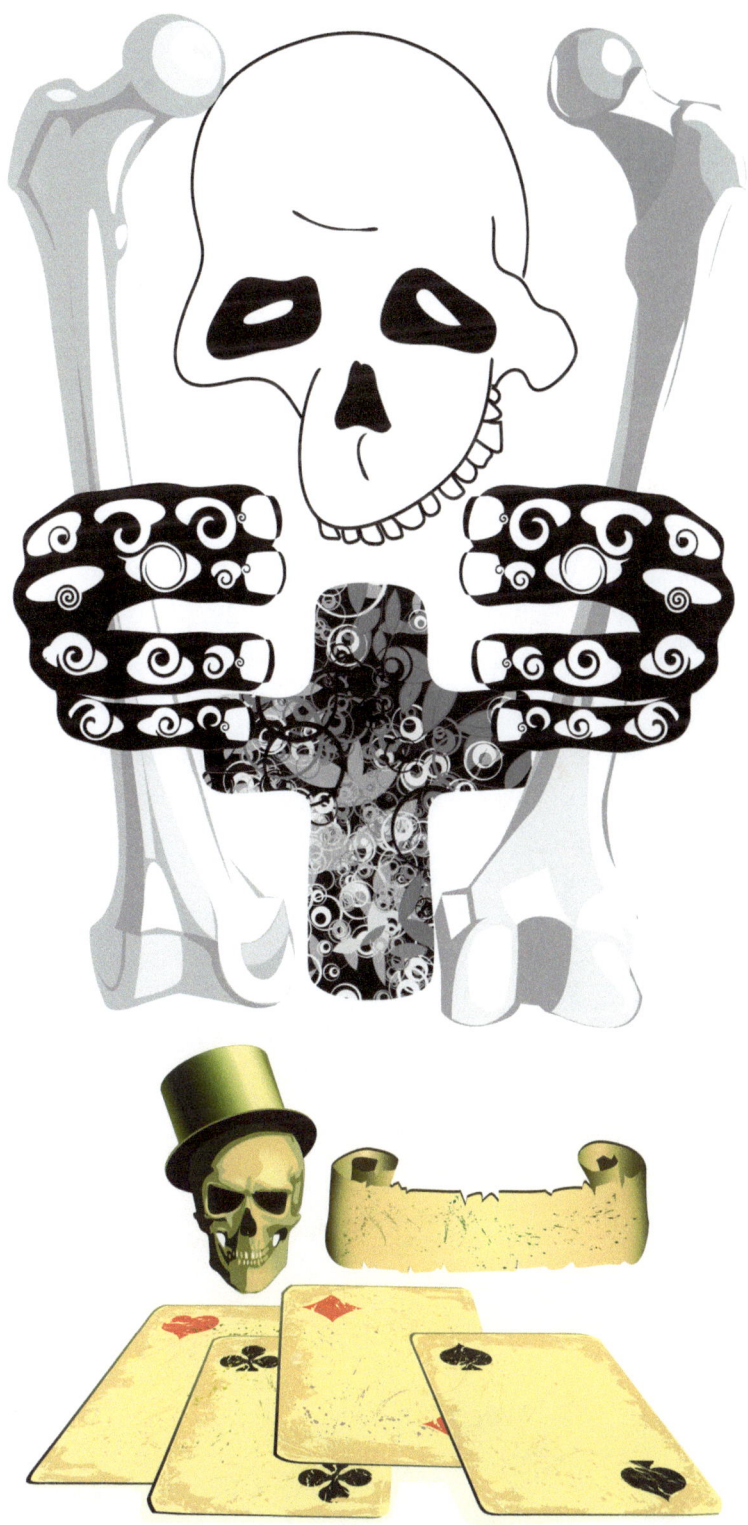

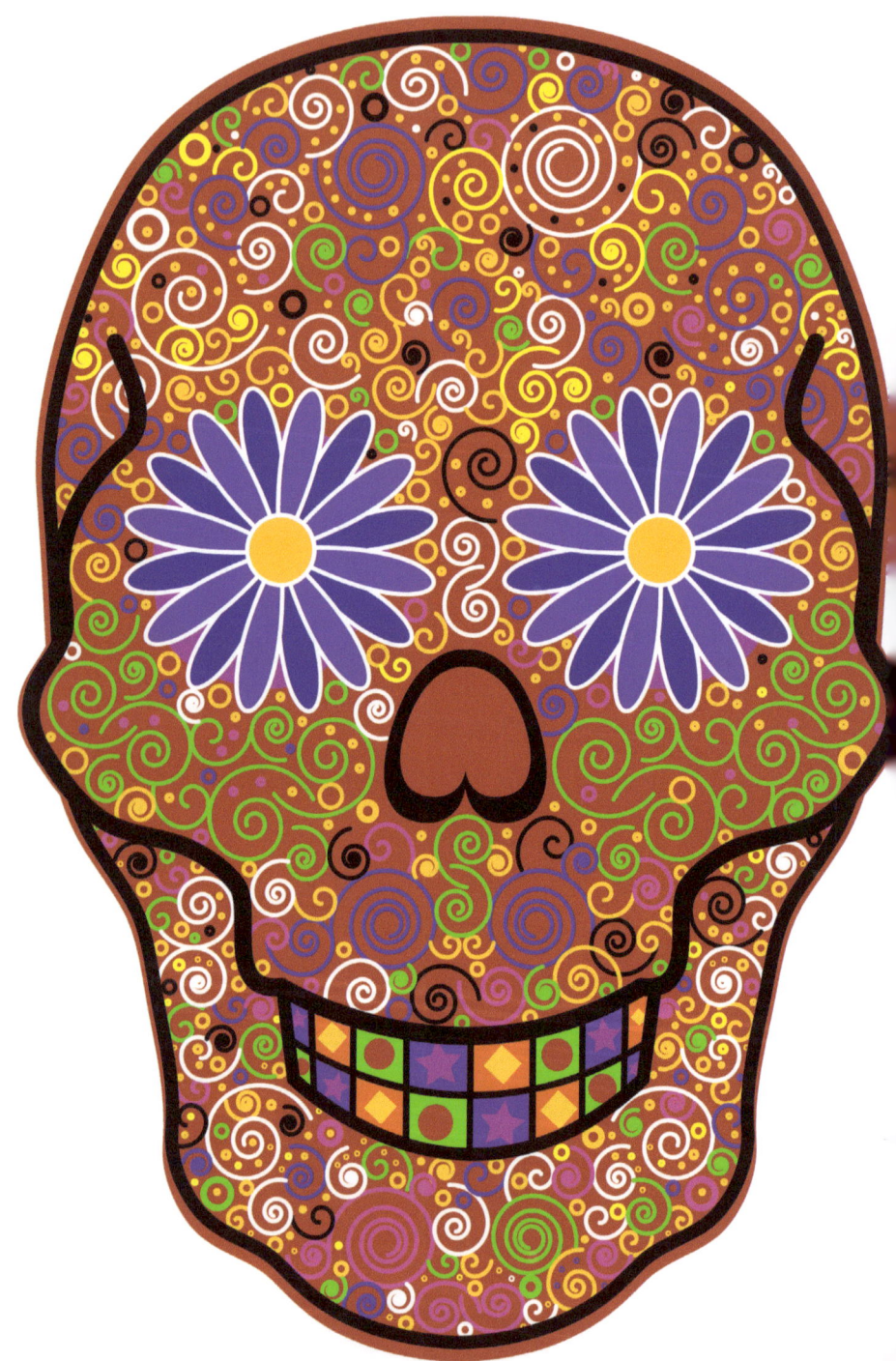

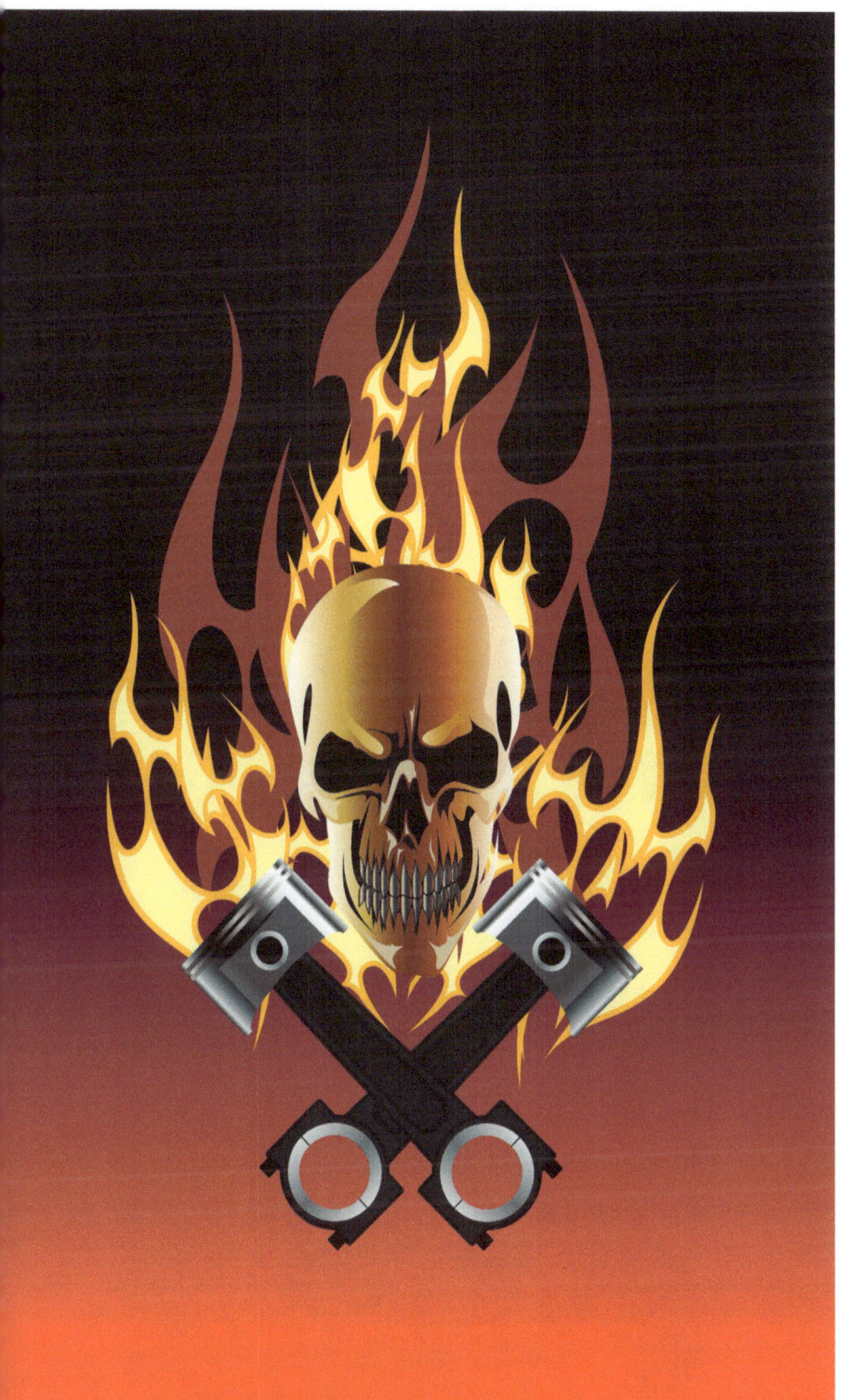

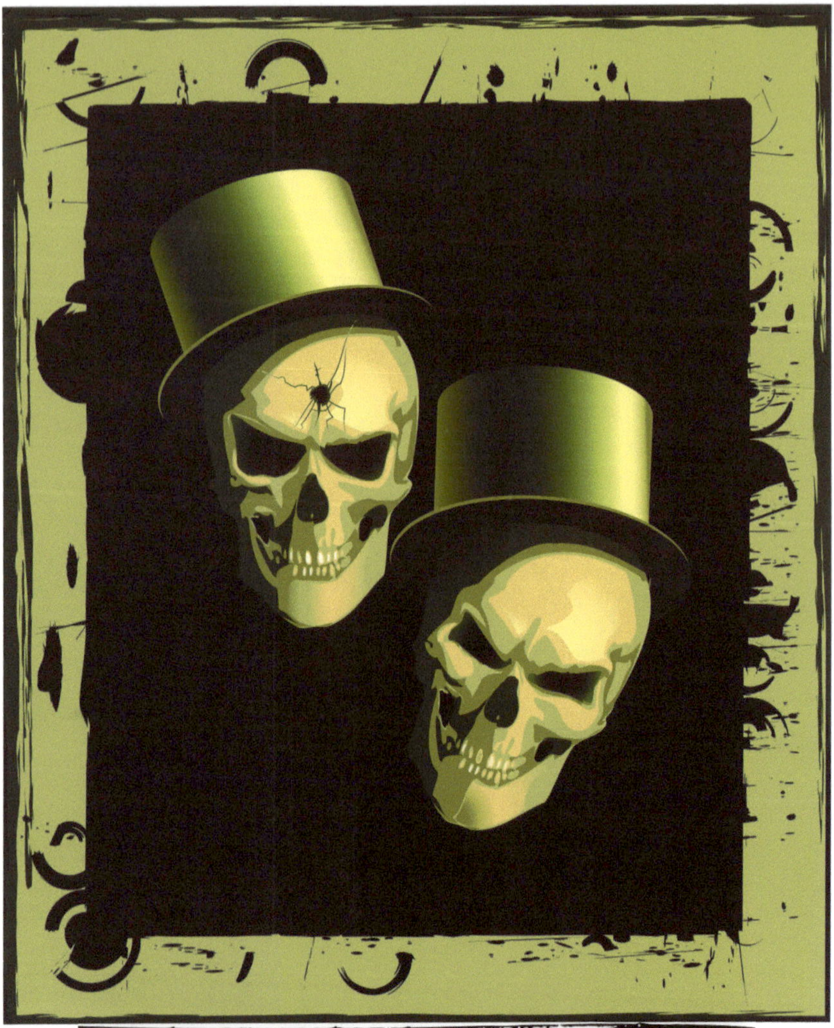

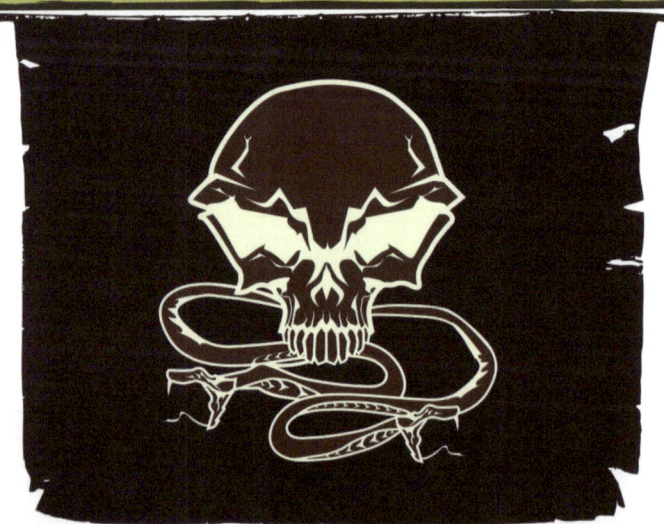

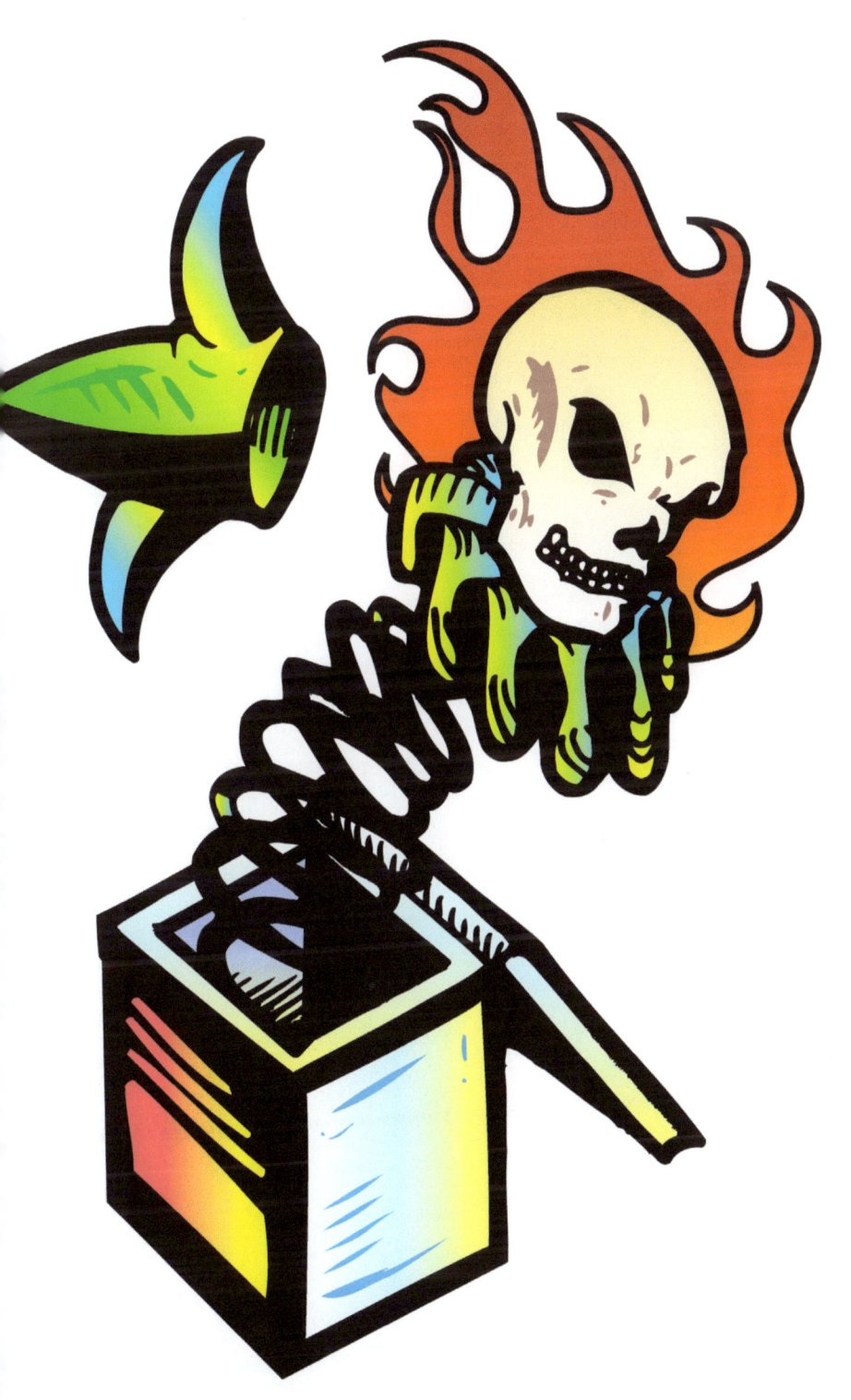

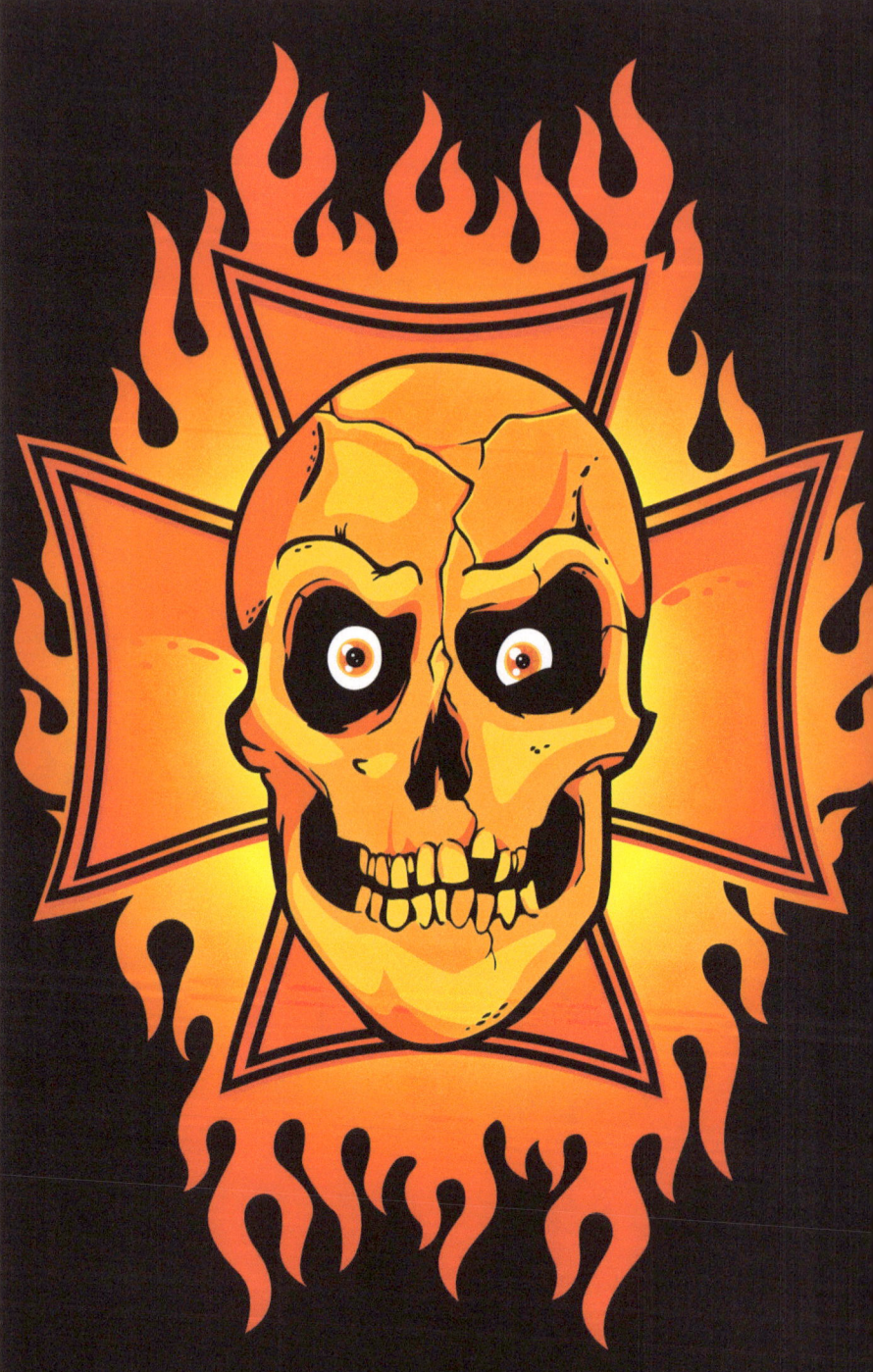

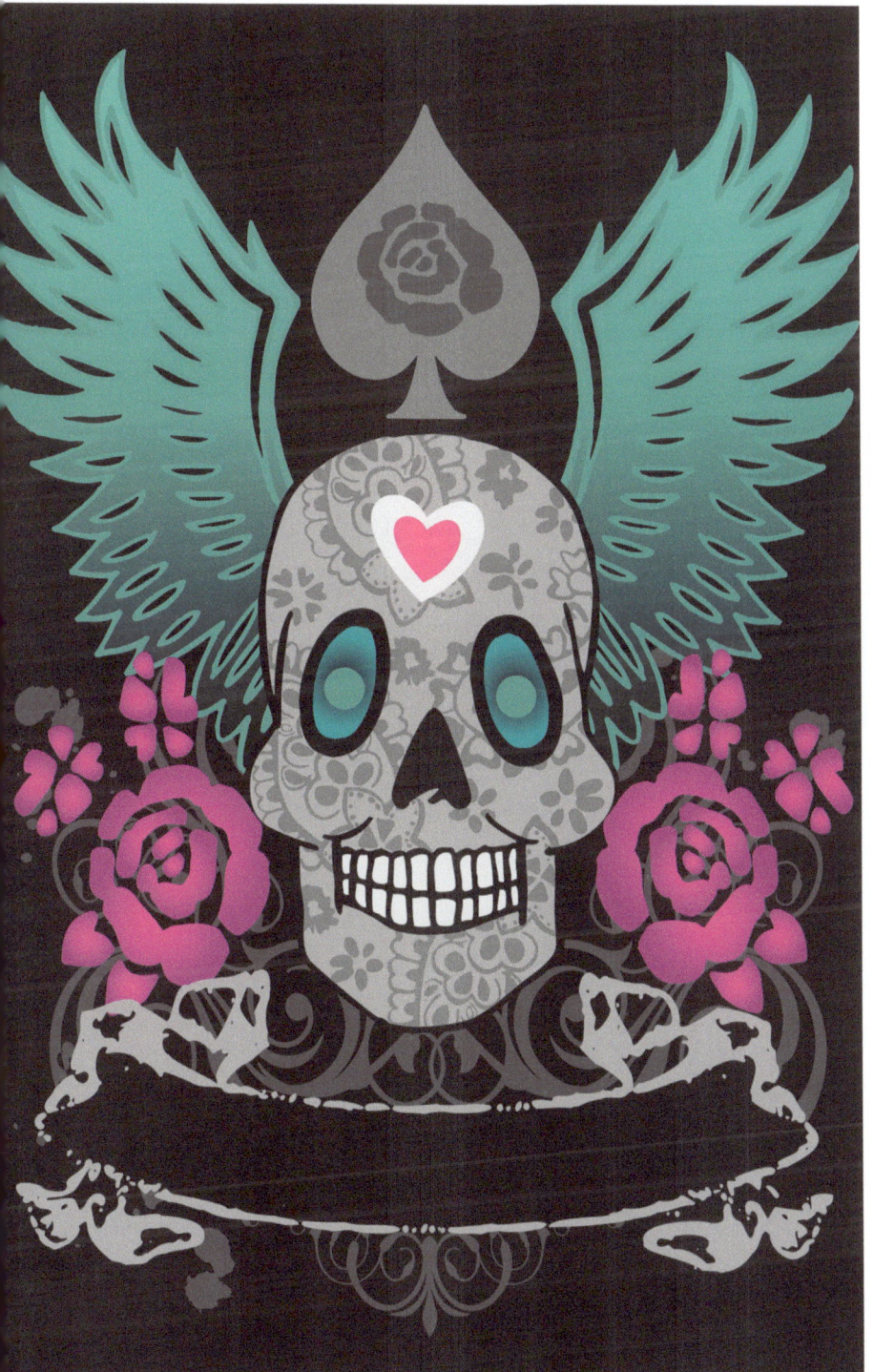

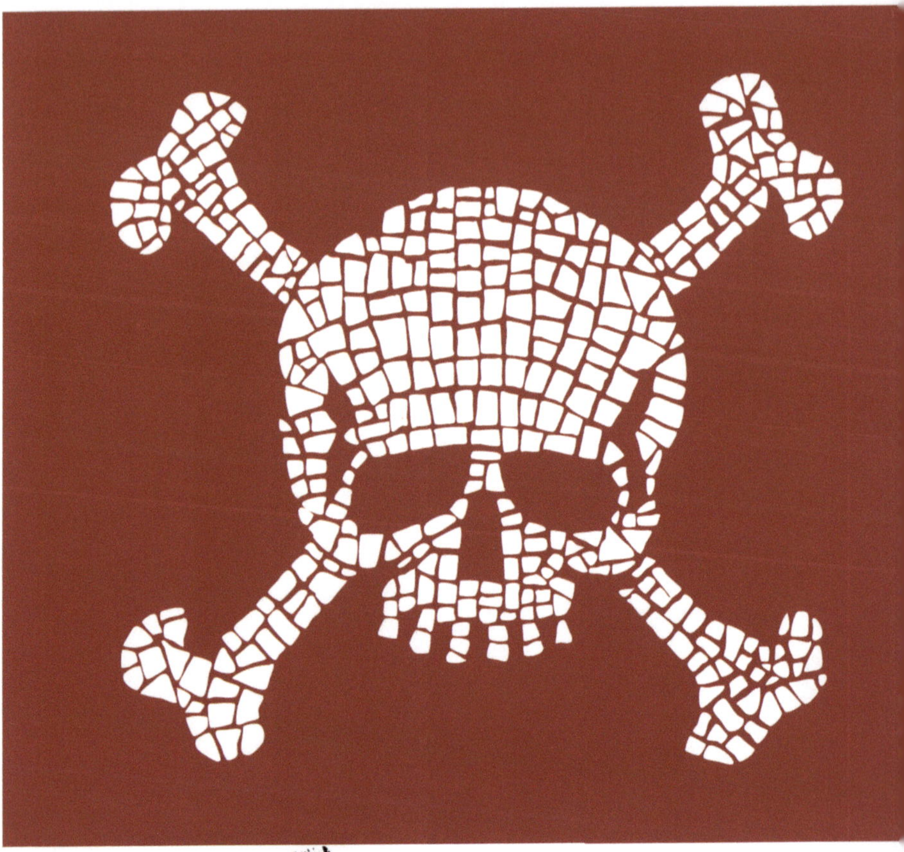

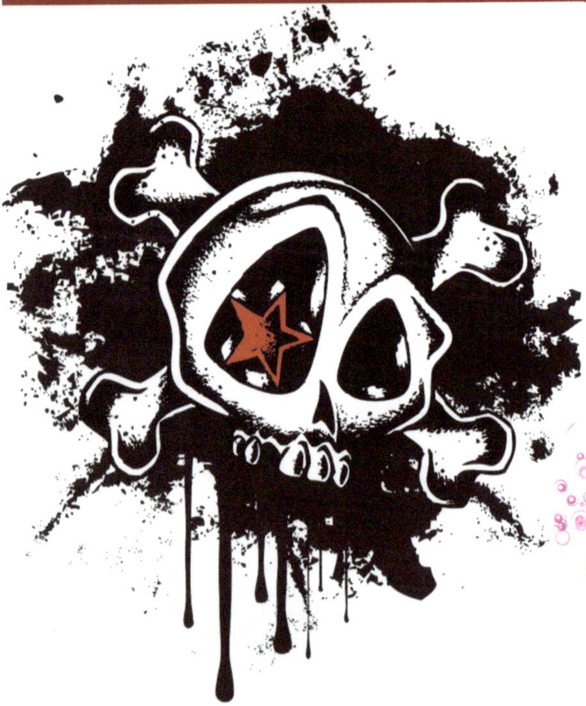

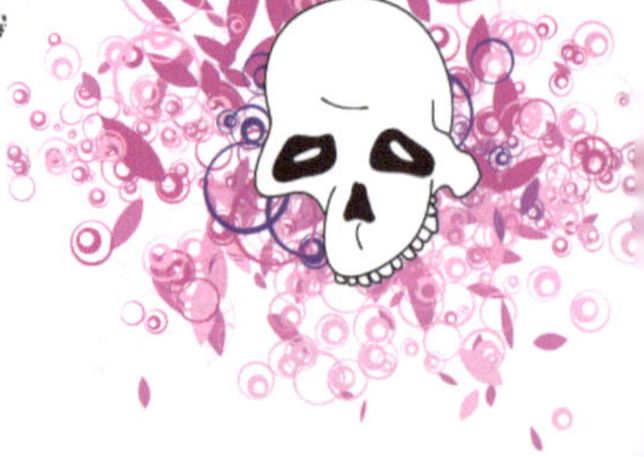

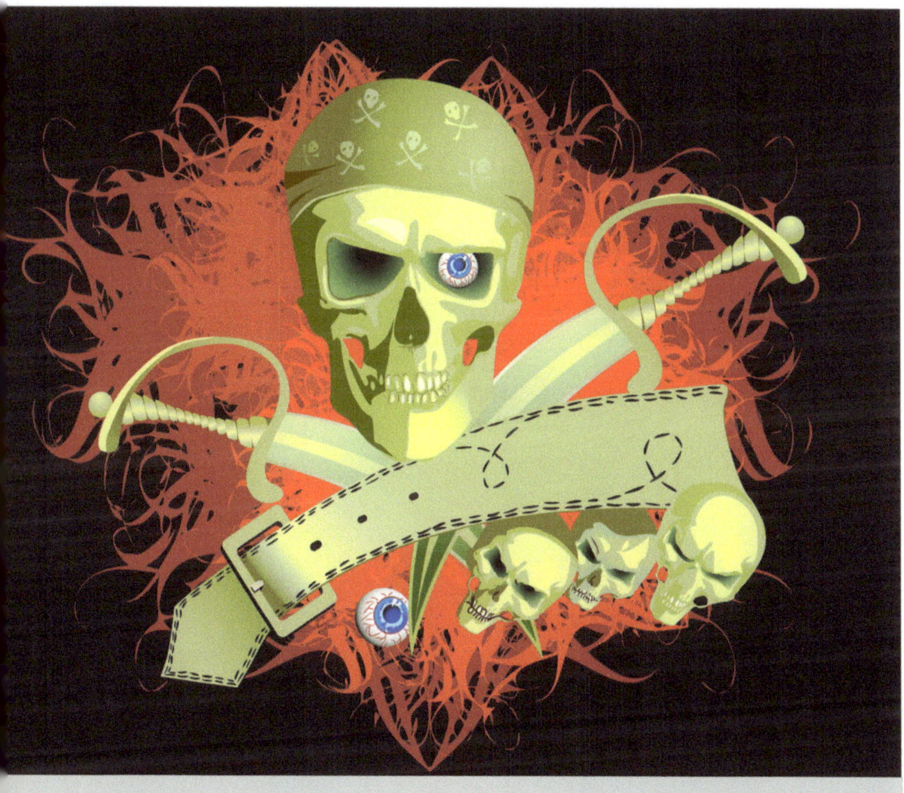

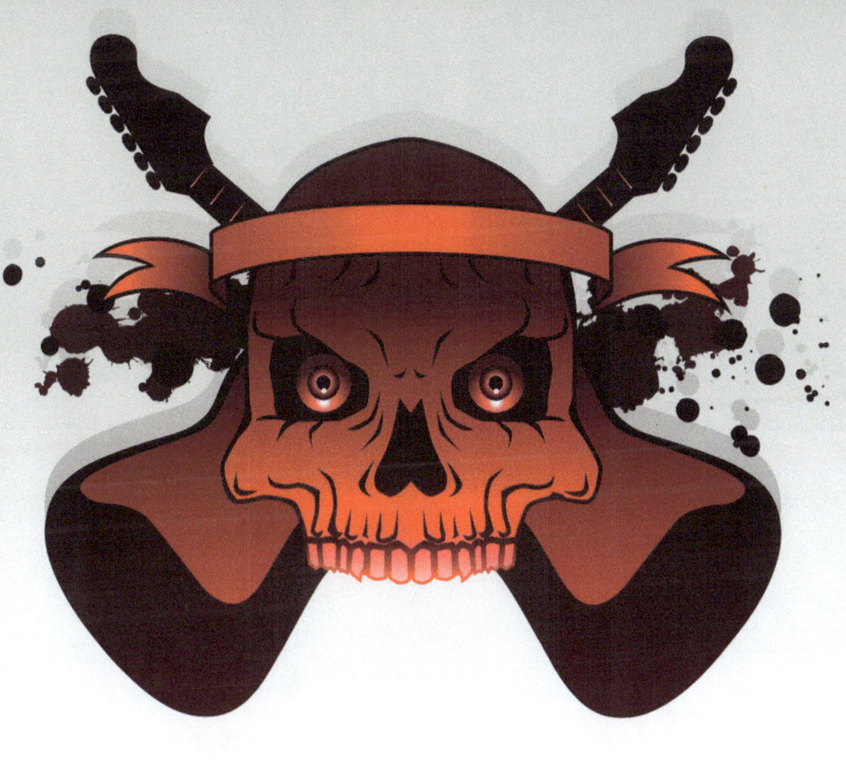

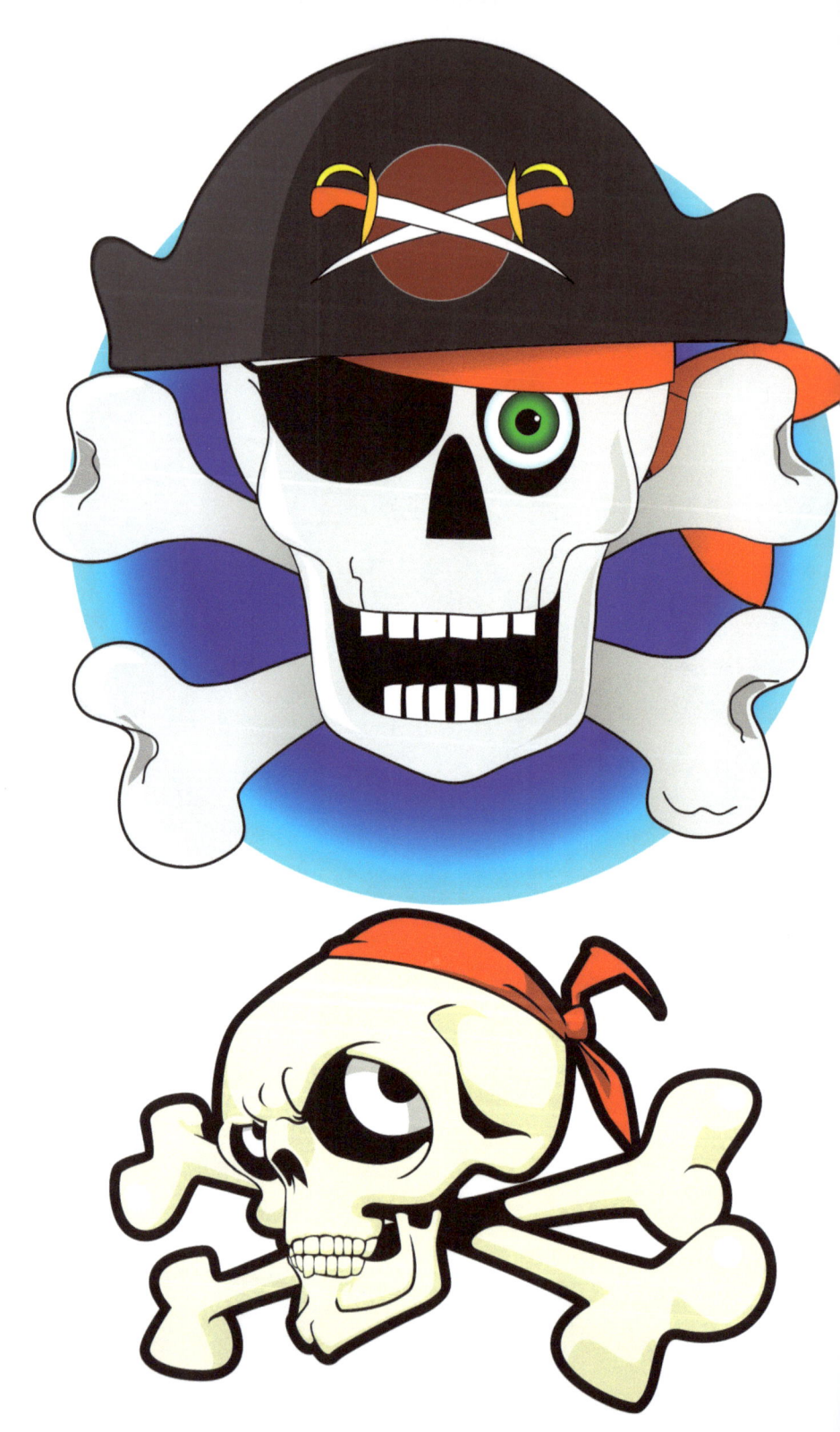

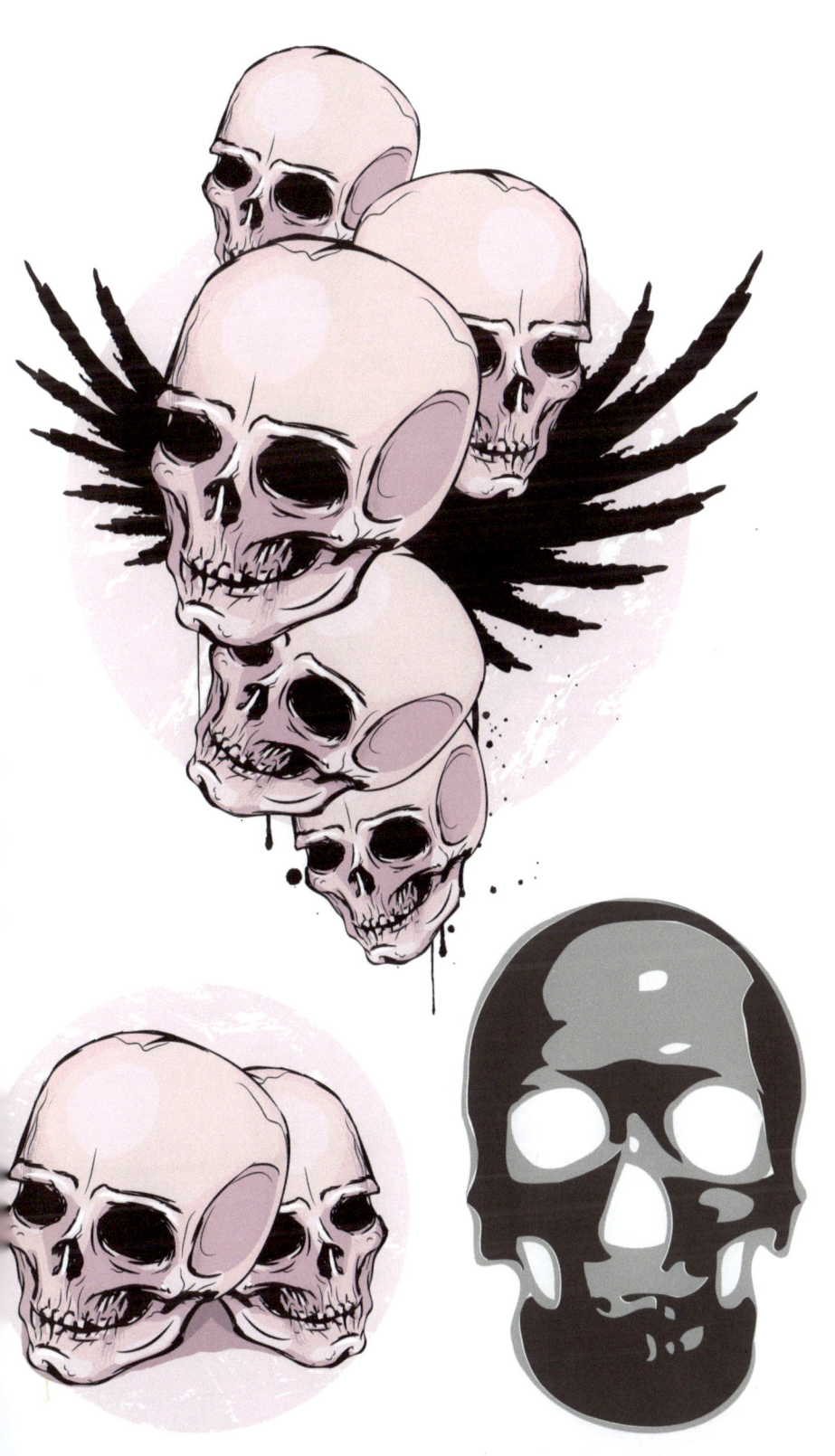

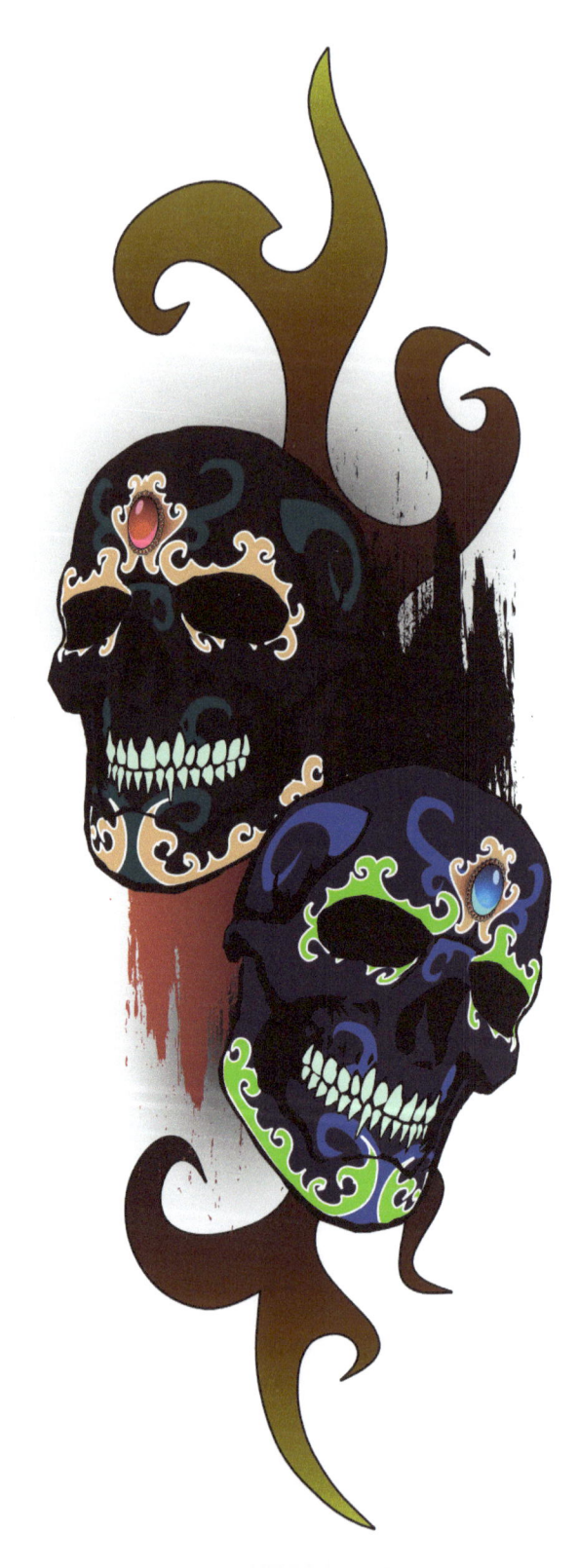

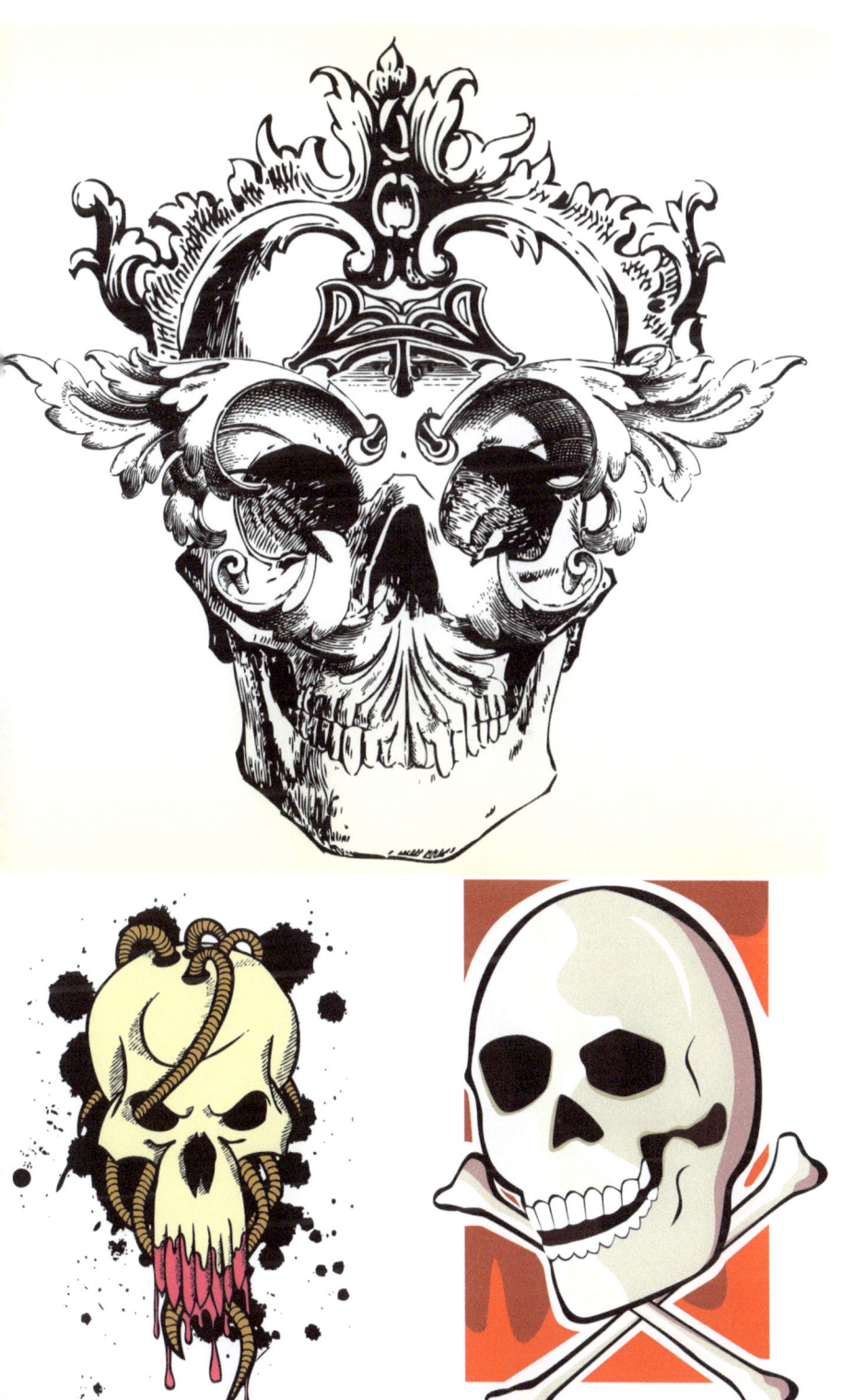

Other Books in the Series

- Cross Tattoos
- Angel Tattoos
- Butterfly Tattoos
- Fairy Tattoos
- Zodiac Tattoos
- Lettering Tattoos
- Scorpion Tattoos
- Hummingbird Tattoos
- Dragonfly Tattoos
- Kanji Tattoos
- Dolphin Tattoos
- Cherub Tattoos

Other titles are in preparation.

www.ingramcontent.com/pod-product-compliance
Lightning Source LLC
Chambersburg PA
CBHW040220220526
45473CB00001B/56